ISBN: 9781314096293

Published by:
HardPress Publishing
8345 NW 66TH ST #2561
MIAMI FL 33166-2626

Email: info@hardpress.net
Web: http://www.hardpress.net

NARRATIVE

OF A

SECOND VISIT TO GREECE,

&c.

[illegible] T H E N S

Drawn by J. D. Harding, from an Original Sketch [illegible] Esq. [illegible]
for Blaquiere's second Visit to Greece

NARRATIVE

OF A

SECOND VISIT TO GREECE,

INCLUDING

Facts connected

WITH

THE LAST DAYS OF LORD BYRON,

EXTRACTS FROM

CORRESPONDENCE, OFFICIAL DOCUMENTS,

&c.

BY EDWARD BLAQUIERE, Esq.

AUTHOR OF

"THE ORIGIN AND PROGRESS OF THE GREEK REVOLUTION," &c.

"Publicity is the soul of justice."—BENTHAM.

LONDON:
PRINTED FOR GEO. B. WHITTAKER,
AVE-MARIA-LANE.

1825.

LONDON:
SHACKELL AND ARROWSMITH, JOHNSON'S-COURT, FLEET-STREET.

INTRODUCTION.

My sudden departure from England, last year, having obliged me to leave a number of facts connected with Greece, and her Revolution, untouched, I have in the following pages, endeavoured to fill up the void; and I hope thus to redeem a pledge, without which I should not have considered the task proposed to myself, as by any means completed. In acknowledging the numerous imperfections of both my volumes, I may be permitted to say of this, as I did of the former, that the materials were collected on the spot, and from those who have either taken the lead in bringing about the struggle, or been prominent actors during its eventful progress.*

* Being desirous of conveying a correct idea of a place to which such frequent allusion is made in my Narrative, I am in-

A

Having, in my humble efforts to promote the cause of freedom and humanity in the New World, as well as in Greece, felt that a great responsibility was incurred, it has been my earnest study to state such facts as I considered most conducive to the great object in view, without disguising truth, or misleading public opinion. In advocating the Greek cause, I was not ignorant of the difficulties by which it was environed. Convinced, however, from the peculiar circumstances connected with this unexampled struggle, as well as by the experience of history, that a nation is not regenerated without having to encounter innumerable obstacles, it would have been both imprudent and illiberal to check the generous ardour of the European public, in favour of a people who have such irresistible claims on its sympathy and co-operation:—such have been the motives for my not dwelling on those errors of judgment and defects of national character, inseparable from

debted to the kindness of my friend, Mr. Robert Greg, of Manchester, for the view of Athens, which forms the Frontispiece. This is, by far, the most correct and tasteful I have seen of that renowned spot. As no country on earth affords a finer field to artists than Greece, it is hoped my friend may be induced to give the remaining treasures of his portfolio to the public.

every people who are long exposed to a despotic system of government. The course, which has been adopted by so many others, cannot be too much deprecated, for if the defects of a people are ever to be exposed, it is not surely when they are struggling for existence?

In consequence of some observations and letters, contained in Colonel Stanhope's interesting publication, and which could not fail to excite doubts with regard to the character of individuals, whose talents and virtues have impressed me with the highest respect, it has become a sacred duty on my part, to give publicity to statements and documents, which might, under any other circumstances, be devoid of public interest. In performing this duty, I am also bound to bear my humble testimony to the zeal and talent which the gallant Colonel has evinced, from the moment he espoused the Greek cause; his efforts in favour of freedom in other places, is too well known to the public to require any notice from me. As, however, the ultimate triumph of the Greeks, must depend in a great measure on the patriotism and purity of those in whose hands power is placed, I feel assured, that the gallant Colonel will not be displeased with my having followed his example, in giving free utterance to my own sentiments. Though shades of difference in opinion, may have arisen between us, I am convinced no man can appreciate the advantages of candour and truth, in such matters, more justly than the enlightened author of Greece in 1823,—while he does not require to be told, that whatever we possess of freedom and public spirit, is due to that unshackled conflict of opinions, which has at all times been the precursor of public liberty and national independence.

From the fate which has befallen so many efforts in favour of freedom during the last thirty years, and the dangers which still surround every attempt at popular emancipation, it is of the utmost importance that every fact, tending to convey a thorough knowledge of the rise and progress of such efforts, should be made public; for without this, how is it possible to avoid the errors which have led to such disastrous consequences in other countries? In thus alluding to the importance of putting the European public in possession of all the facts necessary to its forming a correct judgment on the nature of the Greek contest, it is impossible to avoid noticing the disappointment and sorrow occasioned by the revival of those dissensions, which have arisen since my Narrative was written, and contrary to the hopes of all the friends of the cause throughout Europe. If I do so now, it is in order to urge more vehemently than ever, the necessity of the great powers coalescing, to rescue a whole people from the imminent danger with which they are threatened by the crimes and follies of a few individuals.

Having espoused this sacred cause on behalf of the million, and made every possible effort to ascertain the sentiments of the Greek people, I have no hesitation in repeating, that the most ignorant among them, would hail such an interference as should place Greece under a regular government, calculated to put an end to rival pretensions, as the happiest moment of their lives, and indeed the goal of all their hopes. In urging this truth on the notice of the cabinets, I also feel assured that I am expressing the sentiments of every man of virtue and patriotism in the confederation. Should the great powers defer some decided measure of policy with regard to Greece, and suffer another campaign to proceed, there will surely be no injustice in charging them with all the consequences which may arise from such unpardonable apathy; while it cannot fail to infer, that the oft repeated insinuations of their conniving at the destruction of a whole nation of Christians, is not an unfounded assertion.

Although it is true, the jarring interests which embarrass the Greek question on every side, may render an arrangement difficult, yet I am convinced with the most enlightened men of Greece, that if the cabinets enter into the discussion, with sincerity, an understanding may be established much more easily than most persons, who have only viewed the matter superficially and at a distance, imagine. As a return to the Turkish yoke is impossible, let the grand question of independence be decided at once. This done, every thing else will follow as a matter of course; and however bright the hopes of the friends of Greece were, when they first beheld the dawn of her regeneration, I feel satisfied they would rather see a monarchy established there, than witness the destruction of the people for whom their sympathy has been called forth.

From a variety of circumstances which have occurred, it is evident that our own ministers are not only actuated by a more liberal spirit towards Greece, but also feel the necessity of putting an end to a conflict, which tends to the mutual destruction both of Greece and Turkey, while it is opposed to every sentiment of religion and humanity. It is needless to add, that such is the tide of popular opinion in favour of an arrangement, if they insist, their efforts will be crowned with success. Without this, all the succours we could send will, it is feared, be insufficient to attain the grand object in view.

Having thus declared my firm conviction, on a subject which is so deeply interesting to civilization, some circumstances, which have taken place since my return from the Morea, render it necessary to say a few words with regard to the part I have taken in the affairs of the confederacy. By referring to the correspondence and official papers, which are offered to the public as the most important portion of the present volume, it will be seen with what anxiety I urged such measures as were most likely to enable the Provisional Government to prosecute the war with increased and becoming vigour; but more especially, to commence the fifth campaign before the season was too far advanced. I have stated the flattering manner in which all my propositions on this subject were received; it remains for me to add, that by a letter of the Secretary-General, the executive body conferred on me the high honour of co-operating with its deputies in this country. Judging, from my previous connection with the friends of Greece, that the former would derive some little facilities from the assistance I might be enabled to give. Having, in consequence of this proof of confidence, felt it my duty to engage that the utmost expedition should be used in carrying the instructions of which I was the bearer into effect, my whole attention was directed to this object on reaching London.

A combination, which I could not possibly anticipate, having prevented me from fulfilling any one of those engagements, I feel it a sacred duty, due not only to the Government, but the people of Greece, to declare, that neither have had any share in the unforeseen obstacles that have been thrown in the way. My sole object being that of thus publicly justifying myself from what a people, to whom I am bound by the strongest ties of sympathy and affection, might justly conceive a betrayal of their interests, at a peculiar crisis, I shall abstain from a variety of minor details connected with this subject, and which would reflect but little credit on the parties more immediately concerned. I do not want to bring individuals unnecessarily before the public: what I wish, in common with every friend of Greece, is, that her cause, by far the most glorious that ever graced the page of history, should not be sacrificed at the unhallowed shrine of avarice, envy, or ingratitude!

A variety of additional circumstances which have occurred since the above observations were written, not only justifies, but renders the publication of the letter* alluded to in the preceding page,

* The following is a translation of the letter in question:—

"PROVISIONAL GOVERNMENT OF GREECE.

"SECOND PERIOD, NO. 264.

"Napoli di Romania, Aug. 12, 1824.

"SIR,

"MY Government having sent instructions to its Deputies in London, by which they are charged with various affairs concerning the well-being of the Greek people, it does not doubt but you will also do all that depends on yourself to be useful to Greece, necessary, in order to prevent the effects of those insinuations, if not direct calumnies, to which it would appear I have been exposed, in common with many others. Having proved, both in my account of the Revolution, and in the present volume, that the resources of Greece entitle her to a high credit on the London Stock Exchange, I may surely be permitted to deplore those arrangements, which have placed the loan recently contracted for, in a situation nearly similar to that into which the former fell during my visit to the Morea. In lamenting a circumstance which cannot fail to be materially injurious to the Greek

in conjunction with our Deputies, who are ordered to apply to you in all the affairs with which they are charged, as their counsellor and co-operator; you will, therefore, act in such a way as to ensure their prompt and happy termination. You will on this occasion afford new proofs of your ardent zeal and your philellenic sentiments. Conceiving it needless to dwell on this subject any longer, I conclude by wishing you a fortunate voyage; and I take the liberty of subscribing myself,

"Your very devoted Servant,

(Signed) "P. G. RODIUS.

"Sec.-General, *ad interim*.

"*To Mr. Edward Blaquiere, Napoli di Romania.*"

cause, I owe it to myself, and those with whom I have acted, to state, that had our advice been followed, Greece would have obtained her second loan on much more advantageous terms, and at least two months before the second was negociated. Nor, had those entreaties, written and verbal, which I addressed to the Deputies, not long after my return, been attended to, would four months have been wasted in negociations that might have been concluded in as many weeks. If, therefore, the interests of Greece have either been sacrificed or neglected, the fault is not attributable to her early friends. It is said, that a party has been formed against the second loan; if this be the case, those whose conduct gave rise to its formation, and which they might have so easily prevented, are surely as much to blame as its opponents, if such there be?

London, March 25th, 1825.

CONTENTS OF THE VOLUME.

PART I.

PART II.

EXTRACTS FROM CORRESPONDENCE, &c.

ERRATA.

Part ii. page 27,—*for*, a soldier grave, *read*, a soldier's grave.

NARRATIVE,

&c.

PART I.

NARRATIVE,

&c.

As there is scarcely any incident, however minute, connected with a Revolution, destined most probably to influence the future fate of a large portion of the globe, which can be altogether uninteresting to the European public, it may be proper, before alluding to the naval and military events of the fourth campaign, to give some account of the circumstances which led to my detention at Zante, instead of immediately proceeding to the seat of the Provisional Government, as I fully intended on reaching that Island.

While the friends of Greece associated in England, were making every effort to awaken sympathy in favour of the cause, and promote subscriptions throughout the country, the comparative want of success which attended their frequent appeals to the public, convinced them, that the only effectual mode of aiding the patriots, was by negotiating a loan which should enable the government to organize a good system of internal polity, and assume the offensive on a scale commensurate with the exigencies of the confederation. It having been shown that the resources of Greece were such as to justify the proposed measure; the arrival of Deputies in London was followed by the long wished for negotiation. Those who are conversant with such matters, assert that the Greek Loan was obtained on very advantageous terms. It may, at all events, be justly regarded as giving rise to a new epoch in the cause; for nothing could more clearly demonstrate the confidence of British capitalists as to the future triumph of the Greeks, while it was justly considered as a virtual acknowledgment of their independence.

Deeply impressed as I had all along been with the claims of Greece, and the importance to the whole civilized world of supporting her unexampled struggle, it is needless to say with what heartfelt satisfaction I hailed the accomplishment of a Greek Loan, or how readily I accepted the proposal of those friends who suggested the propriety of my accompanying the first instalment to the Morea. This being shipped on board a vessel taken up for the occasion, I embarked on the 31st of March, and reached Zante on the 24th of April, after the unusually short passage of nineteen days from Spithead, where we were obliged to take shelter during a strong westerly gale, soon after our departure from the Thames.

While filled with exultation at the prospect of immediately giving new life and vigour to the operations of the war, a combination the most distressing and untoward, rendered it impossible to transfer any part of the money to the Provisional Government. Some accounts being received in England after the loan was negociated, and by which it appeared that the military faction had obtained a temporary triumph over the people and their representatives, measures of precaution were taken to prevent the funds from falling into improper hands. These consisted in the nomination of three Commissioners*, who were to meet in Greece, and after examining the state of affairs, to decide as to the time and mode of transferring the loan to the government: although, as it unhappily turned out, this part of the arrangement was liable to various inconveniences, the most unfortunate decision of all, was that of sending the money to one of the Ionian Islands. It was consigned to Mr. Samuel Barff, a highly respectable English merchant of Zante, and M. Logotheti, a native of the island, to be

* The Commissioners were:—Lord Byron, Mr. Gordon, of Cairness, and Lazzaro Conduriotti, of Hydra. Colonel Leicester Stanhope was to act for Mr. Gordon, until the latter could proceed to Greece.

retained by them until they received an order for its delivery from the Commissioners.

Although it was natural to expect that some difficulties would arise as to the transfer, I was far from anticipating what actually occurred; my fears were however completely lulled, when I reflected that if even the money was not given up directly, the credit and authority of Lord Byron would obviate every difficulty. Indeed, the fact of my having been among the first to urge the lamented author of Childe Harold to hasten his projected visit to Greece, and considering myself as his harbinger, made me most anxious to second his generous intentions, and I had therefore determined to pass over to Messolunghi, on the very day of my arrival at Zante.* Having

* Since the above was written, Count Gamba, his Lordship's companion and friend, has put forth his journal, which is entitled to every credit, and a very unaffected detail of Lord Byron's visit to Greece.

As the Count has alluded to the part I took in pressing his departure, and states that his Lordship waited till the middle of July, for the further information I promised to send from the Morea, it may be proper to state, that I addressed a long letter to his Lordship immediately after my arrival at Tripolitza, in the early part of May. This was followed by another, in which I suggested that, in consequence of my intending to return to England by way of Italy, it would perhaps be as well for his Lordship to defer his intended journey until I had an opportunity of communicating personally with him on the state of affairs, and the best mode of accomplishing his plans in favour of Greece.

anchored there late at night, we had no communication with the shore until the following morning. On our being visited by the pratique master, my first question was, whether Lord Byron was well, and if he still continued at Messolunghi? "His Lordship is dead," was the reply. I will not attempt to describe the shock occasioned by this ominous and unexpected announcement. I rushed back to the cabin, and remained for some moments without the power of reflection. To have heard that the greatest benefactor of Greece had been thus snatched away, just as his life was of such incalculable importance to her cause, and when I anticipated the satisfaction of seeing him in a few hours, was a blow for which I felt totally unprepared. But severe as it was, I confess I did not, at the time, foresee half the irreparable mischief of which it was destined to become the source.

My plans being thus completely deranged, I had no alternative but that of disembarking at Zante, there to await replies to the expresses which were instantly dispatched to the Provisional Government, Prince Mavrocordato, and Colonel Stanhope. It was during this interval, that I ascertained the following particulars relative to the state of affairs in the Morea.

From the facts stated in my account of the former stages of the revolution, and more especially those connected with the seditious movements of the refractory chiefs during my visit to Tripolitza, in 1823, it might be readily imagined there was no probability of their encouraging the establishment of a regular Government, while the resources of the Executive were insufficient to enable it to organize a permanent military force, independent of those irregular bands which had hitherto looked for support to the captains. Accordingly, Colocotroni and Mavromichalis, prompted by the influence of Delijiannopulo, Primate of Caritena, and aided by the counsels of Metaxa, an adventurer from Cefalonia, having determined to place themselves at the head of affairs, formed a party which enabled them to transfer the legislative assembly from Tripolitza to Salamis. Although this was done under the plea of its being in a better situation for superintending the operations of the third campaign with greater vigour, it had no other object than that of dissolving the Government formed at Astros, and driving Mavrocordato, the declared opponent of their schemes, from his situation of Secretary General. Perceiving that all his efforts to restrain their violence and ambition, proved abortive, the Prince was induced to accept the presidency of the legislative body to which he was unanimously elected early in July: aware, however, of the motives which suggested the transfer to Salamis, and convinced that there was a design to impede all his endeavours in favour of the Nation, without his having the power to prevent its execution, he determined to retire to Hydra, where his influence might be most usefully exerted in urging the sailing of the fleet, which had now become of the utmost importance. Zaimis, Primate of Calavrita, and a member of the Executive, also excused himself from proceeding to Salamis, alleging that his presence was necessary before Patrass, to the blockade of which place, General Yatrako was to proceed with a corps of three thousand men, while another under Colocotroni, should occupy the passes between the Isthmus of Corinth and Livadia.

The legislative body proceeded to their new destination early in July, and were soon after followed by Mavromichalis, Colocotroni, Sotiri Carolambi, and Metaxa, as members of the Executive. The deliberations had only been carried on for a few days, under the Bishop of Bresthene, as vice president, when it was plainly perceived that the military chiefs merely wanted to make the representatives of the people the blind instruments of their ignorance and caprice. This state of things soon led to an open breach, which ended in a determination on the part of the former, to throw off the mask at once, and establish a government of absolute force, without any regard to the law of Epidaurus, confirmed as it was by the national will at Astros. Thus shackled in their patriotic labours, it was resolved that the Executive should be left to itself, while the members of the legislative assembly transferred its sittings to Cranidi, a village of the Morea, in the vicinity of Hydra and Spezzia. On reaching Hydra, and conferring with the Primates of that island, Mavrocordato found them highly indignant at the conduct of the refractory chiefs of the Peloponnesus, and ready to support the legislative assembly in maintaining the constitution, and carrying on the war. Having extended his enquiries, it appeared that the sentiments of the Hydriotes were warmly participated in by the whole population of the Archipelago. The utmost cordiality being thus established between the legislative body and the islands, the naval operations were conducted with as much spirit as at any former period of the contest. Besides, the fleet of observation sent to cruise off the Dardanelles, and on the coast of Asia Minor, a squadron was placed at the disposal of Mavrocordato, who repaired to Messolunghi, in obedience to the repeated applications of the leading inhabitants there, to assume the government of western Greece. Although a great part of the troops who had been sent to the blockade of Patrass, were forced to disperse, owing to the severity of the season and an epidemic disease that carried off numbers; those who remained, prevented the Turkish garrison from leaving the walls. A large division had been dispatched to Negropont, under Odysseus, who invested Carysto, the key of that important point, when a Turkish squadron, taking advantage of the absence of the Ipsariots, whose fleet co-operated with the troops on shore, came to its relief, and obliged the Greeks to retire.

The legislative body had not been assembled many days at Cranidi, before it was determined to declare Mavromichalis, Colocotroni, and Metaxa, as well as their adherents, enemies of the state. This necessary measure was followed by the nomination of another Executive, of which Georgius Conduriotti, of Hydra, was elected president. One of the first measures of the new government was to adopt the most vigorous means of putting down the anti-patriots, the epithet by which the factious chiefs and their followers were now designated. A corps of Cranidiotes were sent to blockade Napoli di Romania, in which Colocotroni had placed his son, Pano, ever since its capture, without admitting the troops of the government, and in defiance of repeated orders to give up the fortress. Instead of proceeding to the passes as had been settled, he repaired to Tripolitza, where it was attempted to establish a government totally distinct from that of Cranidi. Andreas Lundo, Primate of Vostitza, was therefore sent at the head of another corps to reduce that place. With respect to the legislative assembly, it removed to Argos in the beginning of April, while the members of the Executive established themselves at Lerna, now called the Molini, about six miles from the former city, and situated so as to admit of an easy communication with a squadron under Miaoulis, which blockaded Napoli by sea.

Such was the state in which I found the affairs of the confederation on reaching Zante. To those who were unacquainted with the real nature of public opinion in Greece, the above state of things might have appeared too unsettled to justify the immediate transfer of the loan. Knowing, however, that the great mass of the nation, including its most distinguished and enlightened patriots, were united against a mere faction without talent or numbers; recollecting also, that no preparations had as yet been made for opening the campaign, I felt satisfied that no time should be lost in strengthening the hands of the legitimate government. Hence the anxious solicitude with which I urged Colonel Stanhope to repair to the seat of government if not already there, and adopt immediate measures for effecting the transfer. On conferring with Messrs. Barff and Logotheti, their opinion coincided so exactly with my own, that they immediately addressed a letter to the contractors of the loan in London, communicating their determination to give up the money confided to their charge, on the requisition of the gallant colonel and Lazzaro Conduriotti, justifying their conduct on the necessity of the case, and the fact that those who made the arrangements in England, could not have contemplated the death of Lord Byron.

While in hourly and anxious expectation of

letters from the Colonel, accounts arrived which stated that he was attending a meeting convened at Salona, for the purpose of adopting measures of defence for eastern and western Greece, and would be at Zante in a few days. He arrived on the 12th of May, and having had a conference with Barff and Logotheti on the subject of delivering up the money in their hands; the result is so fully detailed in the Colonel's correspondence with Mr. Bowring,* that it only remains for me to state the part I was induced to take on the occasion.

Perceiving that Messrs. Barff and Logotheti had now changed the determination they had formed about giving up the money in the first instance, I could not, after the communications received from Prince Mavrocordato, representing the state of western Greece, and indeed of the whole confederacy, as most deplorable, avoid doing every thing in my power to obtain, at least, some portion of the funds I had brought out; if therefore, the language adopted in my note of the 16th of May to the gallant colonel, should be thought strong, it arose from a conviction that there was no exaggeration in the Prince's statements, and a presentiment that the detention of *all* the money, might lead to some dreadful catastrophe.

Here it should be observed that, as if some in-

* Vide Greece in 1823, page 206, *et passim*.

explicable fatality attended the whole of our wishes, a proclamation issued by the Provisional Government, in which Zante and Cerigo were inadvertently named as the depots for the future instalments of the Greek loan, had no sooner reached the knowledge of the Ionian government, than, as might have been foreseen, it elicited another, by which it was declared that the transfer of the money sent to Zante, would be regarded as a high breach of neutrality, and consequently expose the offenders to all the pains and penalties awarded in an edict promulgated by Sir Thomas Maitland, in 1822. Thus it was, that there was no possibility of extricating a farthing of the loan, while a formidable expedition was preparing at Alexandria, the Turkish fleet actually at sea, and an army of sixteen thousand men marching on Salona, destined to cross over to the Morea, and co-operate with the troops of Mehemet Ali.

Every hope of accomplishing the object which induced me to leave England at a time when, from the nature of a previous engagement with the public, I was by no means prepared for the voyage, being now at an end; it only remained for me to address a letter to Colonel Stanhope, expressing my sentiments both with regard to the loan, and one or two other points on which we were somewhat at issue. In addition to this communication, I wrote to my friend Mr. Bowring, as Secretary of the Greek Committee, in which, after explaining my own views as well as those of the best informed Greeks at Zante, I stated my determination to proceed to the seat of government at once, there to suggest such means of providing for the exigencies of the crisis, as circumstances might admit.

Such was the situation of affairs in western Greece, but more especially at Messolunghi and Anatolico, that Prince Mavrocordato found it necessary to dispatch M. Meyer, the Editor of the Greek Chronicle, with an earnest entreaty that I would join him in the first named place without delay. Being quite ready, I embarked in the Greek boat which brought M. Meyer over, on the evening of the 28th of May, accompanied by Mr. Hesketh, a young English Philellene, who had come to Zante with the body of Lord Byron. Having, however, in consequence of his repeated solicitations, promised to visit Sessini, the Primate of Gastouni, for the purpose of conferring with him on the state of his province, we steered for Chiarenza with a view of landing there on our way. Being driven to leeward by a strong north westerly breeze, we were obliged to take shelter in a small cove called Gliffa* within three leagues of

* Besides affording good shelter to coasting vessels, during the strong north-west winds which prevail in this part of Greece for nearly two-thirds of the year, Gliffa possesses a fine spring of fresh water. By a singular coincidence very rarely met with, this actually bubbles up so near the sea, as to be frequently covered by the surge.

Gastouni. Having sent an express to the town informing Sessini of our arrival, we established a bivouac on the beach, there to await his answer. On receiving my note, the old primate immediately dispatched his son, Chrisanthus, a fine young man, who has been honorably distinguished during the war, with an escort of a hundred men, most of whom were well mounted, to welcome our arrival in Greece, and conduct us to the town. He was also accompanied by the Prefect, Andreas Calamoudarti, an excellent patriot, and formerly one of the Primates of Patrass. After the first salutations were over, we mounted some superb chargers, brought down for our accommodation, and proceeded to the convent of St. Eleusis, it being too late to reach Gastouni before dark; and in compliance with the wishes of Sessini, who felt anxious that our entry into the town should be as public as possible. While riding through this part of the coast, which is extremely wild and beautiful, frequent volleys of musquetry were discharged by the escort, as when they first approached us on the beach, this being a common practice whenever the Greek soldiery are desirous of honouring any new visitors.

We reached the Convent about nine in the evening. It is romantically situated in a deep glen, surrounded on every side by lofty hills, and, like all the religious asylums of the Morea, is so constructed as to serve as a place of defence as well as devotion. The form of these buildings is generally square, there being no communication except at the grand entrance. The gates were thrown open by two monks with long beards and rosaries suspended from their girdles. On entering, the first object which attracted our attention was the shrine of the saint, a small structure of the middle ages, and round which the spacious casements of the Convent seemed to have been raised at a much later period. A number of women were busily occupied under a fine group of fig and walnut trees that rose in the centre of the court yard, in preparing supper. We also observed a large flock of sheep and goats attended by some peasants, who appeared to have retired within the walls for the night. On alighting, we were ushered up to the balcony of the Superior, who happened to be absent. Having taken our seats on carpets spread for the occasion, pipes and coffee were served till the hour of supper should arrive. This interval was filled up with a long conversation, during which I had to answer innumerable questions as to the state of public feeling in Europe with regard to the Greek struggle;—whether they had any hopes of aid from the Christian potentates,—and various others of a similar tendency. While many deplored the apathy hitherto manifested, the whole party were unanimous in their expressions of gratitude to those British capitalists who had contributed to a loan, from which they looked forward to the certain triumph of their cause.

Supper was announced soon after ten o'clock; it was served in a room adjoining the balcony, and consisted of the usual dishes of pilaf, a capital preparation of rice and fowls well spiced, boiled mutton and *paramaisto,* or in plain English, a lamb roasted whole, stuffed with a variety of ingredients, among which almonds, raisins, rice, and garlic, were the most predominant. This is indeed considered by many good judges as one of the greatest luxuries furnished by the culinary art, either in Greece or any other country. Though the wine was strongly impregnated with rosin, a practice continued from the earliest ages by the Greeks, it did not prevent us from drinking many bumpers, as well to the cause of the cross as to its friends and supporters all over the world.* Having passed a most jovial evening, we retired to our respective couches, which were laid along the floor of the balconies and in the unoccupied cells of the monks; while the soldiers, who had also been liberally regaled, betook themselves to their Albanian capotes, and lay down in the open air, with stones for their pillows.

Being anxious to visit Castel Tornese, which was only a few miles out of the road to Gastouni,

* In giving an account of the modern Greek repasts, I ought not to omit noticing the practice of consulting the blade bone of the victim, which being divested of the flesh, is handed round and examined by each of the party, who decide the fate of the campaign according to the marks they happen to discover on this novel source of divination.

we rose at day-break, and after attending mass in the chapel, mounted our horses again. On leaving the Convent and ascending a winding path on its northern angle, Calamoudarti pointed out a spot from which it was attacked in the first days of the Revolution, by a large body of Turks, who were beaten off and forced to retreat, by the monks and about seventy Greek peasants who had taken refuge there with their families. As on the preceding day our road, or rather pathway, led through a rich and interesting country, of which only a small portion was cultivated, but we passed numerous flocks, and reached the castle at six o'clock. Tornese stands on a commanding eminence, directly opposite to Zante. It is a gigantic work, raised by the Venetians, and though now very much dilapidated, must have been impregnable in its day. On gaining the battlements, we enjoyed one of the finest prospects in Greece. To the west, an immense expanse of sea, studded with several of the Ionian islands, spread before us. Looking towards the east, we plainly descried the Gulph of Lepanto, between which the rich and beautiful plain of Gastouni intervened. The range of mountains, including those of Arcadia, Calavrita, Acarnania, and Epirus, which bound a great portion of this splendid amphitheatre, is perhaps unequalled in any part of Europe, for the variety of its contour and picturesque effect.

The principal object of my visit to Castel Tornesc, was to ascertain from personal observation, whether, in the event of a landing being effected on the plain of Gastouni, by the expédition of Mehemet Ali, this point could not be advantageously occupied by the Greeks. Having satisfied myself that they possessed no adequate means of rendering it tenable, and that it would therefore be better to lay the adjoining country waste, and repair to the mountains, we set out for the town, and arrived there about noon. As we entered, the whole of the troops and a great part of the inhabitants came forth to greet our arrival; as to Sessini, he received us with open arms, and seemed to be highly gratified by the visit. A long conference ensued, in which the old man drew a melancholy picture of his own wants and those of the province. I told him to be of good cheer, and adhere to the government, to which, I assured him, the money deposited at Zante would soon be transferred.

After a repast which only differed from that of St. Eleusis, by its being served up in the European style instead of the small round table raised about two feet from the floor, so generally used in Greece; the General proposed that we should accompany him in his evening's walk through the town, to which we readily assented. Gastouni is built near the southern extremity of the plain, the town is large, but owing to the ravages of the war, during which it has been frequently given up to fire and sword, the present population does not exceed eight thousand souls. When the contest ceases, and commerce begins to flourish, it would be advisable to select a more eligible position; this will be easily found on the heights near Chiarenza, which are admirably calculated for becoming the site of such a place. Should this plan be realized, Gastouni could not fail to become both prosperous and opulent. Its plain, extending forty miles in length to the walls of Patrass, and varying from six to fifteen in breadth, is one of the most fertile and productive tracts of land in Europe. It is watered by the Peneos, which descending from the mountains of Achaia, passes through a charming valley, in which the ruins of Elis the ancient capital are seen, and after meandering through the centre of the plain, join the Ionian sea near Gliffa. The eastern portion of the plain is watered by the Vergo and several minor streams. With scarcely a tenth part of this fine plain brought into cultivation, and a proportionately scanty population, yet is it from the district of Gastouni that Zante and Cefalonia are supplied with cattle, sheep, poultry, and various other necessaries of life. There are some valuable salt works, and a lagune on the northern shore of the plain, which supplies a large quantity of the finest fish. Independently of its numerous herds and flocks, the cultivated portion of the plain produces corn, maize, currants, wine, oil, flax, and cotton. But the riches of Elis are not confined to these productions alone. There is reason to believe that some valuable minerals exist in the vicinity of Castel Tornese; and, although the friends of Greece would much rather encourage the improvement of her agricultural resources, the time may come when it might be expedient to seek for more hidden treasures.

Anxious to prosecute my journey to Messolunghi, I reluctantly gave up my intended visit to the ruins of Elis and its neighbourhood, where Sessini assured me there are some very interesting remains to be seen, Having, however, heard that the heroine of Mistras, Costanza Zacari, to whom I had occasion to allude in my correspondence from the Morea last year, was residing in the town, I determined, while the horses were getting ready to ascertain something more of her history, and I was fortunately enabled to gratify my curiosity through the aid of a M. Baronzi, of Zante, who happened to be acquainted with her. We accordingly proceeded to the place of her retreat, a small cottage on the suburbs. On entering the wicket leading to it, I observed a very interesting looking young female sitting on the ground, and playing with a child who stood before the door. It was Costanza herself. On our approaching, she suddenly rose up, upon which Baronzi introduced me as the English traveller who had expressed a wish to see her, she immediately took my hand and kissed it in the usual manner of the Greek salutation towards those who are regarded as superiors, and after welcoming me to Greece, invited us into the cottage. Ascending a rugged staircase, we entered a room which, though it had no other furniture than some cushions and a carpet spread in one corner, was both neat and cleanly. Here, Baronzi and myself were asked to sit down, Costanza placing herself near us. She was dressed in the costume generally worn by the Greek women of the middling class ; her head-dress consisted of the small cap of white cloth, which merely covers the top of the head, round this she had tied a small blue and white handkerchief as a turban ; her hair, which is of a jet black, flowed in profusion over the neck and shoulders. Although the hardships to which she had been exposed, have tended to impair Costanza's personal attractions, it is evident to perceive, from her large dark eyes, still full of brilliancy and lustre, as well as the general vivacity of her features, that she must have been very fascinating. Being chiefly desirous of discovering the motive which first induced her to forsake the more natural pursuits of her sex, for the horrors and turmoil of a warlike life, she answered the question put to her on this subject, by saying, that her hatred to the Turks began with the loss of her father, who was put to death in 1813, by the Governor of the Morea.* And though very young

* Zachariah or Zacari, of Mistras, was one of the most formidable of those chiefs known under the name of *Klepthis,* with whom the Turkish tyrants of the Morea ever had to contend. His intrepidity and stratagem, had in fact become proverbial; enabling him to be for many years the terror of Cheli Bey and other Pachas. He left two sons, of whom one was killed at the siege of

at that time, she had ever after ardently wished for an opportunity of avenging his murder. There seemed, however, to be no prospect of gratifying this desire, for she became a slave in the family of a rich Turkish proprietor of Epirus, and was at Yanina when the Revolution broke out. It is probable Costanza might have continued an inactive spectator of the struggle, had not an incidental circumstance roused energies of which she was till then unconscious. Being in the habit of going to a public well, near the house of her task-master, which was also frequented by numbers of Greek women and children, Costanza witnessed such instances of violence and barbarity on the part of the Turks, that she was worked up to an excess of indignation, which could no longer be contained within ordinary bounds: she had contrived to conceal some money which was received from her relatives previous to quitting Calamata, the place of her former residence; having added the produce of a few trinkets to this, Costanza was enabled to form a Heteria, at the head of which, she proceeded to the passes of Macrinoros. It was among the precipitous crags of this dreary region

Napoli di Malvasia; the other, Zacharopulo, is the leader of an irregular band of Mainotes; and greatly distinguished for his bravery, he has also adhered steadily to the government. I saw this excellent young man very frequently during my stay at Napoli di Romania, and was particularly struck by the justness of his remarks and reflections on the state of his country. The wife of Nikitas, a very amiable woman, is also a daughter of the late Mainote chieftain.

that she encountered all the privations and sufferings attendant on the campaign, until the winter of 1822, when she was severely wounded. Thus disabled, for a time, Costanza passed over to Gastouni, whence, she soon after proceeded to Patrass, and was present in all the engagements which took place under the walls of that place in the following campaign. A second and still severer wound, received while in the act of levelling her musket at a party of the Turks who had made a sally from the town, and with whom the advanced posts were closely engaged, obliged her to return once more to Gastouni, where she had remained ever since, and was as yet, in a state of convalescence; on asking what her future intentions were, she replied that, as there were still so many enemies of her religion and race in the Morea, she could not reconcile herself to withdrawing from the war while a Mahometan remained unsubdued, and in the hope of being able to return to her post, she was preparing a more suitable dress of which we saw the half embroidered vest lying beside her. Having terminated the foregoing details, and collected some other facts relative to her family, I took occasion to observe, that however laudable the motive which induced her to fly to arms at the commencement of the struggle might have been, it was no longer either becoming or suited to her enfeebled state of health, to resume such a mode of life. She then said in a tone of great deference and submission, that her only wish was to see Greece freed from its oppressors, but that she would be guided by any advice we thought proper to give

Determined to take advantage of this disposition, and which I was by no means prepared to expect, I told her that some English ladies, who had heard of her devotedness to the cause, expressed a warm interest in her fate, and would, I was sure, be rejoiced to hear she had escaped so many perils; adding, that if she consented to relinquish her project of returning to Patrass, I should have no hesitation in affording her some trifling pecuniary aid, on the part of the Greek Committee, until something more permanent should be decided in her favour. On her acquiescing in this proposal, I requested that, as a proof of her sincerity, she would give up her arms; to this she also consented, though with evident regret; and going into an adjoining room, soon came back, with her musket in one hand, and a case of pistols in the other; the former, she observed, was loaded, and turning to the window, discharged it with the utmost dexterity, after which she handed it to me. Further enquiry enabled me to ascertain she was living very respectably with the family of an old chief. Costanza had been attended by a female ever since the time of her being wounded before Patrass; on presenting the latter to us, she said, "But for poor Maria Dudena, (this is her name,) I should have long since perished." The last topic on which we touched related to the propriety of her joining

Madame Nikitas and her brother. She said nothing would afford her more happiness; but the circumstance of their being separated at so early an age, and left without the protection of their parents, had most probably made them forget her, and they might also be angry with her for having given way to her enthusiasm in favour of her suffering country. I therefore promised to make a point of seeing them, and doing all I could to bring about a reconciliation, if necessary; adding my conviction that this would not be a matter of any difficulty. Having arranged a monthly allowance, which was to be paid in advance by Baronzi, I took my leave of Costanza, and on returning to Sessini's house, related what had occurred. The old man was loud in his praises of the heroine of Mistras, and said he was convinced her fearless conduct in the field had often produced the most salutary effects on the soldiery, by whom she was implicitly obeyed, and even considered as one inspired; for she was always foremost in battle, and had given numberless proofs of intrepidity. I ought not to close this sketch of Costanza Zacari, without observing, that though finely formed, she is rather of a slight and delicate frame, and has not yet attained her twentieth year. Both Baronzi and myself were particularly struck by the unaffected simplicity and the precision of her replies to all our questions, as well as the extreme modesty of her general demeanour. The impression left on our minds by the interview was, that had this extraordinary young woman been destined to occupy a more elevated station in society, and possessed the advantages of a liberal education, she would have displayed talents of the very highest order.*

Having repeated my injunctions and advice to Sessini, that he would in future adopt a less tortuous system with regard to the government, as chosen by the representatives of the people, for his conduct had hitherto been doubtful and wavering, I left him, with a promise of doing my utmost to liberate the money which he regarded as a panacea to all the evils of Greece, while, on his part, he made a number of the most patriotic professions, assuring me that he would dispatch Chrisanthus to assume the blockade of Patrass in a few days. Our escort, or, more properly speaking, guard of honour, was the same as before. Crossing the Peneos, which is fordable about two miles north of Gastouni, we had a very pleasant ride through vineyards, cornfields, and meadows, to Chiarenza, which is seven miles from the town. This is a small bay, where vessels take in their cargoes for

* Lest it should operate to the prejudice of Costanza, in preventing the extension of individual sympathy or benevolence towards her, I am bound to say, and I do so with considerable regret, that it has yet been imposssible to realize the hopes I had entertained with regard to her obtaining some more permanent proof of British generosity. I have, however, reason to believe, that in consequence of the communications I made to Zacharopulo and Madame Nikitas, she has been taken under their protection.

Zante and the neighbouring islands. The remains of the ancient port of Elis are close to it on the west, and might be easily restored, for the foundations of the mole are still perfect. Several ruins near the spot indicate that it was once a place of considerable importance, both in a military and commercial point of view.

Our felucca, which we had ordered round from Gliffa, being in readiness, we embarked on the afternoon of the 30th, accompanied by two gun-boats, which the prince had sent to convoy us across the gulph of Patrass, and reached Messolunghi at day-light on the following morning.* As the letters I received while at Zante had fully prepared me for the state of things in western Greece, it merely remained for me to confer on the best and speediest mode of remedying existing evils. Although Mavrocordato possessed no adequate means of marching troops to the frontiers, or indeed of placing the town in a state of proper security, the great source of uneasiness was derived from the Souliotes, so that our whole attention was now directed to the steps most likely to tranquillize those brave but insubordinate

* On landing, I was conducted to the very house in which Lord Byron died: the proprietor, a merchant of the town, offered me the room in which, but two months before, the lamented bard breathed his last. The melancholy associations inspired by a mere sight of it, were however such, that I declined his offer, and begged to be allowed to occupy any other part of the house in preference.

mountaineers. Without attempting to excuse the violence which had previously marked their proceedings, the misfortunes and sufferings to which both themselves and their families had been exposed, ever since the commencement of the struggle, certainly affords some palliation of their conduct.

More perplexed than I can describe, by the difficulties of my situation, and total inability to improve it, I was most agreeably surprised on the second morning after my arrival, and while conversing with the Prince, to hear that Lord Charles Murray had just landed from an Ionian vessel, and might be expected every moment to deliver some letters of introduction which he had brought. The messenger had scarcely made their communication before his Lordship came in, and presented his letters, together with some packets of which he had taken charge at Ancona, the place of his embarkation. I had heard of Lord Charles' arrival at Corfu; but could learn nothing which led me to suppose he intended to join the standard of the cross. As will be seen by one of the letters addressed to me by this amiable and lamented young nobleman, it seems that though sincerely attached to the Greek cause, his object in leaving England, was to complete a tour which he had commenced a few years ago, in Asia Minor, by traversing Greece; but he had too much virtue and sensibility, to witness such a spectacle as that now presented, unmoved,

Nor had this first interview proceeded long, before Lord Charles declared his readiness to co-operate in any way his services might be deemed useful. Nothing could be more opportune than the appearance of his Lordship at such a moment; for, as it afterwards appeared, no philhellene, who had hitherto joined it, possessed greater zeal, or talents more likely to be of general utility.

The prince lost no time in availing himself of the proffered services of Lord Charles. It being of infinite importance to tranquillize the Souliotes, and prevail on them to take the field, his Lordship was requested to join me in a mission to Anatolico for this purpose, and he immediately consented. As the particulars of our visit to that place and its result, including some miscellaneous matter, were communicated to a friend in London, a reference to the correspondence will render it unnecessary for me to repeat them in this place.

On our return to Messolunghi, we had the satisfaction of finding that a courier had arrived there a few hours after we set out in the preceding day, with despatches from the Government, announcing the total discomfiture of the anti-patriots. When the leading facts connected with this signal triumph, are coupled with the account I have already given of the origin of the dissensions in Greece, a tolerable notion may be formed on the subject. Those who reflect on the execrable system of rule established by the late oppressors of the Greeks, and their invariable plan of exciting hatred between the people, the more easily to govern them, cannot be so unreasonable as to expect, that perfect harmony could follow such a chaos of cupidity and crime ; and yet, the number of those who have opposed the people in their efforts, to establish a regular government, bears so small a proportion to the great mass of the nation, as to be really insignificant.

Having freely alluded to the errors of the government formed at Epidaurus, in not conciliating the captains, and traced the disasters which resulted from them, it is scarcely necessary to say, that I am far from approving the policy pursued towards men, without whose gallantry and perseverance, the revolution would neither have broken out, or succeeded in its object. What I blame in the conduct of the refractory chiefs is, that insatiable love of plunder and ambition to trample on the laws, which have characterised their proceedings as well as that of nearly all the Primates. Should these observations ever reach the knowledge of Colocotroni or Mavromichalis, a circumstance by no means probable, they will do me the justice to acknowledge, that not only in our personal interviews, but the various letters addressed to them by me, I invariably urged them to uffer inconveniences, or even oppressions, that could only be temporary, rather than oppose the representatives of the people; for in this they were only hurrying towards a precipice and destroying the edifice which they had themselves contributed to raise. How often too, have I reminded them that they should have some regard to the interests of their children, since, from the ordinary course of nature, they could at best only expect to appear on the scene for a very few years, whilst it could not be doubted that their crimes against the nation would be visited on their offspring and relatives. The result of their conduct will furnish the best justification of the counsels I ventured to offer, when there was still time to repair all the errors of the past. I can give no better proof of the strict impartiality in which I stand with regard to both parties, than in publishing the letter of Mavromichalis, in reply to one I wrote to him from Napoli di Romania, in July.*

One of the great objects of the anti-patriots was to prevent the negotiation of a loan in England, convinced as they were, that its success would at once destroy their means of perpetuating anarchy.

* My first care on recovering from the fever with which I was attacked after my arrival at Napoli di Romania, was to address two letters to Mavromichalis and Colocotroni, pointing out to them the ruinous consequences of their not coalescing with the government, and such other reasons as I thought most likely to bring about a reconciliation among all parties. The letter to

In order to dissuade the British capitalists from listening to the proposal of a loan, an emissary named Peruca, had been sent to Zante, before the arrival of the Florida, and thence proceeded to Corfu, in the hope of obtaining a passage to England in the Falmouth Packet. Owing, however, to some circumstances which transpired relative to the character of this individual, the authorities would not suffer him to land, and he was therefore constrained to pursue his way to Ancona. Nor had the money been many days landed at Zante, before a M. Flavianus, and who called himself the secretary of Mavromichalis, came there from Calamata, evidently with no other view than to persuade the depositaries not to give up any part of it, alleging that matters were not yet sufficiently arranged between the captains and government to justify such a measure. But from the failure of Peruca's mission, it may be readily imagined that the arrival of the first instalment was considered as a death blow to the refractory chiefs, who now felt that their only hope of success was in a last effort to obtain that by force, which they had failed to achieve by violence.

Colocotroni remained unanswered, but on my return from Athens, I found one from the Mainote Chief; it was delivered to me by my friend Panutzo Notará, a member of the Executive, and in the Hall of its Sittings; so that I instantly handed it to Conduriotti, the President, for his perusal. A literal translation of this letter will be found in the extracts of my Correspondence.

Accordingly, Nikitas, whose weakness of character rather than want of virtue or patriotism,* had induced him to listen to the insidious suggestions of Colocotroni, aided by Coliopulo, to whose military talents I had occasion to allude on a former occasion, succeeded in collecting an irregular band of armed men at the village of Cutzopodi, within a few miles of Argos, on the morning of the 17th of May, and began to advance towards that place, while another party sallied forth from Napoli di Romania, to dislodge the Cranidiotes, forming the blockade of the fortress, under General Scurthi. On hearing of this double

* The disinterested conduct and generous ardour shown by Nikitas, in the early stages of the revolution, gave rise to his being called the modern Aristides. Many traits which are related of him, seem to justify this high honour, while his bravery in the field has given him the appellation of *Turcophagus*. Nikitas is perhaps the only captain who has abstained from participating in any of the rich booty made during the war. His only trophies, are the arms which he may have taken from a fallen enemy: but even these have, on more than one occasion, been offered to the government in lieu of a subscription to the wants of the state. I shall only cite a single fact connected with this subject, and which occurred a short time previous to my first visit to the Morea. Having heard that the Turkish fleet was out, and threatening various points of the confederation, while that of his own country could not sail for want of funds, Nikitas sent a magnificently mounted sabre, which he had taken from the Pacha of Drama a fewmonths before, to the Primates of Hydra, begging they would dispose of it, and appropriate the money in aid of sending out the fleet. This generous trait produced effects which were but little contemplated by the donor. It electrified the Hy-

movement, Colonel Notara, nephew to the venerable Primate of Corinth, marched from Argos at the head of a large party, and accompanied by several members of the legislative body as volunteers. He soon dispersed the band assembled at Cutzopodi, many of whom came forward to implore pardon, alleging as an excuse for their conduct, that they had been inveigled by their leaders. As to the sortie from Napoli, it appeared that these who composed it only wanted a pretext for quitting the fortress, for the whole, with scarcely any exception, came over to the government. Nothing more was heard of the anti-patriot faction, until the 24th, the day of its final discomfiture. Here it should be observed, that the principal means possessed by the refractory chiefs of gaining partisans, were derived from their minis-

driotes; a subscription was immediately commenced; and the fleet sailed in a few days. Nikitas had probably forgotten an act which placed him on a level with the most celebrated hero of Greece, in her best days, when a messenger arrived with a letter from the Primates, in which, after expressing their gratitude for his late proof of patriotism and public virtue, also adding that their fleet was at sea, they requested he would take back his sword, as it could not be wielded by a braver soldier, or more generous patriot!

In alluding to the part which this chief has unfortunately taken with the anti-patriots, it should be observed that he is the nephew of Colocotroni, and probably indebted to him for frequent pecuniary assistance. The former fact was, however, the principal motive assigned by him for his conduct, when I saw him at Napoli, in August.

tering to the irresistible wants of those whom the Executive had been hitherto unable to pay, and consequently organize as regular corps. Thus it was that another armed band, hired in the small district of Presthiotos, near Mistras, by Mavromichalis and Metaxa, contrived to advance towards the Molini, where the members of the government continued for the convenience of keeping up a communication with the fleet, while Colocotroni marched on Tripolitza, not indeed with any hostile design, as he afterwards said, but to treat in an amicable manner with the Executive. Having, however, appeared at the head of a much larger force, than had been prescribed by the government, when it offered to treat with him a short time before, on approaching the walls, Andreas Lundo, who commanded there, refused to admit more than fifty of his followers; upon this, Colocotroni endeavoured to induce his men to force a passage, and some of them attempted to obey the order, but were repulsed and fled together with most of those who had come with the refractory chief. Thus abandoned, and without any hope of carrying his point, he had no other alternative but that of appealing to the clemency of the Government. This being accorded, Zaimis, the Primate of Calavrita, who had hastened to Tripolitza, on hearing of Colocotroni's approach, was associated with Lundo, for the purpose of receiving his submission. They were also fully authorised to adopt such measures as should prevent him from being again enabled to disturb the public tranquillity. The parties met on the 1st of June, when, after a long deliberation, it was agreed that the refractory leader, and those whom he had induced to abandon the lawful authorities, should retire to their respective provinces, and Napoli di Romania be immediately delivered up to the government. If some circumstances which I heard at Napoli, connected with this negotiation, be true, there is reason to fear that Lundo and Zaimis did not act up either to the letter of their instructions or the wishes of government; at all events, it is more than probable that if they had been less lenient towards the offenders, or even taken the precaution of retaining a few of them as hostages for the good conduct of the rest, there would have been an end to the fresh disputes which have since unhappily broken out.

With respect to the Prosthiotes, they came in sight of the Molini, fully expecting to be supported by a simultaneous movement on the opposite side; but, on advancing somewhat nearer, a discharge of grape from the ships of Miaoulis threw them into the utmost confusion, while a detachment under Colonel Cristo, sent out by the Executive, completed their discomfiture, Cristo having seized their leader, and took those, who could not escape by flight, prisoners. When brought before the members of the government, they followed the example shown at Cutzopodi, and solicited permission to renew their oath of fealty; from which they had been alone induced to swerve, by the emissaries sent to corrupt them from the refractory chiefs.

In addition to the above gratifying intelligence, the Prince received a copy of the law recently passed by the Legislative Assembly, relative to the appropriation of the loan, and which provided, that the whole amount should be exclusively employed in carrying on the war, without reference to former claims. The despatches proceeded to state, that, agreeable to the invitation of Colonel Stanhope, M. M. Xeno and Kalergi, two patriots of known integrity and talent, had been sent to Zante to confer with him and receive the money, as well as to deliver up the contract, which had been formally ratified. The despatches also contained a letter to myself from the secretary of the government, detailing the measures which had been adopted with regard to the loan, and calling on me to facilitate its transfer by all the means in my power. By referring to the correspondence, it will be seen with what anxiety this was looked for, as well as the disappointment occasioned by the delay that had already taken place. It having occurred to Mavrocordato, that my presence at Zante might be of use under existing circumstances, I did not hesitate to meet his wishes by offering to proceed there at once, and having embarked immediately, I reached that island the following day. On communicating with Mr. Barff, I found that Xeno and Kalergi had appeared off the town two days before, in a Hydriot schooner, but that owing to the regulations concerning neutrality, the captain was ordered away, so that he had no course left but to steer for Chiarenza, there to await the result of letters which were despatched to Messolunghi, where the two Greek commissioners heard I had proceeded. It being of the utmost importance to obtain permission for them to land at Zante, I lost no time in despatching a messenger, requesting that they would come over in one of the trading boats, and merely give their names into the pratique office, as merchants, not doubting that they would be thus enabled to come on shore. My hopes were soon realized, for on presenting themselves in the manner proposed, they were admitted and also allowed to enter the lazaretto, where they joined me on the next day.

On leaving Messolunghi, I anticipated the pleasure of finding letters from England at Zante, which would remove every obstacle with regard to the wished for transfer of the money. I was, however, totally disappointed. The consequences were such as might be expected. A long correspondence was entered into with the depositaries, and every possible effort made to convince them, that as they could not give up the loan itself, there would at least be no impropriety in accepting a guarantee offered by the Zantiotes, for as much of it as would enable the fleet to sail. It being impossible to carry this project into effect, there was now no resource left, but that of waiting the arrival of fresh instructions from London. It was while we were anxiously anticipating these, that a second instalment of the loan reached Zante. When the vessel on board which it had been sent out anchored in the bay, we all began to congratulate each other on the final end of our anxieties, what was our mortification and disappointment, on finding that this money had been shipped on the same terms as the former.

There being no immediate prospect of attaining the object of our wishes, while the want of supplies and pecuniary aid in Western Greece became hourly more urgent, I determined to make a last effort to succour this portion of the confederacy. Availing myself, therefore, of the friendly disposition manifested by three Greek merchants resident at Zante, and whose names I would most willingly record, if motives of prudence did not interpose, I prevailed on them to cash my bills on the secretary of the Greek committee, and had thus the satisfaction of sending ten thousand dollars to Messolunghi in the course of a few days. Trifling as this sum was, it not only enabled the prince to put the Souliotes in motion, but strengthen several points on the northern frontier.*

* I had, during my first stay at Zante, been able to procure, by giving bills, and, on my personal guarantee, a quantity of

As the permission of remaining at Zante, granted to Xeno and Khalergi, was limited, and our presence gave evident uneasiness to the authorities, we felt very anxious to depart, but could not get ready before receiving an intimation that we had exceeded the period, and must therefore quit the island within twenty-four hours. It was therefore settled that they should proceed to Gastouni, there to await instructions from the seat of government, while I returned to Messolunghi on my way to Napoli de Romania. On reaching the former place, I found Mavrocordato actively employed in preparing to open the campaign and assume the offensive. In consequence of a large body of Turks having made a sortie from Patrass, and ravaged a considerable portion of the plain of Gastouni, threatening the town itself, it was decided that five hundred Souliotes should cross over to Chiarenza, under Costa Botzaris, while the remainder, with Javella at their head, were to proceed in the direction of Salona. A large force had already advanced towards Arta, under Zonga, Macri, Rango, and Stornaris, the most distinguished chiefs of Acarnania.

It being of the utmost consequence that no time should be lost in urging the government to adopt some mode by which a temporary supply of money could be obtained, until the loan was

powder and flour, both of which articles were exceedingly scarce at Messolunghi.

transferred, and not less so, that all possible weight should be given to the mission having this object in view, the Prince felt extremely desirous that Lord Charles Murray should also proceed to Napoli, as his presence could not fail to increase confidence, and remove a great deal of the irritation produced by the unforeseen detention of the money at Zante. Ever ready to co-operate in any thing likely to promote the cause he had so generously espoused, Lord Charles accepted the proposal most cheerfully, and said, he was quite ready to proceed whenever the Prince thought proper. The loss of his lordship's services may be easily conceived from the nature of his occupations during the short time I was absent, for although little more than three weeks had elapsed, a lunette* had been raised at his expence and under his superintendence, which renders the town completely impregnable at least to a Turkish force; his Lordship had also prepared a translation of "Landman's Elements of Fortification" into modern Greek, with drawings executed by himself, besides devoting a considerable portion of each day to visiting the sick, of whom there were great numbers, and administering medicines to many.

Some arrangements being necessary before

* The privilege of naming the Lunette, being very naturally accorded to Lord Charles, he called it after one of his Scottish ancestors who fought and bled in the cause of national freedom.

we could set out, a part of the interval was devoted to attending the ceremony of consecrating a fort constructed for the defence of an important point called Procopanistos, situated on the edge of the Lagune near Anatolico. Lord Charles and myself accompanied the Prince there on the morning of the 28th of June. The Gondola, for so they deserved to be styled from their affinity to those of Venice, in which we were embarked, was followed by a number of others filled with clergy and military, also several of the Primates and other civil authorities of Messolunghi. The day was remarkably fine, and from its being a perfect calm, we proceeded with great velocity, the responsive chorusses and patriotic airs of the boatmen as we went along, greatly enlivening the scene, and often reminding us of the Venetian gondoliers.

On reaching the fort about nine o'clock, M. Cochini the engineer who was there to receive us, and had already displayed the national standard on the walls, fired a salute the moment we touched the shore. After a minute survey of the work, which seemed extremely well calculated for the object in view, that of preventing a disembarkation on the side of Anatolico, we crossed the wet ditch, and entered the fort itself. When all the party were assembled, Josephus, the officiating Bishop of Messolunghi, attended by a long train of ecclesiastics, sung Te Deum, and pronounced a prayer to the memory of Lord Byron. This part of the ceremony being ended, the Prince delivered an eulogium on the late benefactor of Greece, by enumerating the various acts of generosity which marked his too transitory visit to her soil, and concluded an eloquent harangue by giving his revered but lamented name to the new work, convinced that this designation, while it perpetuated the name of Byron, would animate those who might be called upon for its defence at any future period.*

On returning from Fort Byron, we landed at a small sand island nearly level with the Lagune, on which a fisherman's hut was raised; here some of the Prince's servants had repaired early

* On the day after our visit to Procopanistos, the venerable prelate who performed the ceremony of consecration, sent me the following attestation, with a request that I would give it publicity on my return to England.

"These are to certify, that on the 16-28th day of June, 1824, the undersigned proceeded to the new fort lately constructed at the fishery called Procopanistos, accompanied by the most reverend Economos, the reverend Andreas, and my deacon, Cyrillus, being all dressed in our episcopal and sacerdotal garments, and bearing with us the holy gospel and the cross.

In the first place, we sung a solemn Te Deum; I then, with head uncovered, addressed supplicatory prayers to Almighty God for the strength and safety of the fort, and for the success of those who may be hereafter called upon to defend it against the enemies of Greece. In the next place, I performed a funeral service to the manes of the lamented benefactor of my country, Lord Noel Byron. And lastly, as a tribute to his immortal memory, this important point was consecrated under the name of FORT BYRON.

"(Signed) the BISHOP ROGOU JOSEPHUS, of Thessaly."

in the morning and spread a tent, in which we found a collation of fish in great variety, both as to quality and cooking. A couple of hours being passed here, we proceeded to another fort, called Vasiladi, built at the entrance of the channel which leads to Messolunghi from the sea. This defence was constructed by order of the late tyrant of Yanina, and when completed, will be a point of great importance, as it protects the anchorage and might be easily converted into a naval arsenal as well as commercial depot. After viewing the works at Vasiladi, a fine sea breeze, which usually sets in at noon in the summer season, soon wafted us to Messolunghi, where we landed at five in the evening, after a most agreeable excursion.

Having in the course of a conversation with the prince, expressed my surprise at the novel mode of catching fish by means of divers, which excited our astonishment so much at Anatolico, he said there was another treat of a scarcely less interesting description in reserve for me, and which Lord Charles had frequently enjoyed during my late visit to Zante ; adding, that as we could not set out before the first of July, he would be happy to afford me an opportunity of judging for myself on the following evening. The prince alluded to the *Pyria*, or fishing by fire, as practised on the extensive lagune before the town, and which is noticed by the earliest historians of Greece. Orders having been given to the fishermen attached to his own establishment, to prepare their boats, two canoes, each about thirty feet in length, and very low, were brought to the door at nine o'clock, upon which the prince rose and invited me to follow him ; we embarked, and were soon seated on two cushions in the bottom of one of the canoes, while the pipe bearers kept close to us in another. On the canoes being put off from the shore, I observed that besides the gondolier at the stern, there was another man close to the prow, busily occupied in placing some dry chips in an iron cramp, that extended about eighteen inches from the prow; he soon after applied a torch to these, which immediately burst forth into a brilliant blaze. This was the signal for commencing, and in a moment more, I saw him stand on the very end of the prow, with a long trident raised in both hands, and ready to strike his prey. The canoe was now set forward with increased velocity, when, instead of being displaced from his position, the trident bearer not only remained, but began to use the instrument of death, and seldom drew it back without bringing up a large carp or bream, which he safely deposited in the canoe without ever moving from his place. On looking over the side, the water seemed teeming with the finny tribe, of which an infinite variety were darting under and about the boat in every direction. Whenever the blaze slackened, it was renewed by a fresh supply of chips. As we advanced towards the centre of the lagune, there were above fifty boats employed in the same way as ourselves ; nor would it be easy to describe the singularly pleasing effect produced by the canoes darting across each other, while some seemed to be running a race, and came so near, that we could often touch them as they glided past us. The darkness of the night added greatly to the general effect of this novel and interesting scene. On returning, after being out little more than two hours, we found that the quantity of fish taken, weighed above forty pounds ; a few of these being selected for supper, the rest became the property of the boatmen. In the conversation which followed at the supper table, I learnt from the prince, that the boats seldom returned with a smaller quantity than we brought back, but that the fish taken in this way, bore no proportion to those which are kept in preserves, of which there are a great number all over the lagune ; he added, that nearly two-thirds of the fish are appropriated to supplying the Ionian Islands, where they bring very high prices, owing to the excellence of their quality and flavour. As it is, the fishery of Messolunghi is a source of considerable revenue, but it is expected to become much more so in a very short time.

On the day preceding our departure, the Prince invited Lord Charles and myself to walk through the town, and visit the fortifications which he had caused to be raised after his memorable defence of

Messolunghi in 1822. These consist of a parapet, several bastions, and a wet ditch thirty feet wide by seven in depth. The whole of the works, which have placed this important point in a state of perfect security against any Turkish force that could attack it, were nearly completed, and rendered still more formidable by the Lunette already mentioned. Near the great entrance, the prince pointed out the tomb of Marco Botzaris. The remains of the modern Leonidas are laid close to a small church, which, by a singular coincidence, he defended with a handful of Souliotes, during the grand assault of Omer Vrioni's army, and when Messolunghi had no other defences than a ditch of six or seven feet wide, dry in most places, and a low mud bank raised about four feet from the ground. On returning to the prince's quarters,* we visited the seraglio, now converted into a

* The prince occupied one of the best houses in the town, and which had been given up for his use by M. Tricoupi, the chief Primate, and father to my valued friend, Spiridion, who represents his native place with no less integrity than talent in the legislative assembly. In naming the Primate, I regret to say that the news of his death reached Napoli di Romania some days before my departure in the Amphitrite. In him, Messolunghi has lost an excellent citizen, and Greece one of her most virtuous patriots. It is, however, gratifying to be able to add, that his place is likely to be well supplied by my friend, who is at once the most active and eloquent member of the legislature. He is a protegé of Lord Guilford, and does the highest credit to his noble patron.

laboratory and artillery depôt. Our last visit was to the printing-office of the Greek Chronicle and Telegraph. The novel spectacle of seeing a number of compositors employed, and two presses actively at work, for the purpose of disseminating the lights of truth and freedom, in a country whence they had been banished for eighteen centuries, could not fail to excite feelings and associations of the most gratifying nature.

The industry and enterprising character of the Greeks, in this part of the confederation, are strongly exemplified by the rapidity with which Messolunghi has been raised from its ruins, in the short space of two years. Besides a number of isolated houses built in different parts of the town, a new and spacious street, destined to lead from the great entrance on the land side, had been traced, and a considerable portion of it was completed at the time of my arrival. There is indeed little doubt of this place becoming an important commercial emporium at some future period. The adjoining plain, which extends from the magnificent promontory formed by Mount Chalcis, now called Verassova, to the head of the Gulf of Anatolico, a distance of more than thirty miles, though neither so rich or productive as that of Gastouni, is well cultivated, and presents a succession of large olive plantations, vineyards, and corn-fields. It has also the advantage of being bounded by a lofty range of mountains, mostly covered with oaks, pines, and other timber, that secure it from the northern blasts, which blow with great violence during the winter months.

Every thing being at length prepared for our intended journey, we took our leave of the Prince an hour before sun-set, on the 1st of July, accompanied by rather a large suite, and an escort of thirty soldiers. After riding along the plain at a gentle pace for about three hours, we bivouacked for the night, on the right bank of the Phidaris, the ancient Evenus, which enters the sea near the western base of Mount Verassova, and forms the eastern boundary of Acarnania. This fine river takes its rise in Thessaly, and meanders through one of the most wild and romantic regions of Europe. We crossed it a mile higher up, at four o'clock on the following morning, though not without some difficulty, as the stream was still both deep and rapid. An enchanting ride of four hours, winding round the northern declivity of Verassova, and overhanging the river, brought us to the valley of Kavroolima, the resting place. This is a charming spot, surrounded by mountains on every side, except towards the south, which presents a grand view of the gulph of Lepanto, bounded by the lofty range of Achaia, whose towering summits were still covered with snow. Here we were met by a fresh escort more numerous than the first, and commanded by Captain Zanganas, an officer of great merit, who had been for some time employed in blockading Lepanto to the west. Having been apprised of our coming, he had sent some of his men to procure refreshments, which they were busily occupied in preparing when we came up. Nothing could be more hearty than the welcome we experienced from Zanganas and his brave followers. They were posted on the roadside, and under the shade of an immense plane tree, which completely excluded the rays of the sun. While Lord Charles and myself were exchanging compliments and inquiring for news, we observed the soldiers cutting the herbs and shrubs which grew around us in great abundance, with their attaghans; several bundles of these were soon formed into separate couches, upon which we were invited to repose ourselves until the dinner was ready. Each couch consisted of a thick substratum of green fern, covered with the leaves and branches of the judas tree and rododaphne in full flower. It would indeed be difficult to conceive a more luxuriant or odoriferous bed than is thus formed in the course of a few minutes. After indulging an hour's nap, we rose and proceeded instinctively to the scene of culinary preparation. It lay in a dell covered by the impenetrable shade of several plane trees, as large as that under which we had just reposed, and was washed by a rivulet of delicious water. A whole sheep and a lamb were turning on each side of a huge fire formed by decayed branches of the planes; and while looking on, a soldier came up, bearing a ramrod, upon which the hearts, livers, and entrails of the victims were roasted, having been previously well seasoned with rock salt. This is always presented to the guests in Greece before the main repast is served, and considered a great luxury. Nor could we imagine, how a portion of the animal, which is thought so lightly of in other countries of Europe, can become a rich treat in the hands of the Greek soldiery. The process of roasting is no less simple than efficacious with these untutored cooks. It is usual for the shepherds from whom an animal is bought, to kill and dress it, an art in which they are remarkably well versed. When the sheep is prepared, a stake is passed through it; this being placed on two short pieces of wood with grooves, and stuck into the ground, a soldier turns the rustic spit, while another attends to the fire. The process of roasting being complete, the spit is borne off, and placed against a tree for the purpose of carving, which is performed with the greatest precision by the captain, and invariably with his attaghan. As each joint is severed, it is placed on a table usually formed by branches of myrtle, orange, and laurel. In addition to the leading dishes, we were regaled with two large firkins of giagurte and caimaki—the first, composed of coagulated sour milk, and the latter of sweet clotted cream. The ceremony of carving being completed, a distribution of the joints followed, and we sat down with our host Zanganas, while the attendants and muleteers joined the soldiers' party. In the conversation that followed a repast, at which neither food nor appetite were wanting, we were entertained with a variety of anecdotes illustrative of the war in Etolia, and more especially concerning the blockade of Lepanto, which has been sustained by the Greek soldiery, under privations and hardships, that must long since have appalled men who were not engaged in a struggle for freedom and national independence. During a period of eighteen months, in which our host, Zanganas, had occupied different points round the Turkish fortress, he assured us that his men had never demanded a farthing of pay; that they were frequently without capotes or shoes, and sometimes for whole weeks without bread, forced to subsist on meat and such roots as they could pick up in the fields or on the mountains.*

We set out again at three o'clock, this being the hour at which the sun begins to lose its more scorching power, and leaving the valley, continued to ascend the remainder of the day. Our road lay through a mountainous district, thickly covered with trees and shrubs of various hues and dimen-

* A corps which was employed to invest Neo-Patra, in 1823, being unable to procure any corn for some weeks, tried many substitutes, until they at length began to employ fern roots, which were found to yield more nutriment than any other succedaneum. Captain Zanganas, who had often partook of this new species of bread, describes it as being very palatable.

sions, and followed the course of the Phidaris, whose meanderings were frequently seen to the left, and gave a peculiar charm to the landscape. It was just as the sun began to gild the western horizon, that we reached the highest point of this day's journey. The prospect on every side which now presented itself, was by far the most striking and magnificent I ever beheld, possessing all those attributes of sublimity and grandeur, to which neither poet nor painter could do justice. On looking back in the direction we had been travelling, the gulf of Lepanto and mountains of Achaia were seen far to the south; to the west we saw the Arcadian range, plain of Gastouni, Castel Tornese, Zante, Cefalonia, and Ithaca, with the distant windings of the Phidaris and Messolunghi for a middle ground. Towards the north, the beautiful lake of Vrachori bounded by the heights of Macrinoros and the Acroceraunian range engaged our attention, while Pindus and Ossa rising in all their picturesque glories, were lost in a mass of silvery clouds to the east. The middle ground in this direction was different from the other; it consisted of a thickly wooded country, with here and there a village or ruined Acropolis built on the pinnacle of a rock, or overhanging inaccessible precipices. After gazing with mute astonishment and admiration on this grand spectacle of nature, till the mists of evening began to gather round us, we again pursued our way, and descending through a dense wood for two hours more, did not reach our second day's bivouac, also close to the Phidaris, before it became quite dark. Being excessively fatigued, from our ride laying over a very rugged path-way, we were glad to spread the carpets at once, and seek refreshment rather from sleep than supper.

Rising before the sun, we had not proceeded far before we met the prefect of Lidoriki, who had been informed of our approach. He came to offer his services, and expressed a hope that we were satisfied with our escort. From the shortness of his stay, and an air of mystery which seemed to attend his replies to several questions which we asked relative to the blockade of Lepanto, we suspected that he knew something more than he wished to communicate. Though the scenery of this day's ride did not by any means equal that already described, either in beauty or grandeur, yet it had its attractions. Like the former, it was full of contrasts, being sometimes through smiling vallies, in which the oleando, lachenaria, phylareas, arbutus, wild mastic, and myrtle, of an unusually large size, obstructed the road at every step, while at others, it led us over rocks and precipices so destitute of vegetation, that they seemed to be the result of a recent volcano. Our noon-day bivouac lay on a spot of this description, which formed a terrific contrast with the lovely scenery of Kavrolima. Nor was its natural gloominess much improved by a piece of intelligence which two soldiers, who arrived soon after we alighted, came for the express purpose of communicating to Captain Zanganas. They had been dispatched from the force blockading Lepanto, on its eastern side, to collect all the troops they could find in the neighbourhood, for a very obstinate rencontre had taken place on the preceding day between a party of Greeks, under a chief named Triandophilos, and a large body of Turks, who made a sortie from the castle, in quest of forage and plunder. As the messengers could not say whether the enemy had been beaten back, or was still in the open country, the circumstance of our not being more than two hours march from the scene of action, gave us some excuse for feeling a little alarm. Though this was evidently participated in by Zanganas, who felt most anxious to obey the call of Triandophilos, yet he told us not to indulge in useless fears, as there were enough of us to defy any force the Turks could send from Lepanto. Notwithstanding these consoling assurances, the remainder of this day's ride was not passed very tranquilly. The most remarkable part of the road was that which led us through the celebrated forest of Calydon, on the skirts of Pelion and Ossa; it covers a very extensive region, and nothing can exceed the beauty of the timber, which consists principally of ash, elm, and oak of the largest dimensions, and admirably calculated for naval purposes. Some peasants whom we met informed us, that this fine forest is full of wild animals, among which, wolves, jackalls, rein-deer, roe-bucks, and the wild boar, are the most remarkable. On reaching the village of Velvinitza, where we again came in sight of the gulf, we heard that a Turkish flotilla, which had sailed from Patrass a few days before, was cruising between Vostitza and Trisonia, the point at which we proposed to embark for the first named place. Happening to find more abundant resources here than at our last bivouac, and being assured by the ephor, a venerable old chief who had passed his seventy-fifth year, that we had nothing to apprehend from the Turks, as they had been forced to retreat with great loss, the remainder of the evening was passed under a fine group of plane and walnut trees, in feasting and merriment, having previously attended mass in the church of the Holy Trinity, close to the spot. Among other national sports, we saw the phyrric, or war dance, uncommonly well executed by ten of the escort, that being the usual number. This singular dance, one of the most ancient in Greece, and which does not seem to have experienced the smallest variation, is performed by the dancers forming a line and joining hands. It commences by one of the party singing a species of hymn, and leading off in a slow and measured style, which is at last converted into the most humorous and grotesque gestures, in which all the ring join, until it becomes a tumultuous orgie. Upon the whole, the phyrric dance is highly entertaining, and must be well calculated to give buoyancy to the spirits, as well as keep up the martial spirit, which it was doubtless intended to create by the inventor. With respect to our repast at Velvinitza, it differed very little, either in the quality or mode of its being served up, from those which Homer describes in the first book of his immortal epic, more than three thousand years before.

Although we were not entirely free from some perplexing thoughts as to the best line of march to pursue, for many alarming reports were in circulation; this did not prevent us from sleeping very soundly, and every scruple having vanished with the rising sun of the following morning, we set out at the usual hour, with a determination to take events as they might come. A ride of two hours on the side of a deep ravine brought us to the banks of the Morno, another rapid stream. Here it was that our friend Zanganas took his leave to resume his station before Lepanto, having been relieved by another officer and party, who waited for us on the opposite side of the river. We separated on the best possible terms; and, what does not always occur between travellers and their escorts, we were perfectly satisfied with each other.

There was nothing very striking in the local scenery after we passed the Morna, but this was amply compensated by a fine view of the gulf, including the castles of the Morea, Lepanto, and opposite shores of the Peloponnesus. The evening's ride brought us to the heights of Klima, where our bivouac was established on a terrace which overhangs the waters of the gulf. The prospect from this spot, comprising a great part of the gulf and the surrounding mountains, was scarcely less interesting than any we had hitherto witnessed, and we had the double advantage of surveying it as the sun was setting in great brilliancy, and by a placid moon, which rose soon after dark.

A lofty pinnacle within little more than a mile of our bivouac, had been recently fortified, and made the head quarters of the military commander of Venetico. On seeing us approach along the coast, the soldiers appeared looking towards us from their rudely constructed battlements; and we soon after heard the discharge of several vollies of musketry, intended as a mark of honour for the strangers. Our horses, however, were scarcely unloaded when a party was seen descending from the heights, and coming towards us; it consisted of the aid-du-camp and secretary of Captain Triandophilos, who came to welcome our arrival, and inform us that the chief would himself wait on us the next morning. He accordingly came about five o'clock, accompanied by a number of his officers and soldiers. This visit was quite unexpected; but he accounted for his absence from before Lepanto, by saying that, being convinced he had given the Turks a lesson which would prevent their making another sortie for some time, he had returned to his head quarters, for the purpose of despatching a part of the troops to join the commander-in-chief, General Dimo Scaltza, on the frontier near Nea-Patra. From the details he gave us of the skirmish which took place two days before in the plain of Lepanto, it appeared that there were not more than a hundred and fifty Greeks opposed to above five hundred of the enemy, of whom the greatest number were cavalry ; yet were they put to flight with a loss of sixty killed, besides a number of wounded ; while the loss of Triandophilos did not exceed seven. We were much struck by the expressive physiognomy of this chief, as well as his conversation, which was both dignified and sensible. His whole ambition seemed to be that of seeing the christian standard floating on the walls of Lepanto. He expressed a hope that the government would soon place such means at his disposal, as should enable him to achieve an act to which he looked as the reward of all his labours ; for he had been more than two years constantly before that fortress, or in its immediate vicinity. The modest strain in which Triandophilos spoke of actions that have made him the admiration of his soldiers, as well as the natural elevation of his sentiments, while speaking of the Greek struggle, made a deep impression on our minds, and we left him with an assurance that both the wants of the troops, and his own distinguished merits, should be represented to the government. It may not be irrelevant to add, that this promise was fulfilled after our arrival at Napoli de Romania.

I omitted to state, that on reaching Klima, a part of the Turkish flotilla was pointed out to the eastward of Vostitza, having been blown farther up the gulph, by a strong westerly wind that prevailed during some days; we therefore hoped to reach Trisonia and cross over, before they could resume their station to obstruct the passage.

We had only about ten miles to proceed from Klima along the shores of the gulph: the road presented a constant variety, as we sometimes found ourselves on a fine beach and at others on high promontories. The gulph in this part seemed to be abundantly stocked with fish, of which we saw large shoals at every step. The appearance of the enemy, seemed, however, to have frightened away all the fishermen, as we did not observe a single boat on the water. We arrived at Trisonia about noon. There is scarcely a vestige of the town remaining, nor does the plain, which rises gradually from the gulph, till it is encircled by an amphitheatre of lofty mountains, show any great marks of cultivation. There is an excellent harbour here, formed by a small island, between which and the Continent, vessels of any size may freely pass. The port is sheltered from all winds, and would contain a large fleet.

Lord Charles, to whom all the classical associations of Grecian history seemed quite familiar, reminded me as we descended the hill that led into the ruined village of Trisonia, that it was the Trœzene of antiquity, whose inhabitants afforded such an hospitable asylum to the fugitive women and children of Athens, when that city was threatened by the unwieldy army of Xerxes.

On entering a small hut close to the beach, where several boats were drawn up, we understood that the Turkish flotilla were only six miles farther to the east in a small bay called Vidrinitza, and that the guns we then heard, were discharging by them against a village which they wished to destroy, but that a party of Greeks occupied a height near the spot, and would not suffer the infidels to land. On asking whether it was possible to hire a boat, our informant replied, that not one of the men who usually plied the passage would venture across, as two of the Turkish vessels were then in sight. Having afterwards questioned the parties themselves, we found them quite inflexible; nor was it till late in the evening, and when the enemy had disappeared, that we succeeded in prevailing on one of the boatmen to take us over. The breadth of the gulph at Trisonia is not more than twelve miles; and as the wind happened to be quite fair, we got over in less than two hours. Having landed on a fine beach, we were joined almost immediately by Demetrius Adomopholis, the Eparch, and friend of Lundo. A ludicrous incident occurred soon after we disembarked: it being quite dark, for the moon had not yet risen, a bugle which we brought from Messolunghi was no sooner sounded, than a report which spread among the inhabitants of the town that a Turkish boat had effected a landing, gaining ground with the rapidity of lightning, an alarm was instantly given, and in less than ten minutes we saw flashes and heard volleys of musketry in every direction: several hundred armed men also rushed down to the spot; nor was it without some difficulty that the Eparch convinced them we were friends instead of enemies. As to Adomopholis, he begged that we would consider all this needless firing as a salute intended to welcome our arrival.

Vostitza is very beautifully situated; and at the western extremity of a plain, sixteen miles in length, and varying in breadth from six to ten. Nearly the whole of it is devoted to the culture of currants, and may be regarded as one of the most productive tracts in the Morea. With respect to Vostitza itself, such have been the frequency of the attacks it has experienced during the war, that scarcely a single house remains without exhibiting some signs of dilapidation. It however possesses so many advantages, that there is no doubt of its speedy resuscitation. With the exception of some tombs discovered a few years ago, and supposed from the gold and bronze ornaments found in them when opened, to have contained the ashes of Royalty; there are scarcely any vestiges of antiquity to be seen at this place. Its seventeen sources of the finest water in Greece, and which burst forth close to each other within a few yards of the sea, are, however, well worth a visit. The famous plane tree which rises to a height of more than a hundred feet on the beach near these fine springs, is also a great curiosity; the circumference at the base, exceeding forty feet, while its umbrageous foliage has often afforded shelter to a whole battalion of Greeks. A chapel, dedicated to St. Nicholas, has been formed in the hollow of the trunk.

We were lodged in the Eparch's house, and he did all he could to render our stay agreeable. Having discussed whether we should proceed to Corinth by land, or embark at the end of the plain, and thus save two days of a very fatiguing ride, the latter plan was decided to be the most prudent, so that our only difficulty was in hiring a vessel; this our worthy host promised to do his utmost to remove. He accordingly accompanied us on the afternoon of the following day, when we quitted the town attended by a numerous guard of honor, and after a very pleasant ride along the plain, whose southern side is bounded by a range of mountains, presenting the most fantastic and picturesque forms, we alternately passed corn fields, vineyards, and olive groves, and reached a small cove where the Eparch found some boatmen, whom, after a long altercation, he persuaded to receive us on board. We would have willingly remained another day to see Andreas

Lundo the Primate, and who was on his way from the seat of government; but our anxiety to reach Napoli di Romania, would not admit of any farther delay. We therefore addressed letters of congratulation to the general on his late triumph at Tripolitza, and took leave of Demetrius, full of gratitude for his attentions.

Being highly favoured by a fine breeze from the north west, we saw Corinth with its towering battlements at day light, and were soon enabled to descry the Temple of Neptune, as well as one or two Minarets, the only vestiges remaining of the numerous Mosques which lately formed the chief ornaments of the town. While we satiated our eyes with the truly magnificent spectacle of the Acrocorinthus and neighbouring scenery, we could not avoid the melancholy reflection arising from the desolation presented as we sailed along the plain, which seemed to be quite deserted, and its numerous villages all in ruins. On landing in a cove within three miles of the town, and which was formerly the commercial depôt and port, not a soul was to be seen; while the whole beach was strewed with the bones of men and animals, indiscriminately mixed together, and forming large heaps in different places. Although we lost no time in dispatching one of our attendants to the town for horses, it was with some difficulty they were procured, owing to nearly all the inhabitants having abandoned their dwellings a few days before, in the expectation that Dervish Pacha might send a part of his army across the Isthmus. The feelings inspired by a view of the desolate and gloomy scene we witnessed on the beach, were rendered still more acute as we approached the town. The whole way was also strewed with bones and sculls, of which those of our own species formed by far the greatest number. On entering the town, the first object that attracted our attention was the Palace of Kyamil Bey, the late tyrant, with its dilapidated wall and towers, of which but an inconsiderable part remained to point out the former scene of oppression and crime. Without attempting to describe all the contending emotions, to which this scene gave rise, I confess that on looking up towards the Acrocorinthus, and seeing the banner of the Cross waving over its walls, I could not refrain from involuntarily exclaiming, "There is a God! and there is retribution for his oppressed creatures!" *

My old and gallant friend Georgaki Kitzo, whose name appears more than once in my account of the revolution, was still in the command of the fortress. In addition to his having ordered a house to be prepared for us in the town, his secretary and aide-de-camp met us as we entered, and apologised for the General's not coming down to receive us—every moment of his

* From information received in the town, of which all the environs are covered with bones, the loss of the Turks in the neighbourhood of Corinth alone, cannot have been less than ten thousand men.

time being taken up in putting the citadel in a better state of defence: he insisted, however, on our coming to his own quarters, where every thing was ready for our reception. It being still excessively hot, we deferred our ascent till towards sun-set; while resting at the house, to which we were first conducted, we were agreeably surprised by a visit from Anastasius, of whose intrepid conduct on the banks of the Pruth I had occasion to speak, in detailing the operations in Moldavia. He had just arrived from Napoli di Romania with a detachment of four hundred men, and was going to occupy the Dervenachi, or Passes of Livadia, north of the Isthmus. I was much gratified at this unexpected meeting of a man, whose gallantry throughout the whole of Ipsilanti's campaign is still a subject of the highest panegyric in Greece. Anastasius is a gladiator in figure and countenance; though quite unlettered, he is evidently formed to command; and I could perceive from his conversation that, with the exception of his love of country, which seems to be the ruling passion, he indulged no thought or reflection which was not immediately connected with his profession. He appeared to be very popular with his soldiers, and was implicitly obeyed.

Previous to mounting our horses, in order to ascend to the Acrocorinthus, Lord Charles proposed that we should visit the Temple of Neptune, and another massive ruin, said to have been the residence of Lais, the celebrated courtesan of Corinth. The temple is finely situated, and commands a view of the gulph, extending beyond Salona on the north, and to Sycion on the west. There are not more than seven of the columns standing, and only five entire. The order is doric, and composed of fell-stone, which has suffered greatly from the ravages of time. There are numerous other ruins seen in different parts of the town, but all in a state of undistinguishable dilapidation. While going over them, Lord Charles observed on the singularity of there not being one solitary pillar of the most elegant architectural order, on the very spot whence it derives its name, and in which, as Dryden says—

> " All below is strength, and all above is grace !"

I replied, that by a scarcely less singular coincidence, the same observation applied to the raisins of Corinth, as we saw no appearance of vineyards, the whole of its extensive plain being either sown with corn, or covered by olive plantations, which extend for some miles on the western side of the town.

We reached the quarters of General Kitzo about six in the evening, and were honoured with a salute of heavy guns from the fortress. As to the General himself, he received us in the most friendly manner, and only regretted that the circumstances of the war prevented him from entertaining us in a different style. Our supper did not very materially differ from what we had seen during the preceding portion of our journey; but there was a much greater approach to comfort. The repast was also seasoned with some excellent wine of Samos. In the conversation which followed, there was scarcely a subject connected with the Greek revolution that we did not discuss. As our gallant host had been foremost in a hundred battles, none could be better able to give us valuable information on a great variety of occurrences.

Before taking our leave for the night, I adverted to a report circulated at Zante before I left it, and which stated that his sister Vasilica had been enabled to effect her escape from the house of the patriarch at Constantinople, where she is confined as a hostage, with several relatives and attendants. The General said he was sorry to be under the necessity of undeceiving us; she was still a prisoner, nor did he see any hope of her liberation, except through the interposition of Heaven; adding, that the flattering report originated in the conduct of an impostor, who had succeeded in extorting a large sum of money from himself, on a promise that he would extricate Vasilica, and convey her to Odessa. When I asked whether he had received any accounts of his own wife and children, a yet more tender chord was touched. Without, however, giving way to those feelings which this question must have awakened, Giorgaki informed us they were still at Valona, and in the hands of the Pacha of that district.* Lord Charles took a deep interest in this part of our conversation, and with his characteristic humanity, promised to write to the Lord High Commissioner of the Ionian Islands on the subject. The letter written by his Lordship soon after, from Napoli di Romania, and of which a copy will be found in the correspondence, does equal honour to his head and heart.

Though our stay was so limited, I determined to take advantage of it, and not depart without enjoying the grand view presented on every side from the Acrocorinthus. For this purpose Lord Charles and myself ascended a tower, on which the commandant has constructed a Kiosk. This rises to a considerable height on the western angle of the fortress, and affords a cool retreat in the summer evenings. The sun was setting in great splendour over Parnassus, just as we reached the station from which the manifold beauties of the surrounding scene were to be observed. There is something indescribably beautiful in a setting sun among the mountainous regions of

* Madame Kitzo, who is remarkable for her beauty, was taken out of a vessel bearing the Papal flag about two years ago, and while on her way to Corfu from Ancona, where she took refuge in the first year of the revolution. The letter addressed by Lord Charles Murray to Sir Frederick Adam, gives a list of those who were captured with this unfortunate lady.

Greece. Large masses of clouds generally rest on the summits of the highest peaks—these, varying in tint and form every instant, fill the mind with the most pleasurable sensations. I have frequently remarked that just before the God of day descends, the heavens in its vicinity appear as if in a state of conflagration, this effect continuing till long after its having sunk far beneath the horizon. Such indeed was the effect which we witnessed on this occasion.

The highest point of the Acrocorinthus being on the eastern side of the fortress, I rose at daybreak to gain a watch tower, whence I could enjoy the prospect to most advantage. Being favoured with a very clear atmosphere, I was enabled to trace objects for a distance of more than eighty miles on each side. To the south-east, I saw Salamis, Ægina, and the Piræus, bounded by mount Hymettus, while the gulph of Lepanto, Salona, and Parnassus occupied the opposite portion of the picture. The prospect to the east and west, consisted of lofty mountains, rising over each other in amphitheatric pride, many of their summits being covered with snow which never melts. Besides the grandeur of its situation, the Acrocorinthus is one of the strongest military positions in Europe, rising, as it does, above a thousand feet from the plain, and inaccessible on every side. Like all the fortresses constructed by the Venetians, the works are by far too extensive; so that, were it not for their magnificence and the veneration justly attached to a spot, to which so many glorious recollections are associated, it would, perhaps, be desirable that they should either be demolished altogether, or so reduced, that a few hundred men might be able to defend them. At the entrance, and in several other parts of the works, we observed that the ancient walls serve as foundations to those of the Venetians, by whom the Acrocorinthus was placed in its present state of repair.

As there is no part of ancient Greece in which arts and commerce flourished so much as at Corinth, it is doubtless destined once more to become a place of great importance. Nothing, indeed, can be better calculated for a grand central emporium of trade and manufactures. As an entrepôt, between the coasts of the Levant and Italy, by which a long and often dangerous navigation would be avoided, this place presents advantages that cannot possibly escape the future rulers of Greece. There is, perhaps, no situation in Europe so well adapted for the establishment of a great annual fair, like that of Leipsic, or Sinagalia.

We found the country between Corinth and Napoli di Romania much less interesting than we expected, until approaching the plain of Argos, it was neither so fertile or well cultivated as the same kind of soil in Acarnania and Etolia.

We stopped for a short time within six leagues of the Acrocorinthus, to survey the pass in which Nikitas so greatly distinguished himself in the summer of 1822, against the army of Drâmali Pacha, and when he destroyed above two thousand Turks, whose blanched bones are yet unburied, and strewed about the heights over which we rode. Previously to entering the plain of Argos, which is not inferior to that of Gastouni in fertility and extent, the walls of Mycene, the capital of Agamemnon, were seen on the left.

We entered the plain within five miles of Argos, and continued our route towards Napoli, eighteen miles farther to the south. This plain, like nearly all those of the Morea, presents a perfect level. It produces corn, maize, olives, wine, and fruit in great abundance; and also feeds numerous flocks and herds. The plain of Argos and its vicinity presents one of the most interesting sources of research to the antiquary, in any part of Greece; and whenever excavations can be made, I feel assured that the harvest will be most productive. The surrounding scenery is such as must afford equal delight and profit to the poet and painter. It is, indeed, impossible to conceive any thing that partakes more of the sublime and beautiful, than the sun setting over the grand range of mountains which rise to the north of the ruined citadel of Argos, as seen from the battlements of Napoli di Romania; a scene to which no description could do justice, or painter imitate.

Having sent an attendant in advance to provide quarters, we entered the gates of Napoli at noon, on the 8th of July, and were invited to take up our abode at the house of M. Coletti, a member of the Executive. We lost no time in presenting ourselves before the government. Our reception was of the most welcome description: besides the president and four assistant members, we found the whole of the legislative body in the hall; they had just been summoned to confer with the Executive, relative to the frightful catastrophe of Ipsara, from which ill-fated island, two deputies had that morning arrived to confirm the news of its destruction, and demand immediate succours.

It is almost needless to say that the above disastrous news spread general consternation, approaching to panic, among the members of the government and legislative body; its effect was not less acute when circulated among the people. If ever the patriots entertained a doubt of the final success of their cause, it was probably at this moment. As if, however, that Providence which had enabled Greece to triumph over so many difficulties, was still watching over her, the intelligence from Ipsara was accompanied by the announcement of two other events, which could not fail to afford infinite consolation to all parties.

These were the sailing of the fleet from Hydra; and arrival at Zante of a person sent out from England, with instructions to Barff and Logotheti, to deliver up the money deposited in their hands.

The great obstacle to the departure of the Greek fleet has always arisen from the inability of government to make the usual advances of pay to the seamen for the support of their families while absent. The capitalists of Hydra, and its sister island Spezzia, had made such frequent sacrifices in this way, that they were no longer able to continue them, and it is probable that the arrival of the money at Zante may have rendered them somewhat less inclined to do so. Thus it was, that although fifty ships were ready for sea soon after my arrival in the Ionian Islands, the necessary funds could not be procured to meet the demands of their crews. No sooner, however, had the catastrophe of Ipsara been made known, than the whole population of Hydra assembled at the port, and proceeding in a body to the convent where the local government meets, vehemently insisted on the primates, and other rich men of the island, coming forward, and that, by way of example, they had already made a beginning among themselves. This appeal was irresistible, the funds were instantly forthcoming; and from this moment up to the period of my quitting Napoli di Romania, the Greek seamen appear to have been animated by a degree of energy and spirit altogether unknown during any previous year of the war.

Having stated the object of our visit to the government, and received its thanks for the interest we took in the Greek cause, Lord Charles and myself returned to the apartments which had been kindly prepared for us by M. Coletti. The first object of our solicitude was to ascertain all the particulars we could of the attack on Ipsara. As these I am about to relate, were communicated by deputies, who had witnessed the event, they are probably the most authentic yet recorded relative to that direful tragedy.

It having been fully proved by the experience of the preceding campaigns, that nothing but the destruction of the naval power of Greece could ever enable the Porte to regain any part of its former ascendancy, the whole of its attention was directed to this point, so that, as stated in the letters I received from Prince Mavrocordato while at Zante, an attack on the naval islands was to form the primary object of the campaign.* For this purpose, a large naval and military force had began to collect at Mytelene early in April. Owing, however, to the slowness of their opera-

* Previous to the grand attack on Ipsara, a smaller armament had been sent against those islands which, without being very formidable, had been distinguished for their hostility to the Ottomans. At Scopolo, near the Gulf of Volos, the enemy was repulsed with great loss, and after several attempts to land. The infidels were, however, more fortunate at Cassos, a small island

tions, the Turkish armament did not complete its preparations before the latter end of May. The activity and boldness displayed by the Ipsariots during the contest, no less than their vicinity to the Dardanelles, made them singularly obnoxious to the Porte; nor would it have been prudent to leave such a formidable source of annoyance in the rear during the projected naval campaign. It was therefore determined that this island should be the first point of attack. Of all the naval islands, the military organization of Ipsara made it least vulnerable to the enemy. Besides the whole male population capable of bearing arms, amounting to nearly two thousand five hundred men, there was a corps of Albanian Greeks, and about fifteen hundred of the fugitives from Scio, formed into companies. Batteries had been constructed on every point of the island at which a landing was thought possible, and as very early information reached the local authorities, of the intended attack, every means within their reach were adopted to repel the assailants. The whole of the ships being recalled, their rudders were taken away, and a few Sciots placed on board to take care of them, in order that the seamen might

near the east end of Candia, which, like Ipsara, had acquired considerable wealth by the enterprising industry of its inhabitants. Here the Turks succeeded in effecting a landing; and though subsequently forced to retreat, they were enabled to carry off a large quantity of booty, and destroy several of the vessels which lay in the harbour.

be able to devote their exclusive energies to the defence of their native island. Besides the batteries, which were provided with ammunition and well manned, Cotta, a chief of Olympus, was posted at the most accessible point, though one at which it was not expected that any attempt would be made to land.

Aware that nothing but an overwhelming force could make any impression on the island, the Capitan Pacha's preparations were of the most formidable description. The Turkish fleet was descried from the heights on the 1st of June, in the forenoon : on approaching somewhat nearer, it was found to consist of two ships of the line, eight frigates, four corvettes, forty brigs, and nearly 200 smaller vessels fitted up as gun boats, and with mortars, a species of force which the enemy are said to have adopted at the suggestion of some of their friends comprising the foreign legations at Constantinople.

The whole of the ships and vessels were filled with troops, and it had indeed been communicated by a Greek resident at Mytelene, that not less than 24,000 picked men were embarked in the expedition.

The firing from the enemy commenced on the northern side of the island, at four in the afternoon, and was returned with considerable effect from the batteries ; it ceased on the part of the Turks about eight o'clock, after which they seemed to be retiring ; this did not, however, prevent the islanders from taking every precaution, and increasing the means of defence; the posts were visited, and all the leaders enjoined to be vigilant. It was while the inhabitants, placed for the defence of the town, fancied the enemy had in reality withdrawn, that numbers of the troops stationed in the remote points came rushing in, early the following morning, and stated that owing to the treachery of Cotta, the Turks had effected a landing in the night, and having divided into three columns, one of these was at that moment approaching the town. It appeared, on further inquiry, that the enemy contrived to disembark with such silence, that a large body of troops posted on a height not far from the spot, knew nothing of the circumstance until daylight, when, to their great astonishment, they beheld the Turks drawn up in great numbers on the neighbouring hills. While one of the divisions marched towards the town, the other two advanced to attack the batteries, and from taking them in the rear, they found very little difficulty in carrying them, and putting the Greeks to the sword. Those destined to attack the town did not reach it before noon; on entering, they began to cut down all who came in their way, so that neither men, women, or children were spared in the first onset. There has been no exaggeration in the statement that numbers of the Ipsariot mothers, rather than fall into the hands of the barbarians, rushed to the nearest rocks, and dashing their infants into the surge below, plunged after them, and thus ended their own sufferings, as well as those of their offspring. *

After a contest of some hours, in which the Ipsariots, seeing their wives and children perishing without any hope of saving them, they at length determined to try and gain their ships. Accordingly, a part of the inhabitants rushed towards the port, while the rest, together with a body of 500 Albanians, shut themselves up in fort St. Nicholas, which formed the principal defence of the town. What was the surprise and horror of the former, on perceiving that those who were left in charge of the ships, panic-struck by what they saw passing on shore, had cut the cables and suffered the vessels to drift before the wind out to sea, without sails or rudders. It may be readily imagined how much this added to the confusion. There was not, however, a moment to be lost, and as it was out of the question to attempt saving all the fugitives, those who succeeded in reaching the port, rushed into the first boats they could find, while hundreds of the women and children were seen stretching out their hands vainly calling upon their husbands and fathers for succour. Many plunged into the

* Among the many proofs of heroism displayed by the women, my informants related that one, who had been married only a few months, seeing her husband engaged with two or three Turkish soldiers, rushed in between them, and fell with the object of her affections, covered with wounds.

waves and were drowned in attempting to reach the boats as they left the harbour. As a portion of the enemy's fleet were outside, it intercepted and took several of the vessels which had no means of getting away. There were, however, several instances in which the Greeks determined rather to perish even after they had effected their escape from the island, than surrender to the Turks. The captain of a brig which came to Napoli di Romania a few days after our arrival, had laid a train for blowing her up, and when approached by the Capitan Pacha's ship and two frigates, he actually set fire to it. On seeing the fire ascend, and part of the vessel's rigging in a blaze, the Turkish ships retreated in all haste, thus enabling the Greeks to extinguish the fire and make their escape. Another vessel having only five men on board, hailed two of the enemy's frigates which came up with an evident intention to board, and vociferated, that if they came a yard nearer, they would set fire to the powder magazine: this menace had the desired effect, and they were allowed to proceed.

While this scene was passing at the port, another still more harrowing was preparing in fort St. Nicholas. Those who took refuge there were pursued by a part of the Turks, while the remainder were occupied in cutting down the inhabitants who fled towards the ships, and in plundering the houses. On entering the fort, the Greeks had barricaded the gates, and commenced a fire on the infidels, which obliged them to retreat with the loss of half their number. After having satiated themselves with the blood of more than two thousand victims, night came on, and suspended the carnage. The Turks, who had been sent to attack the coast batteries, and two of which were blown up by the Greeks rather than surrender, having concentrated themselves in the town, the Capitan Pacha sent a peremptory order on shore, that the whole of the troops should be employed in reducing fort St. Nicholas. Accordingly they advanced while it was yet dark, preparatory to a general assault. The attack commenced at day-break, and gave rise to prodigies of valour on the part of the Christians. Perceiving, however, that it was in vain to contend against such numbers, they formed the desperate and heroic resolution of burying themselves in the ruins of the fort. Pursuant to this determination, those who remained, placed themselves close to the gate, having previously ranged the women and children in the rear; a soldier being placed at the powder magazine with a lighted match, the gates were thrown open, upon which about two thousand of the enemy rushed in; when the fort was so full that not a man more could enter, the signal was given, and in another instant every soul within its walls were buried in the ruins, or blown into the air by the explosion.

Such was the fate of Ipsara, which may be

fairly attributed to the delay in the sailing of the fleet; for had it been possible to effect this in time, there is no doubt whatever but the enemy would have abandoned his project, or been foiled in the attempt. How prophetically Prince Mavrocordato anticipated some such disaster, will be seen from the extracts of his letters to myself while at Zante.

The loss sustained on this occasion was immense and irreparable. Upon a moderate computation, four thousand Christians of every age and sex perished. When to this is added the loss of all property, personal and public, and about a hundred vessels of different sizes, some notion may be formed of the catastrophe of Ipsara. During the first moments of dismay, the fugitives sought shelter in any of the neighbouring islands they could reach, but it was afterwards thought advisable to establish themselves at Napoli di Malvasia, on the coast of Maina, until the period arrived either for their returning to the place of their birth, or being settled in some other point of the confederation.

A fever with which I was attacked on the day after my arrival at the seat of government, having confined me to my bed for nearly a fortnight, I was prevented from following the progress of events so exactly as I could wish. When enabled to return to the consideration of passing events, I understood that the division of the fleet, which sailed from Hydra under the brave Miaoulis, on the 4th of July, could not, owing to contrary winds, approach Ipsara before the 8th. Impelled by a spirit of vengeance, hitherto unknown to them, the Greek seamen eagerly rushed into the boats, and landed while the fleet hovered off the port to intercept all the enemy's vessels that should attempt to escape. The only object of the Turks, being that of removing every possibility of Ipsara ever holding up its head again, they were busily employed in taking away the cannon and plundered property, of which a considerable portion, together with the women and children they had reserved for slavery, had been already sent to Scio and Mytelene. On hearing that the Greeks had landed, the Turks immediately rushed towards the port, and put to sea. They were pursued by the fleet, and numbers either run down or captured.* Those who could not get out of the harbour, were taken possession of, and conducted with the spoils that had been embarked, to Hydra and Spezzia. The most horrid spectacle that can be imagined presented itself to the Greeks who landed; they found the town still smoking and the streets full of dead bodies,

* It was known that there were a great number of Italian and Maltese seamen serving on board the Turkish fleet and flotilla; of these, not more than fourteen fell into the hands of the Greeks. I need hardly say they did not escape the indignation of the Christians; indeed many of the Greek sailors who were in the action, assured me they felt infinitely more enraged against the Franks than the Turks.

of both sexes and all ages. The putrefaction which had already commenced, rendered it impossible for either party to remain, so that they were forced to retire, leaving the island completely deserted, except by a single detachment of the enemy, who had shut themselves up in one of the few houses that remained standing, and whom the Greeks could not attack, in consequence of their having a number of women and children in their possession.

As a compensation for the disasters which attended the commencement of the naval campaign, many of the patriots assured me, that however calamitous they might be regarded, more particularly that of Ipsara, something of the kind had become necessary to rouse the people from an apathy into which their previous successes had thrown them. Be this as it may, there is no doubt that although the consternation caused by the news from Ipsara, became very general, and continued for a considerable time, the event had really the effect of stimulating all the energies of the nation, and inspiring a spirit of vengeance, which is not only excusable but salutary, when a people are struggling for existence.

The first use made of my convalescence, was that of offering such suggestions to the legislative and executive bodies, as appeared to me best calculated to promote the interests of the confederacy. Lord Charles, of whose ready co-operation and able councils I experienced daily proofs, having come to the seat of government, merely for the purpose stated in a former page, left Napoli in his return to Messolunghi, there to complete the literary labours which he had so successfully commenced previous to our departure. His Lordship set out on the 20th of July, by way of Tripolitza and Calavrita. On taking my leave of him, I little imagined it would be for the last time, or that this lamented young nobleman was also destined to become a martyr to his zeal in the Greek cause.

What with the necessity of changing the air, and my determination not to quit Greece without visiting Athens and the Gulph of Ægina, Lord Charles had no sooner left Napoli, than I prepared for my own departure. On presenting myself to the Executive the day before, I was assured that my propositions would be considered, and the decision of the government made known on my return.

I left Napoli on the evening of the 22d July, and after a pleasant ride over the southern extremity of the plain of Argos, which is thickly planted with olive trees in this place, I slept at the convent of St. Demetrius, within four leagues of the fortress. Our ride on the following morning, lay through a hilly and uncultivated tract, upon which I saw several ruins, and many indications of former wealth, though it is now almost deserted. After resting for a couple of hours at Ligoria, a village very pleasantly situated on a rising ground, surrounded with lofty mountains, we proceeded to visit the ruins of the ancient Hieron, built in a deep valley, within four miles of the village. The remains of this city, consisting of a numachia amphitheatre, and several temples, cover a large extent of ground, so that it must have been a place of considerable importance. From Hieron we had to trace our way over a pathless country for three hours, till we joined the road that leads from Ligoria to Epidaurus. This winds round a thickly wooded mountain, at the base of which runs a stream that was now nearly dry; on reaching the eastern side of the hill, we had a delightful view of the plain and height on which Epidaurus once stood, with Ægina, Salamis, and Attica, in the distance.

Epidaurus, so celebrated for its temple of Esculapius, the most frequented in the days of Grecian civilization, and scarcely less famous, from giving its name, and being the spot at which the congress of modern Greek deputies met to form a constitution, is beautifully situated, and still possesses remains which cannot fail to interest travellers. On approaching the village, which is built on the head of its small but commodious port, we observed a number of huts raised along the shore, and close to the water: from their being covered with boughs still quite green, I concluded these rustic habitations must be the asylum of fugitives, from some other point of the confederacy. Nor was I mistaken, for when we alighted, Athanasius Anagnostaras, the agent of the government to whom I had letters, informed me that above two hundred families had arrived within the preceding month, chiefly refugees from Negropont and Livadia. What was worse, they were in the greatest distress, and he had no means of relieving them. The afternoon was devoted to visiting the ruins, among which we saw several fine fragments of statues and bas-reliefs, which testified the former magnificence of this place. On returning, I crossed the port, and landed close to the huts, whose inmates were mostly women and children, and evidently of the higher classes. They were all busily employed either in cooking their scanty meals, or with distaffs in their hands. Athanasius, who accompanied us, pointed out many of the fugitives who had inhabited palaces, and been nursed in the lap of luxury. Yet did they seem to bear up against their calamities with the utmost calmness, and even cheerfulness. I regret to be obliged to add, that an epidemic disorder, which was now beginning to appear among these unhappy sufferers, carried off numbers during the two following months.

As there is a constant communication between Epidaurus and the opposite shores of the gulph, I had no difficulty in crossing to Ægina, which we reached after a passage of four hours, and landed there about eight o'clock on the following morning. Owing to the advantageous position of this place, it has afforded a secure asylum to numbers from Negropont, Livadia, and Attica.

Like most other parts of the confederation, Ægina possesses very few vestiges of its ancient grandeur. The temple of Neptune and Jupiter, Panhellenius, together with its tombs, which once contained the ashes of many a hero, are, however, still objects of interesting research. I rode to the old town, situated on the highest pinnacle of the island, whence we enjoyed one of the finest panoramic views of Greece, and then proceeded to the temple. Nothing can be more beautiful than the situation of this fine remain; it faces the Acropolis, which, together with the Piræus, plain of Athens, and Mount Hymettus, are clearly descried from its site. Ægina is well cultivated, and celebrated for its almonds, of which several cargoes are exported annually. It is considered as one of the most salubrious islands in Greece.

Understanding that a great portion of the inhabitants of Athens, and among others, some friends whom I wished to see, had removed to Salamis, I embarked for that place and arrived in its spacious and magnificent port on the evening of the 27th. There were a great number of ships and small vessels in the harbour, as it had now become the general rendezvous. On landing, I found the town was also overflowing with visitors, many of whom were living in the open air. I had the good fortune to find a comfortable lodging in the house of my friend, Anargyrus Petrakis, a highly distinguished patriot who has had the advantage of a European education, and is one of the Ephors of Athens, his native city. It was only two days before my arrival, that an account had been received of the gallant exploit of Generals Goura and Marfopolos, the Cefaloniote, on the plain of Marathon, where with little more than five hundred men, they routed a body of four thousand Turks, which had advanced from Negropont, with the ulterior project of investing Athens itself. By a singular coincidence, this rencontre took place on the very spot which is pointed out as having been the sepulchre of the Persians who perished in their attempt to subdue Greece above two thousand years before. The battle lasted twelve hours, and ended by the defeat of the Turkish force, capture of fourteen standards, and a large quantity of baggage.

Ambelachi, the second port of Salamis, and that to which the Athenian fleet retired after the victory of Themistocles, is only separated from the town by a narrow isthmus. We rode there the next day, to embark for the Piræus, about eight miles to the south-east. With the exception of some extensive foundations, Salamis does not present a single ruin worth mentioning. The island is mountainous and barren ; it is, however, a good nursery for seamen, and supplies many to the maritime commerce of Greece. Though small, the Piræus is an admirable harbour, completely sheltered from every wind, and capable of receiving the largest ships. On landing there early on the morning of the 28th, I found the place quite abandoned, with its convent and store-houses in ruins. Having, however, through the assistance of a shepherd who brought his flock down to feed close to the port, procured horses, we set out for Athens, a distance of six miles. The road leads across the plain, and passes through a continued grove of olive trees, which nearly covers its whole extent, the intermediate space being sown with maize and corn, or laid out in gardens and vineyards.

A considerable portion of the road lays between the celebrated double wall which led from the Acropolis to the Piræus, but of which nothing more than a part of the foundations are discernible. The approach to Athens is both grand and picturesque ; and nothing can be more striking than the Parthenon, as seen from the port on which it proudly looks down. On entering the gates and witnessing so many remains of its ancient splendour which have escaped the wreck of time and violence of those barbarous hordes who have by turns possessed the city since the decline of the Roman power, one would be apt to imagine that some divinity has presided over this temple of arts, civilization, and early freedom. As my visit was to be but of very short duration, I determined to profit by it, and see as much of the antiquities as possible. My first care was to wait on the Ephors, whom I found assembled in a large building which had formerly been the residence of the Turkish aga. They were busily occupied in devising means of defence; for the Turkish troops which Goura and Marfopolos had defeated, were soon after re-inforced by double their number, and had now advanced within four leagues of the city, which they threatened with an immediate attack. Goura had arrived two days before to prepare for their reception. I said all I could to convince the Ephors that supplies of men, money, and ammunition would be soon sent to their aid by the Provisional Government, and I offered to be the bearer of any communication they might wish to make. My next visit was to Goura himself. Like the most distinguished of the modern Greek heroes, Goura is young and unlettered. He may truly be styled a matter-of-fact man; for after my dwelling for some time on his late exploits and previous acts of gallantry; instead of entering into any account of them on speaking of himself, he merely replied, that if the government would only send him a supply of ammunition and muskets to arm the peasants, he would answer for the safety not only of Athens, but the whole of Attica.

It being necessary to get a written order to see the interior of the Acropolis, it was readily granted, and I hastened to feast my eyes on that wonder of the world. It would be extremely difficult to describe the mingled sensations of admiration and sorrow which cannot fail to agitate the mind of the most ordinary observer, on visiting this spot, sanctified by so many splendid specimens of art, raised to the majesty of the gods, though now fallen into ruin and decay. There never could be a finer conception than the Propylea, in which, though so disfigured, the marks of its former grandeur are seen through the rudely constructed walls that obstruct this approach, worthy of the glorious edifices to which it led. The present entrance is a covered way, on the right of a lofty tower of defence, built by the Venetians; on each side as we passed, we observed several fine fragments of statues and bas-reliefs leaning against the walls: this passage conducted us to the façade of the Parthenon. It is no exaggerated panegyric of this structure to say, that it is every way worthy of the divinity to whom it was raised. Beauty, grace, and grandeur, all combine to make the Temple of Minerva what it is—at once the wonder and admiration of travellers.

I observed that, as usual, a thousand vulgar names, English, French, and German, were carved on the columns of the façade; surely it was the very essence of bad taste that one which has been coupled with that of Attila and Omar, so far as their predilection for despoiling monuments of antiquity is concerned, should find a place among the rest; it is indeed very unlikely that this name will be forgotten so long as the spoliation of the immortal friezes remains on record. On ascending the shivered wall to examine the solitary remains over the great door-way, I could not help raising my eyes to heaven, and ejaculating a prayer of thanks, that there were a few groups which could not be removed, at the period of spoliation. Should those glorious trophies of art, which lose all their effect on the pigmy walls of the British Museum, never be restored, there is at least something left to show that Athens led the way in art, and has taught it to succeeding nations. Distressing as it was to see the destructive effects of the explosion which took place when the Venetians were besieged here in the seventeenth century, it was still more humiliating to witness the mosque which a late tyrant caused to be raised in the very centre of the temple, and which bears all the marks of that puerile design and barbarous taste which distinguish the modern Vandals. Near the door of this miserable edifice, I found a party of Turkish prisoners hewing shot out of the fragments of pentelic marble and granite columns that were strewed about in such abundance.*

From the Parthenon I proceeded to the temple of Erectheus; this master-piece of art, unequalled by any other in the world, had been converted into a powder magazine by the Turks, nor has it as yet been in the power of the Greek Commandant to establish it in a different spot. A wall of rough bricks and stone has also been built up between the celebrated Caratidæ. Anxious to

* Two of these shot were presented to the Greek Committee soon after my arrival in London.

see the roof, of which I had heard so much, I got up to an aperture in the wall with the aid of some Greek soldiers. I need hardly say that its beauty far exceeded all my expectations. I was surprised, however, to find, that notwithstanding all the efforts which had been made to destroy this wonderful specimen of art, the whole should be in such perfect preservation. I should observe, that the space between it and the bomb-proof covering of the magazine below, about five feet in height, has often served as a quarter for the soldiery, so that the whole of the sculptured ornaments are quite blackened with smoke. Of the next temple, its rival in beauty and execution, that of Minerva Polias, but a few columns remain; these are of the most exquisite workmanship. I should not omit observing that few views in Greece will bear a comparison with that which we enjoyed from the top of the Parthenon.*

The walls of the Acropolis are in a very good state of repair, and owing to the discovery of a well in the northern angle of the fortress, and which had been totally unknown before the

* The happiest attempts hitherto made to illustrate the scenery of Greece, will be found in the work of Mr. Williams, of Edinburgh, in which this able artist and his engravers, have displayed infinite taste. It would seem, however, that a much more important work is preparing by the Chevalier Bronsted, a German traveller, who, to judge from the prospectus of his forthcoming publication, is about to render a highly important service to literature and the fine arts.

revolution, it is now regarded as the most impregnable point of the confederation; for, unlike Napoli or Corinth, the walls are neither too extensive nor complicated. Having heard that there were some Turkish prisoners who had been taken a few days before at Marathon, I made a point of paying them a visit; they were confined very near the well to which I have just alluded. The first party I accosted through my interpreter, were playing cards under a shed, and seemed quite reconciled to their lot. The object of the questions I put to them, was that of ascertaining as nearly as possible, whether the war with Greece was popular among the Turks, and if they served voluntarily; one of them replied, that it was so, because the Sultan represented the Greeks as robbers, and the sworn enemies of the Mahometan race. Another, who seemed much less sprightly than his companions, informed us that he had been taken by force, with many others, from a village about twenty days march from Constantinople, on the shores of the Black Sea; that he had no idea of where he was coming, and felt no inclination whatever to fight against a people who had never done him any injury. Among various other acts of cruelty perpetrated by the troops who had advanced from Negropont, these prisoners informed us, that the Janissaries, of whom a large body came into Greece this campaign, had wrested thirteen peasants from the hands of Omer Pacha, the Governor of Negropont, who wished to preserve their lives, and impaled them alive but a few days before; alleging as a reason, that they had their orders from the Sultan himself to give no quarter to the Greeks. In leaving them, I expressed a hope that when they returned, they would not fail to inform their co-religionists and countrymen of the mild treatment experienced by themselves from the Giaours.

Descending from the Acropolis, we visited the prison of Socrates, the martyr to philosophy and virtue; also the rocky Tribune whence the prince of Grecian orators taught his fellow citizens the value of freedom and national independence. After once more surveying the Parthenon, from the monument raised to the Roman consul Philopapus, we walked down to the banks of Illissus, which, though a considerable stream in winter, was now almost dry. The site of the academy, magnificent columns of the temple of Jupiter Olympus, one of the finest specimens of Adrian's reign, next attracted our attention. Re-entering the town through the gate that leads to Cape Colonna, the excursion terminated with a visit to the beautiful little monument called the Lanthorn of Demosthenes, the famous corinthian colonade of the Pæcile, Tower of the Winds, and Temple of Theseus, by far the best preserved of any of the Athenian monuments, and whose friezes have, by a miracle, escaped the sacrilegious hands of the Goths of the nineteenth century.

I am not aware of the predominant impressions made on the minds of others who have visited the beautiful remains with which Athens abounds. On entering the Acropolis, I was instantly struck by the amazing contrast between its monuments and all that I had seen at Rome, or, indeed, in any part of Italy. This is so remarkable, and so infinitely in favour of the Grecian artists, that it is impossible not to perceive at once, that after all, those of Rome, cannot aspire to any thing more than the merit of mere copyists.

Had the Society of Philomusæ been properly supported by the friends of art and learning, it might have done much towards preserving the Athenian monuments from the ruin into which they are fast falling; as it is, the members resident at Athens, have done their utmost. Among these M. Gropius, the Austrian Consul, stands most highly distinguished, and it is to him I am indebted for the able report which will be found in the extracts from my correspondence. If circumstances over which, it is probable, he could exercise no control, had not placed M. Gropius as an agent and functionary of Austria, I feel satisfied, he would have been as great an enthusiast in favour of Grecian regeneration, as he is in all that relates to the preservation of her ancient remains.

Having promised to return to Ambelachi, I proceeded to that place, and did not leave it before the afternoon of the 30th, when I fully intended to have paid a visit to Miaoulis, who had been lying at anchor under Cape Colonna, but having heard that he put to sea again, I was obliged to relinquish my project,* so that I now determined to proceed to Hydra, being desirous of communicating with the primates.

The caiques or open boats used on the coast of Greece, are much more convenient than larger vessels, since they possess the double advantage of sails and oars, and the latter are in constant requisition during the summer months. Happening to hear of an anchoret, who had resided for many years in a small island, on the coast of Ægina, close to the temple of Jupiter Panhellenius, I requested the boatmen to put in there, in order that we might pay him a visit. On landing and going up to the small church, which stands very conspicuously on the highest part of the rock, we searched for him in vain. The shrine of St. Nicholas, the most popular patron of the Greek seamen, was however lighted up, and the books open ready for the performance of the church service. Whether the old man had left the island in consequence of the alarm which now prevailed, or retreated to some hiding place, we could not ascertain. His absence did not, however, prevent the crew and our attendants from proceeding to

* Two letters, which I afterwards received from the naval hero of modern Greece, will be found in the extracts from my correspondence.

the church and going through a long formula of prayer. On coming away, they took care to trim the lamp which hung before the Saint's portrait, they also filled the censor with incense, and placed a bottle of oil and a few wax tapers in a niche appropriated for their reception. There is, in fact, scarcely a bay or promontory in Greece, that has not one or more of these little shrines for the accommodation of mariners; and it is always customary for those who visit them, to leave an offering like that I have described. In passing on towards Hydra, we sailed through the magnificent Harbour of Poros, formed by an island on the coast of the Morea, by far the most capacious and best adapted for a naval station in Greece. As there are two embouchures, ships may either sail from or enter Poros with any wind. It was suggested to the Ipsariots that they ought to have taken refuge here, instead of Malvasia, where there is no harbour of any kind; and they would have done so, had it afforded sufficient security. Those who are anxious to see the Greek navy assume a more permanent footing, have been constantly urging the government to establish an arsenal in one of the ports of the Morea. The district of Poros is celebrated for its oranges, of which large quantities are exported yearly to Constantinople.

We arrived at Hydra just as a large division of the fleet was preparing to join Miaoulis. It was now intended to augment the fleet to one hundred, including twenty fire ships, with the ulterior project of opposing the expedition of Mehemet Ali, which had sailed from Alexandria in the early part of July.

It was with great difficulty we were enabled to get into the landing place, owing to the little cove, for it hardly deserves the name of port, in which the ships of the Hydriots take shelter, being so extremely full; I had scarcely less trouble in making my way to the convent, for such was the crowd that we could not proceed a step without jostling or being jostled. When the origin of this island and its rapid progress in maritime wealth, are considered, it is, perhaps, one of the most interesting spectacles to be witnessed in any part of Europe.

It is indeed impossible to see the fine population of this and its two sister islands of Ipsara and Spezzia, together with what they have achieved in opposition to the most formidable obstacles, without at once perceiving that they are capable of becoming still more powerful and wealthy; the ferocity of character and impatience of control, not unmixed with a predilection for lawless violence, which have sometimes marked the conduct of these hardy islanders, are the necessary consequences of heir situation: when under a good government and subject to the influence of wholesome laws, I have no doubt of their becoming good citizens.

The principal object of my visit to Hydra, was to ascertain the sentiments of the primates and naval chiefs, with regard to the establishment of a regular navy, and obtaining ships of a larger class. Contrary to what some reports I had heard at Napoli di Romania led me to expect, I was happy to find a perfect accordance in their opinions with my own, in the above important points. Having passed two days most pleasantly in the house of Lazzaro Conduriotti, elder brother to the president, who has also made great sacrifices to the cause, I departed to Spezzia in a boat which he kindly provided for me: in our passage, which lasted only four hours, the crew were incessantly occupied either in singing or recounting their respective adventures during the war; perceiving that most of them were decked out with turbans, and had very good Turkish pipes, it occurred to me that they had just returned from a successful cruize. I was not mistaken; they formed part of the crew of one of the ships sent for the relief of Ipsara, and had all brought away some trophies, besides those which they may have left on the island. Their account of the horrid scene which it presented when they landed, corresponded very exactly with what I had heard from others.

Spezzia is by no means so large or populous as Hydra: its seamen are, however, quite as brave and enterprising as their neighbours and rivals. It has been generally considered that the inhabitants of this island are more urbane and civilised than those of the two others; no person has attempted to account for this difference, nor did the shortness of my stay enable me to enter into the enquiry. The island is governed by primates, with the principal of whom, Gika Botasi, brother to the vice-president of the executive, I dined, accompanied by a very amiable and intelligent papas, Procopius Tipaldi, a native of Cefalonia, who officiates as secretary to the local government. Though small, the harbour of Spezzia, affords better shelter than that of Hydra, but, at best, it is by no means well calculated for the security of large ships. This island's contingent for the present year, was about forty ships and vessels of various sizes. Having found the same facilities with regard to the object of my visit to Spezzia, as at Hydra, I set out on my return to the seat of government, and, after visiting Porto Keli, a very fine harbour of the Morea, within three miles of Spezzia, as also port Vivari, the grand naval station of the Venetians, I reached Napoli on the evening of the 4th of August, after an absence of twelve days.

As a compensation for the anxieties I experienced in the early part of my second visit to Greece, scarcely a day passed during the last three weeks of my stay at Napoli, in which some glad tidings did not arrive, or incident occur to afford satisfaction to the friends of Greece.

On presenting myself before the executive body, I was informed that letters had just been received from Zante, stating that the money was at length embarked and might be expected every day. I also found letters from Prince Mavrocordato, giving very flattering accounts of the progress of the war on the Acarnanian frontier. A letter from my excellent friend Georgius Valtinos, inclosed the details of a battle in which he had himself borne a most distinguished part; that of Ampliani, near Salona, fought the 29th of July, and in which little more than 800 men defeated a division of the army of Dervish Pacha, consisting of about 8000, with a loss of 1000 killed and wounded, also taking their guns, several standards and an immense booty; the loss of the Greeks on this occasion did not exceed twenty men. The name of Dimo Scaltza, Andreas Lundo, Notara, Panouria of Salona, Calivas, and the Souliot chiefs Dagli, Diamanti, Zerva, and Draco, deserved to be recorded, as having by their gallantry and judgment contributed to the victory of Ampliani, one of the most brilliant exploits of the war.

Soon after the above news came, a vessel arrived in the bay, with despatches from the brave Sactouri of Hydra, who with a squadron of only eighteen ships, including six fire-ships, had succeeded in destroying a large Turkish frigate and several other vessels in the waters of Samos. It is needless to add, that but for the heroic and modest Canaris, it is not likely Greece would have to boast of this signal triumph. Amidst all these sources of exultation, the arrival of the money crowned the general joy, and gave a new impulse to all the affairs of the confederacy.

It was while I anticipated the pleasure of receiving a letter from Lord Charles Murray, informing me of his arrival at Messolunghi, and the resumption of his generous labours for the Greek cause, that a courier arrived from Gastouni bringing an account of his death: this melancholy event took place there, on the 13th of August, after an illness of several days. I had such frequent opportunities of witnessing the benevolence of this young nobleman's disposition, and the zeal with which he pursued the interests of Greece, that even if I had not been honored by some portion of his personal friendship, the unlooked for news of his death could not fail to be a source of the deepest regret to me.

Lord Charles's death was occasioned by a fever, contracted in consequence of his being exposed to a heavy storm on the mountains between Tripolitza and Calavrita. It having been arranged previous to his departure from Napoli, that we should correspond, I took care to inform his Lordship of whatever occurred, and had received two letters from himself while on the journey, probably the last he ever wrote; the first was dated at Tripolitza on the 22d of July, three days after he left Napoli, in this he says: "We arrived here in a prosperous state last night; I remained a day at Argos to visit the tomb of Agamemnon, with which I was much struck.—To-day I visited Ipsilanti, he received me with great politeness.—This morning we set off, taking the route through Arcadia, where I believe I am at present. If I had known it in time, I would have written a more pastoral epistle!" Further on his Lordship adds:—"Tripolitza pleases me more than Napoli or Messolunghi. The plain is at so great an elevation above the level of the sea, that the air is consequently more pure, the inhabitants are cleanly, industrious, and therefore prosperous; the fruits here are more backward than at Napoli." The following is an extract from the next letter, dated Calavrita, on the 26th:—"We arrived here yesterday evening, after a most uncomfortable journey. A tremendous storm of thunder, lightning and rain, overtook us in one of the mountain passes of Achaia, indeed, even in my native north, I never saw such a heavy storm. I was mounted on one of the camels, and not having a sufficient supply of capotes, I was soon wet through, and there being no village at hand, I was obliged to continue the journey for four hours in my wet clothes; the consequence has been, a severe attack of fever and rheumatism, but I am better to day, and hope to be able to set off to-morrow." The remainder of my information was derived from the Archimandrite Teseo, of Cyprus, who travelled in his Lordship's suite: from this it appears, that being anxious to reach his destination, Lord Charles left Calavrita two days after the date of his last letter, for Gastouni, but experienced a relapse, when within a few miles of that place, and arrived there in a state of great exhaustion. His Lordship was received into the house of Sessini, who paid him all the attention in his power. On perceiving that the fever increased, an express was dispatched to Messolunghi for Mr. Millingen: that gentleman, who had during a late illness of his own, received the most generous attentions from his Lordship, set out immediately, but came too late, Lord Charles having expired about an hour before his arrival. His Lordship's remains were buried with military honours in the public cemetery of Gastouni. Having waited on the executive body the moment I heard of the arrival of the courier dispatched by Sessini, I was assured that immediate steps would be taken to forward his Lordship's papers and effects to Sir Frederick Adam, the Lord High Commissioner of the Ionian Islands, as the nearest British authority, as well as one of his private friends. In deploring the loss of one who had rendered such services to the cause during his short stay in Greece, and whose talents, as well as his high rank in society, made him a most valuable acquisition, the President added, that he hoped the time was not far distant, when Greece would be enabled to raise a monument to the memory of his Lordship's virtues, and as a mark of gratitude for his devotion to her cause.

I have already alluded to his Lordship's numerous acts of benevolence and charity while at Messolunghi: these were indeed his predominant virtues, for during the time we were travelling together, a day never passed without his ministering to the wants of some poor family, or visiting the bed of sickness. If this part of his Lordship's character excited admiration, it was not less distinguished by the extent and variety of his information. There was, indeed, scarcely any subject upon which he did not converse, as if he had made it a particular object of study, while his classical attainments were of a very high order. In addition to his familiarity with the writers of antiquity, he spoke and wrote the German, French and Italian, with the utmost facility; and I need not give any greater proof of his acquaintance with the modern Greek, than the fact stated relative to his translating an elementary work on fortification, into the Romaic, before he had been a month in Greece. This was to have been followed up by several others.

As a companion, Lord Charles was both amiable and entertaining; nor was he ever at a loss for some apposite anecdote illustrative of the subject of conversation. When I add, that he had but just attained his twenty-fourth year, it is not too much to say, that the nobility has lost a distinguished ornament in the death of this young nobleman, who, if his life had been spared, would have doubtless rendered eminent services to his country.

More deeply impressed than ever with the importance of adopting prompt and efficacious measures for securing the credit of Greece in England, and thereby obtaining that further aid, without which the war might be protracted to an indefinite period, I felt most anxious to lose no time in returning home, in order to contribute as much as I could, to the above objects. It was, therefore, with infinite satisfaction I heard the propositions I had made, previous to my departure for Athens, had been discussed, both by the legislative body and the members of the executive; it was still more gratifying to me to find, that the whole of my suggestions were honoured with the approval of these two branches of the state.*

Convinced that the more civilised nations of Europe, could not better render back a part of that debt of gratitude they owe the ancient Greeks, than in promoting knowledge and encouraging education among their descendants, I eagerly seized a passage in one of Mr. Bowring's letters to Colonel Stanhope, in which he said that that great philanthropist and good man, William Allen, expressed a wish that twenty Greek youths might

* One of my first cares on returning to the seat of government, was, to represent the neglected state in which I found the monuments of antiquity at Athens; this was accompanied with an earnest request, that a commission should be specially named for the purpose of superintending their preservation. From the positive assurances received both from the Legislative body and Executive, I trust this has been done.

be sent to England, to be educated at a cheap rate. I at once determined to bring them home without any condition as to the expence of their education, merely asking myself whether England, in which millions are expended in the pursuit of idle pleasures; a country which is more indebted to the early institutions and learning of Greece than any other, could not afford to pay four or five hundred a year for the instruction of a few Greek youths? Here I should remark that this proposition was received with the utmost satisfaction by all parties; as a proof of which, I had scarcely made it, before some hundred applications were sent in. Owing, however, to the undefined nature of the proposal made by my friend Bowring, I felt some repugnance at charging myself with more than ten, half the number named by Mr. Allen.

My object in the selection of those whom I have brought to England, was that of choosing indiscriminately from every rank, and without partialities of any kind; all I required was that the youths should be of good moral qualities, and apt dispositions for learning. It is most gratifying to be able to add that the result has fully answered my hopes and expectations. I cannot close this account of occurrences at Napoli di Romania, without expressing the satisfaction I experienced, on witnessing the rapid progress of civilization, manifested in all I saw during my visit. In addition to a well regulated police and sanitary regulations, steps had been taken for cleansing the town, in which new houses were daily rising, on the ruins of the old Turkish receptacles of filth and disease. Unable to dispense charity to the extent I could wish among the numberless victims of wretchedness who sought relief from Candia, Ipsara, and other points, at the seat of government,* nothing I saw gave me more heartfelt satisfaction, than the establishment of a Philanthropic Society, at the first meeting of which I had the pleasure of being present. This is of itself, the strongest proof that can be adduced of the right of Greece to re-enter the bosom of the European family; but when I add that it originated with the citizens and was eagerly encouraged, I am sure I shall have established its claims to the admiration, if not the active support of the British public.†

* My first duty on reaching England in the Amphitrite, was to represent the deplorable condition of the fugitives from Ipsara, Candia, and other points, collected in the Morea, to the Greek Committee and Society of Friends. Indeed, I felt most anxious that an appeal should be made to the public in their favour, as nothing can exceed the privations and wretchedness to which they must be still exposed.

I have reason to believe that a sum of £200 was immediately transmitted to Zante, by the Committee of Friends, for the Ipsariots, and I feel assured that the example would have been followed by the Greek Committee, had it possessed funds.

† Several documents connected with the organization of the Philanthropic Society, will be found towards the end of the volume.

By a reference to my address to the legislative assembly, just before I left Napoli di Romania, it will be seen that I did not omit reminding the legislators of Greece, how anxious its friends in this country were to witness the establishment of tribunals, without which the law of Epdaurus must necessarily remain a dead letter. If the progress hitherto made in this respect, is more tardy than could be wished, it arises from a combination of difficulties which nothing but time can overcome; but urgent as the necessity of organizing tribunals for the administration of the civil and criminal codes certainly is, it is perhaps of still more importance to the present interests of the confederation, that an admiralty court should be established; for it cannot be denied that excesses have been committed by some of the Greek cruisers, though, like every thing else, these have been exaggerated. This necessity became more apparent than ever, during the discussions which took place relative to the famous proclamation issued by the provisional government, against the European vessels employed in the expedition of Mehemet Ali. In order to correct the misapprehensions into which the framer of that document had fallen, as well as to prevent future errors of a similar nature, Sir James Mackintosh drew up a masterly paper on the subject of international law generally, and also the draft of a new proclamation, in conformity with the received laws of European nations. These documents, which are distinguished by all the perspicuity of reasoning and elegance of style so peculiar to the writer, were forwarded to the government in October, with a letter from the Greek Committee recommending the adoption of all that Sir James had suggested.*

With respect to the state of religion, public education, and the press, the circumstances of the war, have acted as a great bar to the projects of the legislative and executive bodies in favour of the above corner-stones of the social edifice. Of all those who have visited Greece, Colonel Stanhope has displayed most zeal and perseverance, not only in convincing the Greeks that without education and a free press their liberty would be merely nominal, and unproductive of any benefit. It was, however, quite impossible to give effect to the gallant Colonel's benevolent designs during

* I fully intended to have published the above valuable paper, had my excellent friend, M. Maniakes, of Parga, not signified his intention of preparing a synopsis of public law, selected from the most distinguished publicists of Europe, and in which he cannot fail to avail himself of the authority and elucidations of Sir James. Whether on the score of integrity or talent, my young friend is fully equal to the task he has undertaken; and I should be wanting in justice, were I not to take this opportunity of acknowledging the ready and able assistance I have received from him in my own humble labours to promote the cause of his country. It may not be irrelevant to add, that Mr. Maniakes has obtained a degree at Cambridge, where he went under the auspices of that truly generous and enlightened benefactor of Greece, the Earl of Guildford.

my stay in the Morea; and it is perhaps to be regretted, that the types and printing press which he presented to the Athenians, had not been handed over to the government, as they would not fail to have been of infinite service in promulgating its decrees and public acts during the summer, when they were lying idle at Salamis, to which place the Ephors removed them when the city was threatened by the force from Negropont. I am glad, however, to be able to say, that they are now in full activity under a young patriot of considerable talent, M. Psillas, who has recently commenced a journal entitled, "The Ephemeredes of Athens."

"The Friend of the Laws," has been edited for some months at Hydra, by M. Chiappa, an Italian, who seems to be very well suited to the task he has undertaken. "The Greek Chronicle," the first paper which appeared in Greece, is conducted by Dr. Meyer, a German, who has become a Greek citizen through his marriage with a native of Messolunghi, where his journal is published. Though what the French call *une tête exaltée*, and rather too fond of indulging in personalities, Meyer unites a degree of enthusiasm with a love of improvement, which will make him a very useful citizen of his adopted country. Another paper, entitled "The Greek Telegraph," commenced under the auspices of Lord Byron, and but for his Lordship's death, and consequent departure of Count Gamba, who was its chief support, would have been extremely useful to the cause. This Journal has been conducted in so slovenly a manner ever since, that its extinction will not be a very great loss to Greece.

With regard to education, it has been decreed by the legislative assembly, that a grand central school, on the Lancasterian principle, should be established at Argos, and that each province of the confederacy shall send two pupils for the express purpose of acquiring a knowledge of the system, in order to be afterwards able to establish schools in their respective districts.

The execution of the above plan, will be greatly facilitated by the arrival in Greece of some young men, who have been qualified for the office of schoolmasters by the Society of Friends, and sent out at their expense.

Nothing has as yet been decided concerning a patriarch, so that the affairs of religion remain in the hands of the minister of worship and public instruction. A few hundred copies of the Bible, which were sent to Messolunghi from Corfu, were distributed in western Greece, and received with avidity; but several bishops and priests, whom I met at Napoli di Romania, told me that the translation was extremely defective. I answered, that if they thought proper to send a corrected copy to England, I would be very glad to become the bearer of it. Dyonisius, the bishop of Tripolitza, assured me he would attend to this subject.

Although there is surely no country in the world which has stronger claims on the support and sympathy of the Bible Society, than a people who are struggling to establish Christianity in the fairest portion of the globe, it is a singular fact, that with the exception of the Bibles which were sent from its agent at Corfu, nothing whatever has been done by the Society for Greece.*

* It is peculiarly gratifying to be able to state, that the result of bringing the Greek youths, alluded to in a former page, to England, has even exceeded my expectations. They were received by the Society of Friends and Greek Committee with the utmost kindness; and, pursuant to an arrangement made soon after their arrival, it was settled that they should be educated at the joint expense of the two associations.

It having been decided that they should be placed at the British and Foreign School Society, in the Borough-road, preparatory to their removal to such seminaries as may be best suited to the nature of their particular aptitudes, I can give no better proof of their progress at this excellent establishment, destined as it is to spread the seeds of knowledge throughout the most distant parts of the earth, than in stating the fact of my having been able to send specimens of their writing to the provisional government, when they had been only twenty days in the school. These specimens were such as to excite the surprise of all who saw them, more especially when informed that some of the boys had never held a pen in their hands before coming to England. The following are the names and ages of the youths in question:—Georgious Tombasi, of Hydra, 14; Eustratius Ralli, of Constantinople, 14; Stamo Nako, of Livadia, 13; Costa Sotiri, of Souli, 12; Demetrius Califomas, of Athens, 14; Antonio Lambro, of Smyrna, 12; Pericles Raftopolis, of Tinos, 12; Epatho Marolachi, of Scio, 12; Leonidas Dracakis, of Scio, 13. Two of these youths, Eustratius Ralli and Stamo Nako, have been removed to the celebrated establishment of Messrs. Hill

One of the last visits I paid at Napoli di Romania, was to a Mosque, the largest in Greece,

at Hazlewood, where they are to be educated at the expense of Mr. Bentham. A very fine young man, named Nicolo Vlaco, who travelled with me during my late visit to Greece, and a young Cefaloniote, N. Cacurattos, are also at the School Society in the Borough-road, preparing to become masters.

The friends of the Greek cause, and indeed of civilization generally, will be gratified to hear, that a committee has been already formed for the exclusive purpose of disseminating the blessings of education in Greece. Although the Greek Committee has done its utmost to promote this undertaking, it is but justice to add, that the Directors of the Foreign School Society take the lead, and are most sedulous in their endeavours to promote its success ;—it cannot, indeed, be in better hands.

While the arrangements connected with the Education Committee were yet in progress, a letter addressed to Mr. Bowring, was received from Mr. Patterson of Edinburgh, stating, that a number of ladies had formed an association in the Scottish capital for a similar purpose. It is hoped this example will be followed in England, where an attempt of the same kind has unhappily failed.

Madalena Mavrojenes, the heroine of Myconos, whose sacrifices and devotion to the cause of her country I had occasion to notice in my correspondence from Tripolitza, was among the residents at Napoli di Romania during my late stay there. Having expended the whole of her fortune in the cause, this interesting woman has nothing left but her patriotism and love of country, which I believe to be of the purest and most disinterested description. In the various conversations we had, I was forcibly struck by the justness of her sentiments, as well as the great anxiety she evinced to see all classes of the Greeks united. Her labours as a mediatrix have indeed often proved very successful. Madalena frequently inveighed in bitter terms against the apathy and indifference of the Christian world towards a cause which, she said, was their own. Having, at the close of our last inter-iew, observed, that I should be most happy to become the

and built of hewn stone, upon which the Turks had expended several hundred thousand piastres, but which, by a happy ordination of Providence, is ere now fitted up with galleries and benches, in the European style, and become the place of meeting and deliberation for the legislative assembly.

When every thing had been prepared for my departure, and that Mr. Hastings, whose gallantry and devotion to the Greek cause, I have more than once had occasion to notice, had determined to take his passage in the vessel,* an incident occurred which has since been the subject of very general discussion throughout Europe. I allude to the arrival of the Dispatch, Captain Scott, with a communication from Sir Frederick Adam, relative to the proclamation issued by the Provisional Government, when it was ascertained

medium of any communication she might be desirous of making to the women of England, whom I represented as feelingly alive to the fate of Greece, and the sufferings of its children, she handed me a letter addressed to them, on the day before my departure, and which will be found among the papers at the end of the volume.

* The object of my friend, Mr. Hastings' visit to England, was to superintend the construction of a steam vessel, towards the purchase of which, he had made the singularly generous offer of contributing £5000. If this admirable project has not been carried into execution, the fault does not rest with the able projector. It will, indeed, be a real misfortune to the cause, if it loses the services and talents of an officer who, to an intimate and scientific knowledge of the naval profession, unites the greatest bravery and presence of mind in action.

that the troops destined to invade the Morea, were to be brought from Egypt in European vessels, and belonging to those powers who had declared themselves neutral in the Greek contest. Having been called on to offer my opinion on the course which the Provisional Government ought to pursue, I had no hesitation in recommending that every concession should be made to the ministers of a country upon whose support Greece must in a great measure rely for her future independence. I at the same time, and with as little hesitation, assured the parties who applied to me that whatever the laws of nations enjoined, and the dignity of England required, no proclamation which the executive body could frame, would be sufficiently severe against men who could be so infamous and lost to all sense of religion and humanity, as to lend themselves to the projected invasion.

Embarking on board the Amphitrite on the evening of the 27th* of August, we did not leave the Bay before the 29th. Having occasion to communicate with Mr. Barff, of Zante, we arrived there in three days, and were allowed to lay off and on the Bay for nearly twenty-four hours, when we made sail for England. The only occurrence that

* Having been visited by a second attack of fever immediately after I got on board, and which prevented me from going on shore for the despatches, they were brought off the next day by my friend M. Xeno.

took place worth notice during our passage, was that of our having put into Malaga, where the flag of regenerated and free Greece waved nearly two whole days, while the town itself was in possession of a foreign force, and the people a prey to the persecutions and oppressions of the servile party. The moment we had received the supplies of water and provisions of which the want could alone induce us to venture into a Spanish port at such a time, a peremptory order came from the authorities to depart. Being favoured by the elements, we reached the entrance of the Channel in fifteen days, and had the additional pleasure of seeing the Greek standard flying in the Medway, on the 13th October, 1824. If I am particular in the date, it is because this is an event which certainly deserves to be recorded in the history of our time.

Being desirous of stating no facts of which I cannot speak with positive certainty, I shall leave the task of detailing naval and military events subsequent to my quitting Greece, to those who are on the spot. I may, however, be allowed to congratulate the friends of the cause on those exploits, whether at sea or on shore, which have justly raised the reputation already acquired by the Patriots, while they have added confidence to the hopes previously entertained of its ultimate triumph.

Having, by the various statements made after

my return from the Morea last year, so frequently alluded to the resources of Greece, and her means of fulfilling the financial obligations contracted on the London Stock Exchange, I was truly astonished, while at Napoli di Romania, to receive letters stating that the loan had fallen to a discount of 18 per cent! and this without any adequate cause being assigned, since the catastrophe of Ipsara was not yet known in England. But even a knowledge of that disaster ought not to have produced such a depression. Being absent at the time, I shall not hazard an opinion as to the cause which led to this circumstance; I must, however, both in justice to Greece, and those who may be induced to invest any part of their capital in her loan, express a hope, that in the event of any future financial operation, those entrusted with its management will leave no effort untried to prevent the fate that has befallen the first Greek loan, more especially in its earlier stages.

Knowing, as I do, that the consolidation of the social edifice in Greece, if not the safety of the cause itself, depends on the establishment of her credit in this country, I did not fail, during my late visit, to continue the inquiries commenced in the preceding year, relative to the resources of the confederation; and from the following statement, for which I am principally indebted to my valued friend Nicolo Contumas, the patriotic representative of Tinos, and the celebrated Professor Anthimos Gazi, of Thessaly, whom I found at Napoli, actively employed in representing the district of Olympus.

Pursuant to a law of the Legislative Body, passed during its last session, the Morea is divided into twenty-seven departments, namely—

Napoli di Romania, Argos, Corinth, Lower Nachaguis, Vostitza, Calavrita, Tripolitza, Caritena, Phanari, Arcadia, Pyrgos, Gastouni, Patrass, Mocastro and Modon, Coron, Nission, Mieromani, Andrussa, Emplakika, Calamata, Leondari, Eastern and Western Maina, Menomvasias, Mistras, Prastos, and San Pietro. What with the natives, and those who have been led to the Morea by the circumstances of the war, the number of inhabitants now there, is by the lowest calculation, estimated at 700,000, of these there are 70,000 in arms. As I have already made frequent allusions to the richness and fertility of this portion of Greece, it will be sufficient for the present object to state, that besides its producing every necessary of life in abundance, the exports of the Morea consist of the following articles, viz. olive oil, currants, silk, cotton, valonea, sponges, wool, goat and sheep skins, ship timber, and bees wax. In the article of provisions, great quantities of cattle, sheep, poultry, butter, cheese, and honey, are supplied to the Ionian Islands. The fruits principally exported from the Morea, are figs, oranges, lemons, and almonds.

Anxious to ascertain as nearly as possible the extent of the national domains, I am, from the concurrent testimony of several well informed members of the Legislative Assembly, induced to state that eighty parts out of a hundred of the whole country, will be at the disposal of the Legislature. This property, of which the value is incalculable, consists, of lands, olive plantations, forests, principally of oak and ash, and fir, salt pits, fisheries, public buildings, gardens, villas, &c.

Notwithstanding the impossibilty of cultivating more than a very small part of the soil, the Government was, during the last year, enabled to collect above a million of Spanish dollars merely from a tenth of the produce of private individuals, and its quota of 30 per cent. on what the national domains, of which there is but a very inconsiderable portion in cultivation, produced, together with a trifling duty on imports, and without levying a single tax. I am assured by many, that if the financial department was properly regulated, nearly double the above sum might have been raised in the Morea alone.

Continental Greece is divided into twenty-nine districts, the names of which are as follow :—Athens, Thebes, Livadia, Talentium, Butunitza, andTurkochori, Zeitouni, Almiyros and Cacossi, Magnesia, Salona, Lidoriki, Malandrina, Neopatras, Carpenissi, Cravoari, Venetico, Apocuro, Zigo, Vlocho, Xeromero, Vonitza, Messolunghi, Vrachori, Anatolico, Valtos, Agrapha, Arta, Aspropotamos, Dervenachoria, and Negropont.

The inhabitants of that part of Continental Greece which is in possession of the Greeks, is estimated at six hundred thousand souls, of whom forty thousand are capable of bearing arms. The exported produce consists of cotton, silk, wool, corn, oil, valonea, skins, ship timber, fir, cattle, and provisions of various kinds. With respect to the national property, in this portion of the confederacy, it bears an exact proportion, both as to its extent and value, to that of the Morea. Owing to its having been so frequently the seat of war, and the consequent impossibility of extending cultivation, as in the Peloponnesus, the amount of revenue collected last year is not estimated at more than half a million of Spanish dollars. According to the statements of Anthimos Gazi, who is intimately acquainted with the subject, Thessaly contains above 800,000 inhabitants, of which not more than 35,000 are Turks. There is not a more productive region in Europe, than that in the neighbourhood of Larissa and Zeitouni. The exports of Thessaly are very large, and consist of silk, wool, cotton, flax, hemp, wine, tobacco, wheat, rice, maize, &c. The best manufactures of Greece are also established in this country, particularly those of silk, cotton, and wool.

The Archipelago forms two divisions, that of

the Cyclades and Sporades. In the first are comprised—Tinos, Myconos, Syra, Paros, Antiparos, Sipros, Milos, Khimilos, Cos, Amorgos, Sykiro, Polycandros, Santorini, Astipalica, Anaphi, Zea, Thermia, and Seriphos. In the second; Samos, Patmos, Leros, Colymnos, Icaria, Scopelos, Scyros, Sckiathos, Melindronia, Carpathos, Nissiros, Simi, Chaliki, Episcope, Cassos, Ægina, Salamis, Angistrion, Poros, Hydra, Spezzia, and Ipsara. The inhabitants of these islands do not exceed 300,000 souls, of whom 50,000, including 20,000 excellent seamen, are capable of bearing arms. The revenue raised during the last year in this portion of the confederation, is estimated at 200,000 Spanish dollars. The island produce, consists of wine, silk, wool, valonea, sponges of the first quality, and various fruits. The number of merchant vessels belonging to the islands attached to the confederacy, is computed at about 2,500, of which one-third are ships and brigs.

There can indeed be no better proof of the internal resources of the confederation, than in the fact of its having carried on a successful warfare against the whole force of Turkey and the Barbary states, for three years, without borrowing a farthing, or receiving any assistance of consequence from without; and yet the whole of its debt, including the first loan contracted in this country, does not amount to five millions of Spanish dollars.

Some notion may be formed of the riches of

Greece, when I state, on the authority of the best political economists of the country, and after careful inquiry, that whenever the government shall be in a situation to dispose of the national property, the olive plantations alone will yield a sum of more than fifty millions of Spanish dollars.

Although there is no part of the world in which emigrants will find a more productive soil, or happier climate, than Greece, the time has not yet arrived when emigration to that country can be encouraged. Whenever the Turks are driven from the Morea, and that a strong government is formed, the plain of Gastouni, Vostitza, Corinth, and Argos, will be the most eligible points for settlers to establish themselves. Attica, more particularly the vicinity of Athens, is also a most desirable spot. It is needless to say, that the success attending emigrants to Greece, must depend on the protection and security afforded by the government.

When the circumstances of the confederation shall admit of it, great numbers will not fail to flock over to the continent from the Ionian Islands. These will be a most valuable acquisition to Greece, from that similarity of language and religion, which will enable them at once to assimilate with the people.*

* I was particularly struck by the eligibility of Port Tolone, which is now quite abandoned, for the establishment of a colony. This beautiful place is within about eight miles of Napoli di Ro-

In marking the origin and progress of this eventful struggle, and contemplating the future destinies of Greece, such is the variety of reflections which arise in the mind, that it is extremely difficult to select what is most worthy of comment. Those to which I am more particularly desirous of calling public attention, relate to the conduct of the christian world and policy of the European cabinets towards the Greeks, as well as to their future prospects of success.

When it is considered that no event of either ancient or modern times ever appealed so strongly to the passions and understanding of men as the Greek revolution; and that notwithstanding all the effects of prejudices arising out of the interests which the advocates of despotism fancied they had in suppressing public sympathy in favour of Greece, an acquiescence in her right to shake off the Turkish yoke, has been gradually gaining ground, until it is no longer disputed, even by their enemies; is it not both melancholy and humiliating to reflect, that with such irresistible claims, claims founded on the double basis of religion and humanity, and which were advocated by the most eloquent writers of the day, the whole sum subscribed by the christian world, to save a nation of christians threatened with exter-

mania, and at the southern extremity of the plain of Argos; it has an excellent harbour, and is well supplied with good water. Port Vivari, which is only four miles from Tolone, is perhaps one of the finest harbours in Europe.

mination, should not have exceeded £90,000; and that of this sum the most opulent nation of ancient or modern times, England, should only have contributed *one-fourth*, the rest being raised in Germany, Switzerland, and the United States, for the sums raised in France and Italy are scarcely worth naming. Should there be any set of persons disposed to account for this incredible apathy, when the motives to action were so imperative and sacred, it would be a satisfaction to hear the reasoning they have to put forth. For my own part, after having considered the subject in a variety of its bearings, I regret to say, that I think the future historians of our time, will attribute our want of sympathy for the suffering Greeks, to a spirit of selfishness, as incompatible with the national character of Englishmen, as it is opposed to the liberal institutions, of which it is our boast to have been so long the possessors.*

* By recent accounts, it appears that the Philellenes of the United States, have sent a steam vessel as large as a sloop of war to the Greeks. Should this be the case, they could not have sent a more valuable offering; and only estimating the value of this gift at £30,000, the United States will have subscribed twice as much to the Greek cause, as the whole British empire. In noticing the liberality of our trans-Atlantic friends and fellowmen, it should be remarked, thatt he subscriptions among them have been open little more than a twelvemonth. The press of America has however been most eloquent, as have the philanthropists of the Union, in support of the cause. I avail myself of the privilege of my valued friend, Mr Barker, of Thetford, who is unwearied in his labours in promoting the cause, to subjoin an admirable letter

While we deplore this lamentable want o charity, in a country which has acted so nobly in

received by him from a highly distinguished American citizen, residing at Washington, and of which the sentiments do him the very highest honour. May they serve as a guide and lesson to those in whose power it is to follow such wise and humane counsels!

"Washington, Sept. 30th, 1824.

"By the last mails we have received the dreadful news of the taking of Ipsara by treachery, and of the massacre of all the inhabitants of that island and Cassos, hanging many, and them to the yard-arms of their vessels! We shudder with horror at the feelings of those sovereigns of Europe who permit such atrocities to exist! for they are as much bound by the laws of God, to restrain such acts of horrible barbarity, in the nations of each other, as individuals in society are bound to notice the aggressions of individuals against their respective societies. It is in vain to plead the policy of nations; for it is a plea that divine justice will not admit, against the dictates of humanity and reason. When the inhabitants of Scio were butchered in cold blood, and their wives and daughters sold into the harems of the Turks, were not the feelings of every virtuous man roused, and did they not call for a dreadful example? But what was done! Not a monarch in Christendom moved a finger in behalf of the Greeks! On the contrary, some of them aided the Turks privately, to support the legitimacy of Governments!

"We felt afflicted at the exultation of Lord Strangford, when he obtained a cession of Moldavia and Walachia to Russia; for we think it will let loose an additional horde of savages upon the poor Greeks, already almost exhausted by the overwhelming numbers of their enemies. If, however, which I do sincerely hope, it was the intention of England to declare the Greeks a free and independent people, and that England would guarantee their possessions, and if it was necessary to obtain the consent of Russia, (whose inhabitants are nearly as barbarous and savage as the Turks), to whatever should be done for the Greeks, and this

other cases, I feel confident, in opposition to the opinion of many, for whose judgment I entertain

cession was the preliminary—then I hope the friends of humanity will not be disappointed in the intentions of England; for of all the glorious exertions that were ever made by a nation, that of Grecian support would redound the most to the grandeur of the British name; and after these inhuman massacres, which are enough to rouse the most cold-blooded politician, who could object to the interference of Great Britain? We have heard that their fleet was sent out to humble or destroy Algiers, because of an insult to their consul; and we do sincerely hope that they will not look with apathy on the murder of thousands of Christians, by their ancient allies, the Turks; but that they will drive them across the Hellespont, as an example to the barbarians of every country. The establishment also of the Greeks as an independent people, would extend the christian religion, and when we consider how much blood was shed, in vain, to establish christianity in the east, now, when it is completely in the power of England alone to effect this great object, we hope most earnestly that the opportunity may not be lost. Power formerly produced more effect in changing the opinions of the barbarians to Mahometanism than reason, and it will probably tend to remove their errors now. You may as well plead pity to the wolf, as try to melt such hardened hearts to kindness.

"We know that the English nation will view with abhorrence the massacre of so many innocent people, and consider it as one of the deepest crimes against the family of man. They were among the first to prevent the continuance of negro slavery, and I am in hopes they will be also the first to stand forth as the champions of christianity, in the preservation of the christian Greeks.

"Were the English, in punishment of such infernal acts against the common laws of humanity, to declare that they cannot longer countenance so barbarous a people, and therefore declare and guarantee the independence of the Greeks, they would prevent the *injurious interference of other nations;* for knowing the immense power of the English at sea; knowing their pecuni-

the highest respect, that it is now too late to expect there can be any considerable funds raised

ary means, and the unconquerable spirit of so gallant a people, no crown would dare to contend against such a force, engaged in the cause of God and of humanity; for the virtuous people of every nation would be on the side of England! What a glorious opportunity for displaying that noble chivalric spirit which prevails so universally in England! It is a nation of virtue, of honour, and magnanimity!

"Our Government are deeply concerned for the Greeks, but they have thought it improper to interfere in the politics of Europe; for, being unwilling that those nations should disturb the repose of this continent, it has been thought proper that this *government* suppress as much as possible all but our sympathies and sincere wishes for the prosperity and advancement of the cause of the Greeks.

"Postscript.—Since writing the above, we have been gratified and astonished by the exertions of the brave Greeks, who have retaken Ipsara, and destroyed a portion of the Turkish fleet! Every event tends more and more to shew them worthy of the aid of civilized christians; for such acts of heroism and devotion to the cause of their country, were scarcely ever exhibited by any other people! Such a nation is indeed worthy of all that can be done for them, for they will be capable of equalling, perhaps even of surpassing, their ancient splendour in morals and virtue. They have given such proofs of magnanimity, that every thing great may be expected from them; and as they have declared that they will die rather than again submit to the Turks, why will christians look on their gradual extirpation, and permit such cruelties as the Turks have committed? If the Greeks be supported, they will offer a barrier against the extension of Russian power. But if the Greeks and Turks, by such bloody conflicts, should be gradually exhausted, they will both become an easy prey to the rapacity of the Russians, who will fall upon them with fresh men and means. It would therefore be humane to aid them in this great work of emancipation.

by subscription in any part of Europe for Greece. With this conviction on my mind, it is natural to inquire how and to what extent the Greek committees of North America, Germany, Switzerland, and this country, can contribute to the cause in aid of which they were established.

Nothing could be more praiseworthy on the part of the committees, during the early stages of their formation, and when there was a reasonable hope that their numerous and eloquent appeals to the public, would have been answered in a far different way to what they were, than sending out warlike stores and volunteers. It is, however, to be regretted, that two causes contributed greatly to diminish the service which might have been thus rendered to Greece; the first of these was, the incapacity and unfitness of many of the individuals unhappily chosen to conduct

"The European nations we know are jealous of the very movements of England, for they justly consider England as at the head of free governments; and the arbitrary potentates find it difficult to make a distinction between a free government (where the laws govern, and where the monarch is subject to law as well as the people,) and a republic. They think the moment a king ceases to be arbitrary he ceases to enjoy the regal rights. Thus were the Spaniards forced by the French to annul their constitution, which would have regenerated the nation; and the late cruel and arbitrary acts of the king have produced a civil war, which must end in his destruction,—for the dark ages have passed, and the lights of philosophy and reason permit not the gloomy horrors of monkish superstition to impose on man with impunity!"

the affairs with which they were entrusted; and the second, that system of warfare and want of organization, which rendered it impossible for the Greeks to avail themselves of supplies that might, otherwise, have been of the utmost utility and importance.

In noticing the incapacity and want of principle which has been but too justly laid to the charge of several individuals who have joined the Greek standard, it would be exceedingly unjust not to say that the number is very limited, while the great majority of the Philellenes, have been distinguished by all those qualities which would, under different circumstances, have rendered them an invaluable acquisition to any cause. Without entering into a detail of the circumstances which have, unhappily, induced so many excellent men to withdraw from the cause, or naming the individuals whose conduct has forced them to adopt that painful alternative; I am bound to add, that no blame whatever can be attached to the Greek nation at large, or those enlightened patriots with whom I have been in communication.*

* It would appear, from the remarks of a recent traveller, that there have been found individual Greeks, so base and lost to every sense of gratitude, as to "ridicule and despise" that Phillellenism, which has induced so many to sacrifice fortune, health, and even life itself in their cause.

The remarks which follow the above statement, are by no means in accordance with the liberal spirit which "peeps out"

But taking it for granted that the establishment of the credit of Greece in the money markets of Europe, will render assistance of the above description less necessary; and that what might be regarded as the political interference of the committees, will cease with this new state of things; have they not a noble field still open in combining their operations, for the purpose of promoting education and a knowledge of the useful arts throughout the confederacy? If to the prosecution of the foregoing objects, they adopt the resolution of appropriating a portion of their funds to the preservation of the ancient remains,*

in several parts of the author's animated sketch of Grecian affairs. Without stopping to examine those other points upon which I think he might be most easily refuted, the Philellenes, with whom he takes such frequent pains to disclaim all connexion, may surely be permitted to ask, whether it be really a proof of "madness," or of the absence of "political virtue, &c." to have espoused a cause like that of Greece?

* If it be too much to anticipate the restoration of these splendid monuments, surely every effort ought to be made to prevent their total destruction. It is on this account and because the Greek committees may be supposed more capable of appreciating them, than the unlettered people of Greece, that I feel anxious to suggest how much may be done in this matter. It is worthy of remark, that among all the travellers of rank and fortune who have visited Athens, from every part of Europe, not one should have ever undertaken either to preserve or restore any of its ancient monuments. It is not less humiliating to think, that the only person who seems to have considered it a merit to despoil the Parthenon, should have been a Briton!

and rescuing those treasures of art, which abound in almost every part of Greece, a truly important service would be rendered to the cause of civilization. When the time arrives for divesting the committees of all traces of their political attributes, every excuse for luke-warmness, which these have hitherto furnished, will be removed, and thus afford the best chance of embracing all parties and opinions; a desideratum which it has till now been found totally impossible to attain.

Were the members of the Continental committees, North America and England, to unite with the Philomusæ society of Athens, and in which many of the ministers, if not some members of the Holy Alliance are already enrolled, and thus form one general association for the

Though it has, as yet, been impossible for the Government either to take any effectual steps for the preservation of the ancient remains, or excavating for those which still lie buried in almost every point of the confederation, the prohibition to export any more statues or bas-reliefs, proves that it is not indifferent on this subject; indeed, I am enabled to state, that whenever the seat of government can be transferred to Athens, one of the first objects of the legislature, will be that of establishing a national museum, convinced, as it is, that this will be the best answer it could give to the aspersions of Sir William Gell, and some German travellers, as well as making the ancient mistress of civilization the centre of modern attraction. The friends of art will be glad to hear, that scarcely a day passes without the discovery of some new treasures. Such is the inexhaustible field left to posterity by the ancients!

above-named purpose; I need not say, what incalculably beneficial consequences the friends of Greece and humanity might not anticipate.

Flattering as it is to England to have led the way in educating a number of Greek youths, who are, I trust, destined to render eminent services to their country, it is most desirable that the committees of other countries should follow our example: convinced, as I am, that this is of all others, the most effectual mode of promoting the great interests of the cause.

I have but little to add to the observations made in another place, relative to the policy of the great powers towards Greece, except some facts that occurred during my late visit, which prevent me from altering a single opinion then offered to the public.

What with the innate justice of the Greek cause itself, and the progress of public opinion in its favour, I naturally expected to find a corresponding disposition on the part of the Austrian and French officers commanding the squadrons of these two powers in the Mediterranean, more especially, as the ministerial journals of France had all along affected to be highly favourable to the cause; while the "Austrian Observer," the avowed organ of the Cabinet of Vienna, had relaxed in its censure of the Greeks, for some weeks before I left London. In noticing the following facts connected with this subject, as a matter of duty, I do not mean to assert, that the aggressors were authorized to act as they have, by their respective governments. Indeed I am particularly anxious, that this allusion to the conduct of a few isolated individuals should not be considered as betraying any wish on my part to implicate either the French nation or its government, convinced as I am, that the Greek cause has found as able and eloquent advocates in France, as in any other part of the world. It should also be observed, that these have been confined to no party.*

One of the first causes of complaint, on the part of the Provisional Government, arose from the fact of a small French squadron arriving at Napoli di Romania in the latter end of May, while that fortress was still retained by the anti-patriots, for the purpose of negotiating the ransom of the Turkish Bey taken at the time of its capture: they had already made considerable progress in the arrangements for their liberation, when a detachment, which had taken possession of a small isolated fort near the town, notified to the French captain, that if he did not withdraw, and address himself to the legitimate government at

* It gives me peculiar pleasure to be enabled to state, since the above was written, a Philellenic Society has been actually formed at Paris, containing some of the most distinguished names in France, and, of all parties. I understand that the principal object of the Society is, to promote instruction in Greece, as well as educate a number of youths.

the Molini, within a given time, the battery would be opened on him. This had the desired effect, and the vessels departed without being able to succeed in their mission. *

It was not many days after the above transaction, that a French brig of war took a chiaox or messenger of the Capitan Pacha, to the island of Naxos; he was sent there for the express purpose of summoning the inhabitants to submit to the Porte. But the most serious charge of all, is that which represents the French and Austrian commanders as having given their opinions, if not advice, as to the best mode of attacking Ipsara. If, as I was assured by several highly respectable inhabitants of that ill-fated island, an Austrian frigate, which appeared on its coasts a few days before the catastrophe, sent her boats to sound and examine every part of the island, and that the result of this survey was conveyed to the Capitan Pacha, then at Mytelene, there is no language too severe for such conduct. Although this statement was made to the government at Napoli, and very generally believed throughout Greece, I merely give it, without vouching for

* The Greeks could not help connecting this anxiety about liberating the Turkish Pacha, with a wish on the part of the French agents to make his services available to the expedition of Mehemet Ali; for it should be observed, that of all the military leaders the Porte had in the Greek provinces, this man was the best acquainted with its resources and localities.

the authenticity of an act which would cover those concerned with merited opprobrium. It was also remarked by the Greeks, that whenever they came in contact with the enemy's squadron, they invariably saw either an Austrian or French vessel in sight, for what purpose they could not assert.*

In stating the complaints of the Greeks, it is but justice to add, that a French corvette came to Napoli, a few days after the arrival of Lord Charles Murray and myself, bringing a hundred and fifty of the Ipsariot fugitives: this act would, however, have assumed a much more disinterested and generous character, had it not been made the pretext for renewing the negociation relative to the Turkish Bey. Indeed M. Brest, the French consul at Milos, who is known for his hostility to the Greeks, came in the vessel, and together with the captain, almost insisted on the government giving up the Turk in exchange for the fugitives. This was very properly resisted, on the plea that they could not consent to the release of an officer, who might be of so much use in facilitating the projects of the enemy, at the moment when the Morea was threatened with invasion.

* A paragraph appeared in the Hydra newspaper, during my stay at Napoli, which stated, I know not how truly, that the captain of a ship of war, I will not say of what nation, refused to assist a Greek vessel which had run ashore at Syra, lest it should be considered as a breach of neutrality!

Influenced by these arguments, the negociation ended by the disembarkation of the Greek women and children, and the departure of the French captain and M. Brest.

While noticing the conduct of the French and Austrian agents, it might well be regarded as an act of partiality, were I to omit stating that the agents of the Levant Company have not relaxed in any of their hatred and hostility to the Greeks or their cause. Having already expressed my opinion on the conduct of those who have been placed to represent England, and watch over her interests in the Mediterranean, as well as on the impolicy of tolerating such a system, I shall merely add, that Patrass still continues, as it has done for the last three years, to be regularly supplied by the British agents of Yousuff Pacha, resident at Zante, and that their vessels had free admission into ports of the Ionian Islands, during my late visit. Were I permitted to name one of them, and the mode in which he has discharged a solemn public trust, I should excite the indignation of every honest and honourable mind. But I will leave him, and others, to enjoy wealth, which has been acquired by the sacrifice of every honourable principle. It is scarcely necessary to repeat, that the ministers of England will be rendering an immense service to their country, by revising the consular system in the Levant, and that the delay in effecting what might be so easily done, is a source of the greatest injury to our political and commercial interests in that part of the world.*

In alluding to the Ionian Islands, it is with infinite satisfaction I am enabled to state, that, notwithstanding the extreme difficulty of the task imposed on the present Lord High Commissioner, Sir Frederick Adam, the neutrality is conducted upon less harsh principles than formerly, though probably without any departure from the instructions of government. When it is considered that these islands belong to the Continent, without whose aid the inhabitants could not exist, there is something truly unnatural in that state of things which has forced them to act in many instances, as the allies of the Turks against their co-religionists and countrymen.

When those who are acquainted with the transactions at the Congress of Vienna, reflect by what an accident the Ionian Islands fell into our hands, after being almost rejected by a late minister, and compare it with the importance they have

* It is most satisfactory to be enabled to state, that since the above was written, a notification is said to have been addressed to the Levant Company, by Mr. Canning, recommending the return of its charter into the hands of government. Although this salutary measure is rendered incomplete, by suffering the consular agents of the company to remain, it is by no means the least important service rendered by the Foreign Secretary since his accession to office.

now acquired, they cannot help exulting in a circumstance which may be rendered so conducive to the interests of humanity in the east of Europe. In order, however, to render these Islands what they might become, an acquisition of the highest importance and value, it cannot be too often repeated, that they must be governed more in the interests of the rulers and the ruled. As all the modifications required to render British protection popular, and the people prosperous, can be done without incurring a farthing expence; it is devoutly to be hoped, that ministers will make up their minds on this subject without loss of time. If they do, the task of inquiry and reform cannot be confided to better hands than the actual Lord High Commissioner, who has, since the reins of government have been in his own hands, proved himself a true friend to the Ionians.

Although there is no direct evidence to prove that Russia has interfered so actively as the two powers just named, it would be ridiculous to suppose that the cabinet of St Petersburgh was less interested than heretofore in the progress of the struggle, or that, notwithstanding its former policy, there were not Russian partisans still in Greece. Having already recorded my humble opinion as to the views and interests of the great powers with regard to what is passing in the east of Europe, and seeing that subsequent events have only tended to confirm what I ventured to assert last year, it merely remains for me to notice the reports in circulation, previous to my alluding to the hopes of the Greeks, and their means of prosecuting the contest.

Those who compare the doctrines held out at Laybach and Verona, with the treatment of the Greek patriots, and general policy of the allied monarchs, do not require to be told, that they were decidedly unfavourable to the success of the cause, as well as the principle upon which it is founded. Whether the non-interference of the sovereigns is attributable to any expectation that the Porte would succeed in re-conquering its christian vassals, or that a prolongation of the contest would not fail to weaken both parties, and thus render them more tractable on a future day, I will not attempt to decide ; but from what has transpired relative to a congress of ministers being assembled at St. Petersburgh or Paris, for the express purpose of treating on the affairs of Greece, it is evident that there is at length a determination to interfere. If this project could be attributed to the dictates of humanity, instead of the dread inspired by the spectacle of a people conquering their freedom through every obstacle, well might the Holy Alliance claim absolution and oblivion of all its aggressions against human liberty. But the experience of the past furnishes such proofs that it arises rather from the fear of the revolutionary principle, than any sympathy for Greece ; as to render it necessary that every precaution should be taken to prevent the consequences which are inevitable, if the projected interference be not closely watched by England.

It has been whispered, that a means, to which one would imagine certain powers could never have thought of resorting, have been adopted to intimidate England, and make her desist from pursuing a policy dictated no less by her own interests than those of justice and humanity. It is said that in the course of some conferences which have taken place in the political circles of Vienna, those who influence the policy of the northern courts, have more than once hinted that if England continued to be the champion of revolted countries, they did not see why others should not follow the example, with regard to those discontents which agitate a portion of our own empire.

Strange as it may appear to those who know how much it is against the interest of Austria to coalesce with Russia, in her projects of aggrandizement on the side of Turkey, there is every reason to believe that all the efforts of our ministers have not enabled them to prevail on the cabinet of Vienna to detach itself from that of St. Petersburgh on the subject of Greece. Should this be really the case, who knows but the new connection of the two great rivals of the north, may have a close affinity to the offensive and defensive alliance formed between Catherine and Leopold; previous to the war of 1790.

When the invariable policy of Russia and Austria, with regard to European Turkey, is considered, a policy which has for its object the extension of their respective frontiers towards the south; can any thing be more opposed to the wishes of these two cabinets, than the establishment of a power which would form a barrier to their future plans of ambition? This is the grand point to which I imagine a British statesman ought to direct his whole attention.*

* Although there are no accredited foreign agents in the confederation, it is not doubted but all the great continental cabinets have minute information of what passes. There is reason to fear that England, the power most deeply interested, is by far the worst informed on the subject of Greece.

Whether the project of restoring the Knights of Malta was abandoned, or merely suspended, I could not ascertain while in the Morea. The two agents who were employed by the projectors of this famous scheme, had visited Messolunghi and Argos during the winter; and after three months fruitless efforts to make the project palatable at either places, they departed for Syra, an island in the Archipelago, under the special protection of France, in March. It was of great importance to the Greeks, that a positive denial should not be given on the subject of their mission, before they knew that the negociation for the loan had been effected. This desire will alone account for the length of Messrs. C*** and J***'s visit.

Previously to the arrival of those individuals, a communication had been made to Colocotroni and Mavromichalis, with a view of ascertaining what their views with regard to the future mode of

The policy dictated by the new position of England with regard to the continental powers is so obvious, that it might well be considered superfluous, were I to attempt offering an opinion on the subject in this place; yet how is it possible to avoid some allusion to that state of things so new in Europe, which has changed her from the ally of despotism to the protectress of freedom and constitutional rights! It is this happy change which has rendered her more especially the friend of regenerated Greece, by far the greatest honour that ever fell to the lot of any nation. Thus it is, that while it becomes the business of the future historian of the present day, to condemn the conduct of the Christian world towards the struggling Greeks, he will be bound to confess, that without the possession of the Ionian Islands by England, they might have remained much longer in bondage; and that whatever may have been the apathy displayed by the wealthier portion of the community with regard to the cause, the loan so happily contracted in this country must secure the triumph of Greece if she be true to herself.

governing Greece were, and whether they would not consent to be governed by Hospodars. This communication, though made on the immediate authority of the Austrian ministry, is said to have been fully approved by all the members of the Holy Alliance.

Owing to the unsettled state of affairs, and consequent impossibility of collecting the opinions of the opposite party, the negociation of which the above communication was doubtless intended to be the prelude, did not take place.

This will indeed be a source of proud exultation to our posterity, while the immense service we have already rendered, is fully appreciated throughout the confederation.

So convinced were the legislative and executive bodies of the paramount importance of cultivating a good understanding with this country, when I left the seat of government, that no measure was left untried to profit by it, or improve a connection on the stability of which, they felt convinced their final success so mainly depended.

The opinions I ventured to give last year, on the total impracticability of renewing, under any modifications, the unnatural connection with the Porte, have acquired more strength than ever from subsequent observation and inquiry. These opinions are founded now, as when first advanced, on the conviction that the Turks would consider no compact with their revolted vassals binding, and that if suffered to occupy a single point of the confederacy, hostilities would only cease with the extermination of one party or the other. Surely with a certainty of this fact before their eyes, the allied sovereigns would not force the Greeks to submit to such conditions, after having abandoned them to their fate,—nay, shewn a predilection in favour of the infidels for nearly four years! It is indeed difficult to conceive upon what principle the Holy Alliance can interfere in the contest, except with a view of establishing the independence of Greece, and thus wiping off a stain, which even such an act of religion and justice can hardly ever wash away.

The payment of an annual tribute, as suggested by some politicians, would be scarcely less hateful to the Greeks than the occupation of their territory, inasmuch as it would make them virtually the vassals of their old tyrants, while the smallest neglect or delay in its payment would at any time furnish the Ottomans with a plausible pretext for declaring war. The only way in which compensation can be given to the Porte, is, in my humble opinion, by the payment of a round sum in the first instance. But would it not be a crying injustice to make the Greeks, exhausted as they are by their heroic efforts, pay this? And ought not the allied sovereigns who interfere, contribute whatever might be thought an adequate compensation to the Porte? Should they refuse to do this, an appeal might be made to the Christian world: that has also the crime of apathy and indifference to answer for; and it cannot redeem the sin more effectually, than by coming forward to ransom its fellow Christians of the east from the yoke under which they have so long groaned.

In the general observations made before my last visit to Greece, I ventured to assert that a federative system of government was that which appeared most proper for Greece. This opinion was founded on the impossibility of bringing about an accommodation with the Porte, and on the isolated nature of the country, as well as the almost total absence of those materials of which the old monarchies of Europe are composed. If, however, additional inquiry, and circumstances which I did not foresee during my first visit to Greece, have led to some modification in my opinion, on the latter subject, they remain quite unchanged with regard to the former point. It will therefore be readily imagined, with what sorrow and surprise I have heard, that it is in contemplation to revive the odious question of establishing Hospodariots in the Greek provinces.

This project, which, while it would completely answer the views of Austria and Russia, and render the condition of the Greeks infinitely worse than they were under Voivodes and Pachas of the late tyranny, is so opposed to the interests of humanity and self-evident policy which this country ought to pursue, that I trust it will be firmly opposed in all its stages. On the other hand, while I maintain that the establishment of a monarchy in Greece, will be attended with the greatest difficulty, I am free to confess, that if a sacrifice is to be made to the monarchical principle, I would, in common with the most enlightened patriots of Greece, infinitely rather see a foreign prince placed over that country, than witness a compromise, by which all the fruits of its glorious struggle would be totally lost. If there are any other arguments in favour of a scheme of which the practicability has so often been doubted, it arises from a conviction on the mind of the leading men in Greece, that the dissensions which were so thickly sown, or rather the natural result of the Turkish system, as well as the difficulties attending the consolidation of a strong government on the federative principle, would be most easily removed by the introduction of a prince into Greece, in the same condition as Charles John has been received by the Swedes. Should this mode of reconciling all interests be adopted, I need hardly add, that the success of such a plan would depend altogether on the guarantees which the great powers offered to the person chosen by the Greeks to assume the reins of the new government. In the course of the various conversations I held on this subject while in Greece, I could perceive that even those who were most in favour of receiving a foreign prince, were quite appalled by the difficulties that might arise. Some of this class of politicians, for whose opinions I entertain great respect, candidly confessed to me that their minds had long wavered between a limited monarchy, like that of England, and the federative system, as established in Swisserland. I have already said, that so far as I could judge of the disposition of the people, all they required was the formation of a government which should put an end to the present state of anarchy. If I observed any change in favour of monarchy on the part of the people, during my late visit, it arose from a dread of the impossibility of reconciling the primates and military chiefs, as well as a firm conviction that one tyrant is preferable to a hundred!

Such, however, is the difficulty of deciding which form of government is most likely to secure the happiness of Greece, and insure its independence, that opinions are naturally very much divided among the Greeks themselves. But of one thing I feel convinced, and which it may not be irrelevant to repeat in this place; it is, that additional observation and inquiry enables me to say, that so far as the representative body is concerned, they are as far removed from wild and visionary schemes on one side, as they are from the revolutionary principles attributed to Greece by the declarations at Verona, on the other. What they ask for, is rational freedom, and institutions which shall assimilate them to the most free and prosperous nations of Europe. Surely the fact of their aspiring to these blessings forms their best panygeric!

It need not excite surprise, if the hostility of some European princes, and the indifference of all, should have rendered the monarchical system unpopular in Greece. If, however, the Greeks could persuade themselves that a prince would be found capable, by his talents and virtues, of governing with probity and vigour, I am inclined to believe they would not hesitate to receive him.*

* It is a singular and melancholy fact, but little creditable to the age, that not one of the crowned heads or sovereign princes of Europe, except Pius VII. and his successor, has manifested the smallest sympathy for Greece. The only instance I have heard of as an exception to the general rule, was communicated

I have, on a former occasion, alluded to the injustice of the politicians of England and France, animadverting too severely on the dissensions of the Greeks; when all the circumstances of their

to me by a Prussian officer whom I met in the Morea. He told me that he had it on very good authority, that his sovereign had one day filled a bumper, and drank to the success of the Greeks!

What a contrast does not this universal apathy exhibit with the noble and generous sentiments of Henry IV. of France, whose great ambition was to gain a battle over the Turks of his day, which should force them to abandon Constantinople and recross the Hellespont!

With the exception of Count Capodistrias, and another, whom it is perhaps rather too soon to name, I fear history will have to make the same reproach to all the leading statesmen and ministers of our day. Here I feel a particular pleasure in having an opportunity of recording the high admiration inspired by the conduct of this upright minister, and able diplomatist,—whose efforts to bring about the regeneration of his country, and sacrifices in its cause, are entitled to the highest panegyric.

If it be rare in this age of egotism and venality among too many of those who aspire to fill the higher offices of state, to find a man possessing the most liberal and enlightened sentiments in favour of freedom, it is still more so to witness the instance of this statesman sacrificing all his rank, honours, and wealth, rather than abjure his principles or abandon his country. When I add, that such a man is Capodistrias, it would be superfluous to say one word more in his praise. The name of such a man cannot, however, be too often cited, or held up at once as an object of public applause, and an example to his contemporaries.

Whatever may be the fate of Greece, or his native islands, which form an integral part of it, I feel assured that the Count will never have to reproach himself with any want of zeal or patriotism.

previous history and sufferings are taken into consideration, it would really be expecting more virtue than human nature is capable of, to imagine that a people, governed as they have been, could possess those elements of union, which have never been found in the best regulated communities of Europe. It is from a conviction of this sort that I have, on more than one occasion, been called upon to express my dissent from those Philellenes who consider it criminal in the leading patriots of Greece to advocate the policy of introducing a foreign prince. In alluding to this subject, I am bound to say, that in the whole of my intercourse with them, I cannot name a single individual who has expressed himself decidedly on the subject; and as the metropolitan Ignatius, and my illustrious friend Prince Mavrocordato, have been more particularly alluded to, I do not hesitate to offer it as my firm belief, that neither of them deserve the imputations laid to their charge on this subject. With regard to the former; having been honoured with his friendship and correspondence from the first moment of my arrival in the confederation, I owe it to candour and truth to say, that to talents of the very highest order, I never saw more probity and disinterestedness in any man holding a public situation.

The difficulties with which the prince has had to contend, were, in fact, such as would have weighed down the stoutest heart; yet, it would seem that privations and persecutions have only tended to give additional vigour to his mind. For if those who have so unworthily endeavoured to depreciate his character in Greece and England, only reflected on the manner in which he has conducted the affairs of western Greece, during the last year, without money or resources, and hourly assailed by a clamorous soldiery, totally impatient of controul, nothing but a determination to censure without cause, or the envy to which public virtue is exposed, would surely have prompted their unmerited slanders.

As to the venerable metropolitan, his whole life has been devoted to the great object of liberating his unhappy fellow countrymen from the barbarous yoke under which they laboured; and it is, perhaps, the highest panegyric of the Emperor Alexander, that he should have extended his patronage and protection to such a man. If Ignatius be favourable to a foreign king, I feel assured that it arises from a conviction, that, by connecting the interests of Greece with that of the other monarchies of Europe, both her internal happiness and external security would be promoted. At a time when the friends of freedom are so justly deprecating intolerance, whether in religion or politics, it is really an act of the highest inconsistency to censure those who happen to think for themselves, on points which must long continue to divide the opinions of mankind.

In thus alluding to the character and conduct

of two individuals who are deservedly the most popular in Greece, I might add a great number of names, scarcely less distinguished for their patriotism and public virtue. Nor, if I chose to reverse the picture, would it be difficult to designate others who have excited the praises and been favoured with the esteem of some Grecian travellers,* without possessing any very consider-

* It will hardly be credited, that individuals who have been notorious for the most cold-blooded cruelties and contempt of law, should have become objects of enthusiastic praise, and been even pointed out as the only men capable of saving Greece. No wonder that those who could thus deceive themselves, have represented Prince Mavrocordato as an intriguing fanariot. His letters to Colonel Stanhope and myself will be the best reply to those who have thus attempted to vilify his name.

One of the heavy charges brought against the prince, was that of his preventing Lord Byron from attending a congress of the chiefs of eastern and western Greece at Salona, for the alleged purpose of reconciling parties and taking measures for carrying on the ensuing campaign with vigour. The legislative and executive bodies no sooner heard of the intended meeting, and those by whom it was to be composed, than they sent couriers both to Athens and Messolunghi, formally disapproving the project, as only calculated to increase the existing dissensions, and endanger still more the public tranquillity. The truth is, there was but too much reason to suspect, that one of the secret objects of the meeting was to discuss whether it would be prudent to join the legitimate government, or the anti-patriot faction. Surely this was a sufficient motive for interdicting the prince from sanctioning such an association by his presence. As it happened, the congress met, and after a few speeches on either side, it dispersed, without being able, for want of means, to adopt a single measure of the smallest utility.

able claims to either. Being, however, satisfied that the greatest injury must accrue to Greece, from every attempt on the part of foreigners to fan the flame of discord among her sons, my whole intention is now, as it has ever been, to reconcile their differences, and make them feel that their interests are the same. It is upon this principle that when I saw individuals, upon whose public conduct I felt myself called upon to animadvert, during my first visit to the Morea, placing themselves at the head of the philanthropic society, I did not for a moment hesitate to hail them as patriots and friends. For in politics, as in morals, I hold it to be the duty of us all to appreciate men solely by their actions.

The object of the meeting and points for discussion, suggested by Colonel Stanhope, were admirable, had there been any person to appreciate their value or undertake their management; but this was unhappily not the case, and the result might, therefore, have been very easily anticipated.

Convinced, as I am, that without being either wild or visionary in his political tenets, the prince *is* a friend of liberty in the fullest sense of the word, I could not help feeling some surprise at the following extract from the nineteenth letter published in the gallant colonel's work: "Prince Mavrocordato is a good man; do not imagine, however, that he is a friend of liberty in a large sense; he is not: but these are no times for the avowal of sentiments hostile to freedom."

The best possible reply to this remark is, the fact of the prince's having had by far the greatest share in framing the law of Epidaurus, and the scrupulous manner in which he has adhered to it ever since.

As to the state of parties in Greece, nothing occurred during my stay in the Morea, to alter the opinion I gave previous to quitting Zante in June. As I had conjectured, I found the great mass of the people and their representatives, steadily bent on making every exertion and undergoing every sacrifice to attain their independence; while those classes, forming but a very small party, who had been accustomed to power, or unsubdued by the Turks, still wished to dominate. In this state of things nothing could be more salutary than the controlling power of the legislative body, and I am bound to bear testimony to the wisdom and prudence with which this was exercised on every occasion. From all I have seen in Greece, I must say, that I do not think the advantages of the representative system has ever been more strongly exemplified, than in a country in which its elements could have been least expected to exist.

In offering my tribute of admiration to the representatives of the Greek people, for the wisdom and firmness they have hitherto displayed, under the severest trials, it is needless to say, that all my hopes of the final triumph of the cause, are founded on their future energies and prudence. Here it may be proper to state, that in consequence of the vague reports about the probable interference of the allied sovereigns, in the affairs of Greece, which reached Napoli di Romania, previous to my departure, I took particular pains to ascertain the sentiments of the leading men in the legislative assembly, as to what their views and opinions were. From the result of my inquiries, I am enabled to state, that while the legislature of Greece admit the necessity of re-examining all they have done, with the view of modification and improvement, it would be not only dangerous to the success of the cause, but pusillanimous to abrogate the laws to which all have sworn, before the enemy is driven from their country. This grand object once achieved, they will be happy to profit by the wisdom and counsel which may have a tendency to the above great end, without particularly adhering to opinions that have not had the test of experience to render them unquestionable.

With respect to the actual state of the Turkish empire; it will be recollected, that in calling upon the allied powers to put an end to the effusion of Christian blood, at the close of the third campaign, I stated that the inevitable result of the contest would be that of exhausting the power of the Porte, until it became an easy prey to the first comer. In suggesting that the too sudden dissolution of the Ottoman empire, might be detrimental to the interests of Great Britain, I argued from an hypothesis, upon which it would now be quite superfluous to dilate. If any doubts were entertained of the observations I made last year, as to the rapid decline of the Ottoman power, it is only necessary to reflect on the events of the fourth campaign, in which the Porte has expended twenty millions of dollars, without gaining a single advantage, except that at Ipsara, while its fleets and armies have met with nothing but discomfiture and disgrace. This, too, when the Greeks were unable to act for above four months of the season best calculated for naval and military operations.

The reverses experienced in Candia last year, were occasioned solely by the poverty of the Greeks, and consequent impossibility of either organising the population, or supplying them with ammunition. The determination of Mehemet Ali, on the other hand, to possess himself of this beautiful island, by far the most productive and valuable section of the confederacy, has rendered it impossible for the natives to organize themselves, so as to keep the field. Whenever the Turks are driven from Patrass, and the central government can turn its attention in good earnest to Candia, there will be no difficulty in rescuing the population, as, from the cruelties to which they have ever been exposed, there is no part of Greece in which the people have so deadly a hatred for their tyrants. I have already stated, that, out of a population of 250,000 souls which Candia contains, not more than one-fourth are Mahometans, and of these, many are called Mussulman-Christians, from its being well known, that a number of families merely embraced Mahometanism from fear, after the conquest of the Island, in 1645, and that while they outwardly conformed to all its rites, they had subterraneous chapels where the religion of their fathers was practised in secret, and whenever they could do so, without fear of detection. Courmouli, the head of one of the most distinguished families in Candia, and who held the place of Grand Aga, had, together with the whole of his family, always retained his faith in secret, and no sooner did the revolt break out, than he declared himself, and devoted the whole of his wealth, which was very considerable, to the cause. Having placed himself at the head of a large body of his countrymen, and displayed great gallantry during the first two years of the struggle, he came over to Hydra last year; and being seized with a fever, arising from excessive anxiety and fatigue, he died there in the early part of May. His family removed shortly after to Napoli di Romania, where they resided during my stay there.

From the inquiries I made, and information received, while in the Morea, relative to this subject, so calculated to interest the Christian world, I have no doubt but that even the Turkish capital itself contains a number of Mahometan Christians. Many well informed Candiots assured me, that there could not be less than a thousand families of the above description in that island.

Whenever the time comes for disclosing all that relates to the Ottoman dominion in Europe, there is no doubt but a great mass of singularly interesting anecdotes will appear.

The number of Mahometan Christians in Epirus is, however, infinitely greater than any other part of Greece, as the persecutions which followed the death of the heroic Scanderberg, left no alternative to the natives between death and apostacy. Although it has been remarked that this portion of the population are, if possible, more vindictive in their hatred of their Christian neighbours than the Turks, there is no doubt but the fact of their forefathers having professed the same religion, would greatly facilitate any attempt to bring about a reconciliation.*

With respect to the sentiments which pervade the Mahometan population of Turkey in Europe, it is the opinion of the most enlightened men in

* Although it will require some time to remove jealousies which were no less the result of clashing interests than the system of government, which encouraged the animosities of different sects throughout the Ottoman empire, I heard some circumstances during my late visit to Greece, which convinces me that the project of uniting the Jews and Christians of the east, is by no means so chimerical as it was at first supposed. That both religions are objects of equal hatred and persecution, to the followers of Mahomet, cannot for a moment be doubted ; and were a few enlightened men to unite on the subject, I feel satisfied, they could do much towards convincing the lower classes of both sects, that they are equally interested in putting down a power which has been a scourge to both, from the period of its commencement, up to the present hour.

Greece, that in the event of any change, by which the country should be governed by a Christian monarch, who guaranteed the free exercise of their religion, and security of property, they would become good subjects. There is, in fact, no doubt, but that these unfortunate people are heartily tired of the dreadful sway of the Sultan and his subordinate tyrants.

However obstinately the Porte, sustained by the Janissaries, may persevere in the war, it is not the less unpopular throughout the whole empire. Nothing in fact but the application of force and bribery, for the Ottomans are liberally paid in advance before they are called on to march, would have enabled the Sultan to collect any troops last year; and with all his efforts, not more than 20,000 could be assembled on the side of Thessaly. The repugnance of the Turks to march is greatly increased by their implicit belief in an old prophecy, which states that the time of their quitting Europe and re-crossing the Hellespont, has actually arrived.

The failure of the first Egyptian expedition, by far the most formidable that has been sent against the Greeks, furnishes the best proof that can be adduced, of the futility of the Porte's attempting to re-conquer his Christian vassals. This armament consisted of 22,000 infantry, 2,500 cavalry, 150 battering guns and field-pieces, twelve frigates, and about fifty smaller vessels of war, together with two hundred transports, of which one hundred and twenty were under the Austrian, Spanish, and British flags, a list of thirty vessels, chiefly Maltese, was sent from Alexandria to Napoli di Romania a short time before my departure.

A French officer, who entered the service of Mehemet Ali a few years ago, and embraced Mahometanism, was second in command, under the name of Soliman Bey. It will scarcely be credited, that some adventurers who had tried their fortunes in favour of the Greek cause, deserted it and joined the infidel standard.

It has justly excited astonishment that Mehemet Ali, who has shown himself so very superior to most of his predecessors, should have entered into a project, on the success of which he knew it was impossible to calculate, and while the prosperity of his own dominions rendered foreign conquest of so little importance. Some say that the motives of Ali have originated from an apprehension that the establishment of Grecian independence would be fatal to his future power; while others assert that his real object was that of securing Candia, of which the possession is of infinite value to Egypt.

The only chance, and this will, I trust, never occur, of the Pacha of Egypt's making any impression on Continental Greece, would be in the defection of the military chiefs: and to effect which, it cannot be denied that the Satraps possesses two powerful engines—in his great wealth, and the dissensions unhappily existing in the Morea. That he is ambitious of establishing a footing in the confederacy, there can be no doubt: and indeed, his whole policy is directed to conciliating the Greeks, of whom great numbers are settled in Alexandria, and other parts of Egypt. One of his first measures after the success of his expedition to Candia last year, was that of remitting all the taxes previously imposed on the Rajahs for three years.

It is not, however, externally, that the Sultan has suffered: discontent and anarchy, within the empire have increased in a corresponding ratio; and what was conjecture, with regard to the feelings of the Christian population of Turkey in Europe, is now matter of certainty. They are also wearied with an intolerable yoke, and only wait the first favourable moment for shaking it off, from the shores of the Bosphorus to the lake of Unna.

With a conviction of the justice of their cause, and after the rapid series of successes which have hitherto marked the progress of the war, the plans and policy of the provisional government may be easily conceived. When I left Napoli di Romania, it was fully intended that instead of following the example of the enemy, by retiring during the ensuing season, a most vigorous winter campaign should be carried on both by sea and land.* The reduction of Patrass, Modon, and Coron, the only points held by the Turks in the Morea, was determined on, and a force had already assumed the blockade of all these places.

Were the Morea once in full possession of the patriots, the whole energies of the government could be directed to Epirus, Thessaly, Negropont, and Candia, where a want of the means of organization, has alone prevented the inhabitants from rising on their oppressors, and joining the confederacy. As yet, there never has been a general or simultaneous rising in any of the above countries, though their partial insurrections have operated as powerful diversions in favour of the central government. When once the train is laid, those who are acquainted with the disposition of the inhabitants, and the imbecility of their Moslem tyrants, feel the most perfect confidence in their speedy liberation.

It is deeply to be lamented that the renewal of those dissensions in the Morea, which the friends

* One of the first measures of the Executive, after the arrival of the money, was that of organizing a regular corps. This had made a considerable progress before I left the seat of government; and though the training may be said to have only commenced, Captain Scott and the officers of the Dispatch, saw a large detachment of the first regiment, dressed in regular uniform, go through all the evolutions of an European regiment in less than a fortnight after its enrolment.

of Greece so fondly calculated would terminate with the negociation of the first loan, should have prevented the prosecution of the winter campaign. These unhappy differences cannot indeed be sufficiently deplored, since they not only retard, but even endanger the final success of the cause itself. Instead, however, of the difficulties and obstacles inseparable from such an unexampled struggle, relaxing the zeal of its advocates, they ought surely to increase their enthusiasm in its favour.

In referring to the arguments which so many eloquent writers of Europe have advanced, to excite sympathy for the Greek cause, I cannot help once more asserting that the whole Christian world is most deeply interested in its success. Nor is it any exaggeration to say, that the emancipation of the Christian population of the east, will be by far the most signal triumph ever achieved by civilization. More need not be said to prove, that this great cause, has an indisputable claim to the support of every friend to religion and virtue throughout the world!

END OF THE NARRATIVE.

EXTRACTS

FROM

CORRESPONDENCE, OFFICIAL DOCUMENTS,

&c.

PART II.

Note.—It may be proper to mention, that a part of the facts stated in the following letter, have been extracted into the WESTMINSTER REVIEW. A natural anxiety to record my own humble tribute to the memory of Lord Byron, induces me to publish the whole communication, as it was originally transmitted to England. E. B.

THE LAST DAYS

OF

LORD BYRON,

COMMUNICATED FROM ZANTE TO A FRIEND IN ENGLAND.

To aid thy mind's developement—to watch
Thy dawn of little joys,—to sit and see
Almost thy very growth,—to view thee catch
Knowledge of objects,—wonders yet to thee!
To hold thee lightly on a gentle knee,
And print on thy soft cheek a parent's kiss,—
This, it should seem, was not reserved for me;
Yet this was in my nature!———

CHILDE HAROLD'S PILGRIMAGE, Canto III.

Zante, May 15th, 1824.

As the hasty lines addressed to you immediately after my arrival here, did little more than confirm the death of Lord Byron, it now remains for me to communicate such particulars relative to that melancholy event, as may tend to satisfy the curiosity of our friends in England, while they will best account for the deep regret so universally expressed by all classes of the Greeks, at having been so prematurely deprived of their late illustrious benefactor and friend.

You are already aware that his lordship arrived in Cephalonia from Leghorn, in the early part of August, attended by a suite of six or seven individuals, and in an English vessel which he had hired for the express purpose of conveying him to Greece. It was however arranged, and I had, indeed, strongly recommended it in my letters from Tripolitza, that he should touch either at Zante or Cephalonia, previously to landing on the Continent. Anxious to avoid compromising the authorities, his lordship determined to remain on board the vessel until information could be obtained from the seat of government, to which Mr. Hamilton Browne, who had accompanied him from Italy, was dispatched soon after his arrival. There being no tidings from this gentleman before the expiration of the charter party, his lordship thought it needless to renew it, as he could always procure Ionian vessels, and therefore at length determined on disembarking. Wishing, however, to live as retired as possible, he proceeded to the small village of Metaxata, within five or six miles of Argostoli, whilst he remained in this retreat, a considerable portion of his time was occupied in reading; he also rode out daily; and though he could only be prevailed on to dine out once, those who came to visit his lordship, were received with the greatest kindness and hospitality. Every account I have heard, agrees in stating, that all who approached his person were highly delighted with the affability and good-humour he displayed during the whole period of his stay in the island. Nor had he been there many days, before several indigent Greek families, exiles and inhabitants, experienced his wonted munificence.

It is reported that one of his visitors at Metaxata, who is in communication with the Societies for propagating Christian Knowledge, availed himself of the occasion to instil the importance of religious meditation and scriptural truth, into the mind of one who had the reputation of not holding either in sufficient reverence, and that although some ludicrous scenes occurred in the course of their interviews, the admonitory party was treated with the utmost kindness, and full credit given to him for the purity of his intentions.

On hearing of Lord Byron's arrival, which he had indeed been long prepared to expect, Prince Mavrocordato who was at Hydra, dispatched his secretary to welcome the distinguished visitor, and when the two Greek deputies now in England, were about to depart on their mission, they were directed to call at Cephalonia, with a letter from the Executive government, thanking the noble lord for his generous devotedness to the cause of Greece, and inviting him to pass over to the Continent, where it was believed his presence would be the best guarantee of their future success. Two vessels of war were at the same time tendered for the purpose of conveying him to any point of the confederation at which he might think proper to land.

Messrs. Barff and Hancock of Cephalonia and Zante, having heard of the difficulties experienced by Lord Byron in procuring money from those to whom he had brought letters of credit from Italy, very handsomely offered to supply him with whatever funds he might require. Every impediment being thus removed, two Ionian vessels were immediately hired, and having directed his horses and effects to be embarked, his Lordship sailed from Argostoli on the 29th of December: anchoring here the same evening. The whole of the following day was occupied in making pecuniary arrangements with Mr. Barff, and after receiving a quantity of specie on board, he proceeded towards Messolunghi, that being the point of Greece most exposed to danger, and destitute of supplies. In this short passage, two accidents occurred, which might have been attended with very serious consequences. Count Gamba, who accompanied his Lordship from Leghorn, had been charged with the vessel in which the horses, and part of the money were embarked; when off Chiarenza, a point lying between this island and the place of their destination, they were surprised at day-light, on finding themselves under the bows of a Turkish Frigate. Owing, however, to the activity displayed on board Lord Byron's vessel, and her superior sailing, she escaped; while the second was fired at, brought to, and carried into Patrass, Gamba and his companions being taken before Usouff Pacha, fully expected to share the fate of the unfortunate men, whom that sangninary chief sacrificed last year at Prevesa, though also taken under the Ionian flag; and their fears would most probably have been realized, had it not been for the presence of mind displayed by the count. Aware that nothing but stratagem and effrontery could now save him, he no sooner saw himself in the Pacha's power, than assuming an air of hauteur and indifference, he accused the captain of the frigate of a scandalous breach of neutrality, in firing at and detaining a vessel under English colours; and concluded by informing Usouff, that he might expect the vengeance of England in thus interrupting a British Nobleman, who was merely on his travels, and bound to Calamos. Whether the infidel chief believed Gamba's story, or that he did not like to proceed to extremities, appears uncertain. Scarcely, however, had the count ceased, and orders been given to put the crew in irons, than the master of the vessel advancing towards the captain quietly demanded, whether he had forgotten Spiro, who fifteen years before, had saved his life in the Black Sea. The Turk looking stedfastly at him for a few moments, exclaimed, "What! can it be Spiro?" and springing forward embraced his former deliverer with the utmost transport, and not only consented to the vessel's release, but treated the whole party with the most courteous attention. As to the Pacha, he not only provided a dinner but invited them to take a day's shooting in the neighbourhood. Gamba gladly accepted these unexpected hospitalities, and sailing the next day, passed over to Messolunghi, where, to his great surprise, Lord Byron had not yet arrived.

Owing to the wind becoming contrary soon after his escape from the Turkish Frigate, Lord Byron's vessel took shelter at the Scrofes, a cluster of rocks within a few miles of Messolunghi; but as this place afforded no means of defence, in the event of an attack, it was thought advisable to remove to Dragomeste, where every preparation was made in case of their being pursued by any of the enemy's cruisers.

Having remained three days at Dragomeste, the wind came round and allowed his Lordship once more to set sail. On hearing what had happened, Prince Mavrocordato did not lose a moment in dispatching a gun-boat to accompany his Lordship, while a portion of the Greek squadron stationed at Messolunghi, were also ordered to cruize in the offing and prevent the Turkish vessels from approaching the coast. On coming up with his Lordship, one of the Greek captains sent a boat on board inviting him to make the remainder of the passage in his ship; this offer being declined, for there was now but a very short distance to proceed, they made sail towards Messolunghi. As if, however, the whole voyage was to be ominous of some future calamity, the vessel had not proceeded many miles before she grounded on a shoal near the Scrofes, and would probably have remained there, had it not been for the activity of Fletcher, his Lordship's valet, and Batista, the courier, both of whom jumped into the water and pushed the vessel off, whilst their master urged the captain and crew to exert themselves, instead of invoking the saints, as is customary with Catholic and Greek sailors on such occasions.

The wind continuing to blow directly against them, the vessel was again anchored between two of the numerous islets which line this part of the coast. Several gun-boats having been dispatched from Messolunghi to accompany his Lordship, he weighed anchor once more, but was under the necessity of bringing to a second time, nor could he reach the anchorage before the following day.

The reception of Lord Byron at Messolunghi, where he landed on the 5th of January, was most enthusiastic. On approaching Vasiladi, each ship of the squadron that lay anchored off the castle, fired a salute as he passed. When he landed, Prince Mavrocordato and all the authorities, together with the whole of the troops and population, were assembled on the beach to greet his arrival; while proceeding to the house that had been prepared for him, a discharge of twenty-one guns took place from the batteries, whilst the welcoming huzzas of the multitude continued long after he had retired. Nothing could exceed the eagerness with which his presence had been looked for at Messolunghi; he could not have arrived more opportunely, and it must be confessed, that his subsequent conduct proved that the inhabitants had not formed an incorrect estimate of him who had so lately quitted all the blandishments of Italy, to join the standard of the Cross in regenerated Greece.

The very first day of his Lordship's arrival was signalized by his rescuing a Turk, who had fallen into the hands of some Greek sailors. The individual thus saved, having been clothed by his orders, was kept in the house until an opportunity occurred of sending him to Patrass. His Lordship had not been many days at Messolunghi, before he had an opportunity of shewing his sense of Usouff Pacha's moderation, in releasing Count Gamba. Hearing that there were four Turkish prisoners in the town, he requested Prince Mavrocordato to place them in his hands. This being immediately granted, they were, on the next day, sent to Patrass, with the following letter.

"Highness;

"A vessel in which a friend and some domestics of mine were embarked, was detained a few days ago and released by order of your Highness; I have now to thank you, not for liberating the vessel, which as carrying a neutral flag, and being under British protection, no one had a right to detain, but for having treated my friends with so much kindness while they were in your hands.

"In the hope that it may not be altogether displeasing to your Highness, I have requested the Governor of this place to release four Turkish prisoners, and he has humanely consented to do so. I lose no time, therefore, in sending them back, in order to make as early a return as I could, for your courtesy on the late occasion. These prisoners are liberated without any conditions; but should the circumstance find a place in your recollection, I venture to beg that your Highness will treat such Greeks as may henceforth fall into your hands, with humanity; more especially as the horrors of war are sufficiently great in themselves, without being aggravated by wanton cruelties on either side."

Messolunghi, Jan. 23, 1824.

Noel Byron.

The above act was followed by another, not less entitled to praise, while it proves how anxious his Lordship felt to give a new turn to the system of warfare hitherto pursued. A Greek cruizer having captured a Turkish boat in which there were a number of passengers, chiefly women and children, these being also placed in the hands of Lord Byron at his particular request, a vessel was immediately hired and the whole of them sent to Prevesa, provided with every requisite for their voyage. The letter which accompanied them was couched in a similar spirit to the former; it was answered by the English council, Mr

Meyer, who thanked his Lordship in the name of Beker Aga, the Turkish governor, and concluded by an assurance that he would take care equal attention should be in future shown to the Greeks who fell into his hands.

The first great proof given by Lord Byron, that his visit to Greece, was not one of mere curiosity, was evinced in his advancing thirty thousand dollars to the provisional Government. This sum was appropriated to the payment of the fleet, and in obtaining supplies for Messolunghi. From the distress which prevailed at this moment, the above supply was of infinite service to the cause. The enthusiasm of his Lordship may be imagined, from the following short sentence, with which he concludes a letter of business to Mr. Barff, not many days after his landing.

"I hope things here will go well some time or other. I will stick by the cause as long as a cause exists, first or second."

It had previously been arranged, that Lord Byron, should be allowed to organize a corps, of which the command was to be given to himself. This now became the object of his most ardent solicitude. Finding that the Suliotes, of whom there happened to be a large body in the town, were anxious to acquire a knowledge of the evolutions of Europe, numbers of them were enrolled, and the English and German volunteers appointed to superintend their organization. Both these operations succeeded with such rapidity, that a corps of five hundred men were clothed, armed, and ready to take the field, before his Lordship had been a month at Messolunghi.

Mavrocordato had long meditated an attack on the fortress of Lepanto, and as the military stores, sent out by the Greek Committee, afforded the means of bringing some field pieces against the walls, it was settled that Lord Byron should proceed on the intended service, at the head of his brigade; and from the preparation that had been made, no doubt whatever was entertained of the speedy surrender of a place, that would render the Greeks masters of the Gulph. In order to facilitate this desirable event, a negociation had been secretly entered into, with the Albanese portion of the garrison, who consented to retire, if paid their arrears. Indeed this matter was quite settled, and his Lordship on the point of marching, when an unexpected accident prevented the execution of his design. One of the Suliotes having presented himself at Lord Byron's door, while he was conferring on some matters of importance, with Prince Mavrocordato, he insisted on being admitted, and being opposed by a German officer, named Sass, who was in waiting, a violent altercation ensued. This was followed by a personal contest in which the German lost his life. As may well be supposed, an incident like the above, unexampled as it was, during the whole war, created a general ferment throughout the garrison. The first movement of the inhabitants and foreigners, was to insist on the Suliote's being given up to justice. The demand was however resisted by his countrymen, on the plea that their companion had been struck in the first instance, and that this was a degradation which no Suliote ever suffered with impunity.

The intention of proceeding against Lepanto, being thus suspended, just as Lord Byron's enthusiasm was at its height; and when he had fully calculated on striking a blow, which could not fail to be of infinite importance to the Greek cause, no wonder that such an unlooked for disappointment, should have preyed on his spirits, and produced a degree of irritability, which if it was not the direct cause, no doubt mainly contributed to the severe fit of epilepsy with which he was attacked on the night of the 15th of February, while conversing with one of his attendants, and when he was apparently in perfect health. After having remained in a state of insensibility for some time, he gradually revived, upon which Dr Bruno, an

Italian, medical attendant, who accompanied him from Leghorn, had recourse to bleeding, by applying a number of leeches to the veins of the temples. From the manner in which this remedy was applied, it was with great difficulty, and only by the application of powerful styptics, that the flow of blood could be stopped.* A person who was present when the attack commenced, and attended while the leeches were applied, informs me that eleven hours elapsed before the bleeding entirely ceased.

No account of his Lordship's illness reached this place, before the 22nd; it was announced to Mr. Barff, by his Secretary, Zambelli, who merely stated that his Lordship had experienced a severe convulsive attack, on the night of the 15th, that though it had left him in a state of excessive debility, nothing serious was apprehended. The paragraph concluded by stating that his Lordship had taken a long excursion on the water that very day, and felt much better. There being some delay in dispatching this letter, the third page contained one from Lord Byron himself, from which the following is an extract:—

"I am a good deal better, though, of course, weakly; the leeches took too much blood from my temples the day

* The following humorous account of his Lordship's illness, by himself, has been shown to me since my return to England, it is an extract from a letter to Mr. Murray, his publisher: "On Sunday (the 15th, I believe,) I had a strong and sudden convulsive attack, which left me speechless, though not motionless, for some strong men could not hold me; but whether it was epilepsy, cachexy, apoplexy, or what other exy or epsy, the doctors have not decided; or whether it was spasmodic or nervous, &c., but it was very unpleasant, and nearly carried me off, and all that. On Monday they put leeches to my temples, no difficult matter, but the blood could not be stopped 'till eleven at night, (they had gone too near the temporal artery, for my temporal safety,) and neither styptic nor caustic, would cauterize the orifice, till after a hundred attempts."

after, and there was some difficulty in stopping it, but I have since been up daily, and out in boats or on horseback; to-day I have taken a warm bath, and live as temperately as well can be, without any liquid but water, and without animal food." His lordship then adds—"Besides the four Turks sent to Patrass, I have obtained the release of four-and-twenty women and children, and sent them to Prevesa, that the English consul general may consign them to their relatives. I did this at their own desire." After recurring to some other subjects, the letter concludes thus:—"Matters here are a little embroiled between the Souliotes, foreigners, &c. but I still hope better things, and will stand by the cause so long as my health and circumstances will permit me to be supposed useful." A marginal note to Zambelli's letter says—"I will do what I can in this affair, and have a promise of his life from Prince M." This sentence relates to a criminal, who had been condemned to death by the tribunals of Messolunghi, but in whose favour intercession was made from this place. The next letter received from Zambelli, contained the following short allusion to the state of his Lordship's health:—"I am obliged to support the Government here at present; my health seems improving, from riding, and the warm bath." The convalescence proceeded so rapidly, that his Lordship was enabled to resume his usual duties by the end of the month; these were divided between the organization of his brigade, and aiding Mavrocordato to heal the dissensions of the Morea.

A letter to Mr. Barff, dated the 5th of March, concerning the Primate of Gastouni, says:—"If Sessini is sincere, he will be treated with, and *well* treated; if he is not, the sin and the shame will lie at his own door. One great object is, to heal these internal dissensions for the *future*, without exacting a too rigorous account of the past. The Prince Mavrocordato is of the same opinion; and whoever is disposed to act fairly will be fairly dealt with. I *have heard* a *good deal* of Sessini, but not a *deal* of *good*. However, I never judge by report, particularly in a revolution. *Personally*, I am rather obliged to him, for he has been very hospitable to all friends of mine who have passed through his district. You may therefore answer him, that any overtures for the advantage of Greece, and its internal pacification, will be readily and sincerely met here. I hardly think he would have ventured a deceitful proposition to *me* through *you*, because he must be sure that, in such case, it would be eventually exposed. At any rate, the healing of these dissensions is so important a point, that something must be risked to obtain it."

Notwithstanding the improvement in his Lordship's health, his friends here felt from the first, that he ought to try change of air; and a letter, strongly urging his returning to Zante, was written to him by Mr. Barff early in March, to which the following reply was received on the 10th:—

"I am extremely obliged by your offer of your country house, (as for all other kindness,) in case that my health should require any removal; but I cannot quit Greece while there is a chance of my being of (even *supposed*) utility; there is a stake worth millions such as I am, and while I can stand at all, I must stand by the cause. While I say this, I am aware of the difficulties, and dissensions, and defects of the Greeks themselves; but allowances must be made for them by all reasonable people."

According as the convalescence of his Lordship improved, his letters became more and more important; that of the 22nd, also to his agent, will best explain the nature of his occupations, as well as the admirable zeal with which he pursued the object of his visit to Greece.

"If the Greek deputies (as seems probable) have obtained their loan, the sums I have advanced may perhaps be repaid; but it would make no great difference, as I should still spend that in the cause, and more to boot, though I hope to better purpose than hitherto. In a few days Prince Mavrocordato and myself, with a considerable escort, intend to proceed to Salona, at the request of Ulysses, and the chiefs of eastern Greece, and to take measures, offensive and defensive, for the ensuing campaign. Mavrocordato is almost recalled by the new Government to the Morea, (to take the lead, I rather think,) and they have written to propose to me, to go either to the Morea with him, or to take the general direction of affairs in this quarter, with General Lundo, and any other I may choose, to form a council. Andreas Londo is my old friend and acquaintance, since we were lads in Greece together. It would be difficult to give a positive answer, till the Salona meeting is over; but I am willing to serve them in any capacity they please, either commanding or commanded; it is much the same to me, as long as I can be of any presumed use to them. Excuse haste—it is late, and I have been several hours on horseback in a country so miry after the rains, that every hundred yards brings you to a brook or a ditch, of whose depth, width, colour, and contents both my horses and their riders have brought away many tokens."

The only allusion to public matters, contained in the remainder of this communication, the last received from his Lordship, is as follows:—

"There is a dissension amongst the Germans about the conduct of the agents of *their* committees, and an examination amongst themselves is instituted. What the result may be, cannot be anticipated. The English are all very amicable, as far as I know; and we get on too with the Greeks very tolerably, always making allowances for circumstances; and *we* have no quarrels with the other foreigners."

It was, however, while his Lordship continued to be the benefactor of all around him, and the successful mediator between each party, that a severe cold, with which he was seized on the 9th of April, after being exposed to a heavy fall of rain, and unable to change his dress for some hours, brought on an inflammatory fever, which was destined to deprive Greece of her most valuable friend, and England of a poet, whom posterity will probably place next to the bard of Stratford-upon-Avon, in all that constitutes originality, strength, and pathos.

Aware of the intense interest which you will attach to the last illness of such a man, I have been most sedulous in my inquiries among those who either attended, or were about his person, from the ninth up to the period of his dissolution. Having more particularly addressed myself to Fletcher, his valet, whose constant attendance on Lord Byron for twenty years is his best panegyric, while it furnishes the surest guarantee for the veracity of his statements *, I cannot do better than transcribe the narrative of this faithful follower, who mourns the loss of his master in a manner the most affecting and unsophisticated. In presenting Fletcher's account it may be proper to add, that with the exception of a few verbal alterations, the whole of the facts are stated as I have received them.

" My master continued his usual custom of riding daily, when the weather would permit, until the 9th of April; but on that ill-fated day he got very wet, and on his return home his Lordship changed the whole of his dress, but he had been too long in his wet clothes, and the cold of which he had complained, more or less, ever since we left Cephalonia, made this

* It has afforded me the utmost pleasure to hear from Fletcher himself, that the executors have acted very liberally towards this honest servant of Lord Byron. Indeed the mere circumstance of his having remained so many years about the person of his Lordship, is highly creditable to himself, while it would be scarcely possible to give a more convincing answer to many of those calumnies which have assailed the memory of his lamented master.

attack be more severely felt. Though rather feverish during the night, he slept pretty well, but complained in the morning of a pain in his bones, and a head-ache; this did not, however, prevent him from taking a ride in the afternoon, which, I grieve to say, was his last. On his return, my master said, that the saddle was not perfectly dry, from being so wet the day before, and observed, that he thought it had made him worse. His Lordship was again visited by the same slow fever, and I was sorry to perceive, on the next morning, that his illness appeared to be increasing. He was very low, and complained of not having had any sleep during the night. His appetite was also quite gone. I prepared a little arrow root, of which he took three or four spoonsfull, saying it was very good, but could take no more. It was not till the third day, the 12th, that I began to be alarmed for my master. In all his former colds he slept well, and was never affected by this slow fever. I therefore went to Dr. Bruno and Mr. Millingen, the two medical attendants, and inquired minutely into every circumstance connected with my master's present illness; both replied, that there was no danger, and I might make myself perfectly easy on the subject, for all would be well in a few days; this was on the 13th. On the following day I found my master in such a state, that I could not feel happy without entreating that he would send to Zante for Dr. Thomas. After expressing my fears lest his Lordship should get worse, he desired me to consult the doctors; on doing so they assured me it was unnecessary to call in any additional medical advice. Here I should remark, that his Lordship repeatedly said, in the course of the day, he was afraid the doctors did not understand his disease; to which I answered, 'then, my Lord, have other advice by all means.' 'They tell me,' said his Lordship, 'that it is only a common cold, which you know I have had a thousand times.' 'I am sure, my Lord,' said I, 'that you never had one of so serious a nature.' 'I think I never had,' was his Lordship's answer. I repeated my supplication that Dr. Thomas should be sent for on the 15th, and was again assured that my master would be better in two or three days. After these confident assurances, I did not renew my entreaties until it was too late.

"The whole nourishment taken by my master, for the last eight days, consisted of a small quantity of broth, at two or three different times, and two spoonsfull of arrow-root on the 18th, the day before his death.

"The first time I heard of there being any intention of bleeding his Lordship, was on the 15th, when it was proposed by Dr. Bruno, but objected to at first by my master, who asked Mr. Millingen if there was any very great reason for taking blood; the latter replied that it might be of service, but added, that it could be deferred till the next day; and accordingly his Lordship was bled in the right arm on the evening of the 16th. I observed at the time, that his arm had a most inflamed appearance. Dr. Bruno now began to say, he had frequently urged my master to be bled, but that he always refused.* A long dispute now arose about the time that had been lost, and the necessity of sending for medical assistance to Zante; upon which I was informed that it would be of no use, as my master would be better, or no more, before the arrival of Dr. Thomas.

"His Lordship continued to get worse, but Dr. Bruno said, he thought letting blood again would save his life, and I lost no time in telling my master how necessary it was to comply with the doctor's wishes; to this he replied, by saying, he feared they were not aware of his disorder; and then, stretching out his arm, said, 'here, take my arm, and do whatever you like.'

* It has been stated, I know not how truly, that his Lordship's objection to be bled was accompanied by the remark, that "more men had died by the lancet than the lance!"

" His Lordship continued to get weaker, and on the 17th he was bled twice in the morning, and at two o'clock in the afternoon. The bleeding at both times was followed by fainting fits, and he would have fallen down more than once, had I not caught him in my arms. In order to prevent such an accident, I took care not to let him stir without being supported. On this day my master said to me twice, ' I cannot sleep, and you well know I have not been able to sleep for more than a week :' he added, ' I am not afraid of dying ; I am more fit to die than many think.' I do not, however, believe that his Lordship had any apprehension of his fate till the day after, the 18th, when he said, ' I fear you and Tita (the courier) will be ill by sitting up constantly, night and day.' I answered, ' we shall never leave your Lordship till you are better.' On the 18th he addressed me frequently, and seemed to be rather dissatisfied with his medical treatment. I then said, ' Pray, my Lord, allow me to send for Dr. Thomas ;' to which he answered, ' do so, but be quick * ; I am only sorry I did not let you send for him before, as I am sure they have mistaken my disease.' I did not lose a moment in obeying my master's orders, or informing Dr. Bruno and Mr. Millingen of it. They said it was very right, as they now began to be afraid themselves. On returning to my master's room, his first words were, ' Have you sent ?' ' I have, my Lord,' was my answer ; upon which he said, ' You have done right, for I should like to know what is the matter with me.' Although his Lordship did not ap-

* There is little doubt but that the presence of Dr. Thomas would have been of infinite use in the early stage of his Lordship's illness. Besides his long experience of the diseases incident to the Mediterranean, the doctor had attended Lord Byron some years ago at Malta, while on his way to Greece, so that the intimacy then formed would have inspired the confidence so necessary between a patient and his medical adviser.

pear to think his dissolution was so near, I could perceive he was getting weaker every hour. His Lordship continued the conversation by saying, ‘ I now begin to think I am seriously ill ; and in case I should be taken away suddenly from you, I wish to give you several directions, which I hope you will be particular in seeing executed.’ I answered I would, in case such an event came to pass, but expressed a hope that he would live many years, to execute them much better himself than I could. To this my master replied, ‘ No, it is now nearly over ;’ and then added, ‘ I must tell you all without losing a moment.’ I then said, ‘ Shall I go, my Lord, and fetch pen, ink, and paper ? ’ ‘ Oh ! my God, no ; you will lose too much time, and I have it not to spare, for my time is now short :’ and immediately after, ‘ Now pay attention.’ His Lordship commenced by saying, ‘ You will be provided for.’ I begged him, however, to proceed with things of more consequence. He then continued,—‘ Oh, my poor dear child ! my dear Ada ! my God, could I but have seen her ! Give her my blessing, and my dear sister Augusta and her children ; and you will go to Lady Byron, and say——Tell her every thing—you are friends with her.’ His Lordship appeared to be greatly affected at this moment. Here my master's voice failed him, so that I could only catch a word at intervals, but he continued muttering something very seriously for some time. I then told his Lordship, in a state of the greatest perplexity, that I had not understood a word of what he said ; to which he replied—‘ Oh ! my God ! then all is lost ! for it is now too late. Can it be possible you have not understood me ? ’ ‘ No, my Lord,’ said I ; ‘ but I pray you to try and inform me once more.’ ‘ How can I ? ’ rejoined my master ; ‘ it is now too late, and all is over.’ I said, ‘ Not our will, but God's be done.’ He answered, ‘ Yes ! not mine be done ; but I will try.’ His Lordship did indeed make several efforts to speak, but could only repeat two or three words at a time, such as, 'My wife!—my child!—my sister! you know all, you must say all, you know my wishes!' The rest was quite unintelligible.

"A consultation was now held (about noon), when it was determined to administer some Peruvian bark and wine. My master had now been nine days without any sustenance whatever, except what I have already mentioned. With the exception of a few words, which can only interest those to whom they were addressed, it was impossible to understand any thing his Lordship said, after taking the bark. He expressed a wish to sleep. I at one time asked whether I should call Mr. Parry; to which he replied,—'Yes, you may call him.' The last words I heard my master utter were at six o'clock on the evening of the 18th, when he said, 'I must sleep now;' upon which he laid down, never to rise again; for he did not move hand or foot during the following twenty-four hours. His Lordship appeared, however, to be in a state of suffocation at intervals, and had a frequent rattling in the throat. On these occasions I called Tita to assist me in raising his head, and I thought he seemed to get quite stiff. The rattling and choking in the throat took place every half hour, and we continued to raise his head whenever the fit came on, till six o'clock in the evening of the 19th, when I saw my master open his eyes, and then shut them, but without showing any symptom of pain, or moving hand or foot. 'Oh! my God!' I exclaimed, 'I fear his Lordship is gone.' The doctors then felt his pulse, and said, 'You are too right—he is gone!'

Thus terminated the life of Lord Byron, at a moment the most glorious for his own fame, but the most unfortunate for Greece; since there is no doubt, but had he lived, many calamities would have been avoided, while his personal credit and guarantee would have prevented the ruinous delay which has taken place with regard to transferring the loan.

In thus devoting his life and fortune to the cause of religion and humanity, when he might have continued to enjoy the enthusiastic praises of his contemporaries, and all the fascinations of society ; his Lordship has raised the best monument to his own fame, and furnished the most conclusive reply to calumny and detraction. Nor is it possible to compare the beautiful allusions to Greece called forth by his splendid genius, with the fact of his becoming a martyr in the cause of her regeneration, without sentiments of the most heartfelt admiration and sympathy.

When all he had done and was about to do for the cause, is considered, no wonder that Lord Byron's death should have produced such an effect; it was, in fact, regarded not only as a national calamity, but as an irreparable loss to every individual in the town, and the English volunteers state that hundreds of the Greeks were seen to shed tears when the event was announced. With respect to Prince Mavrocordato, to whom his Lordship had rendered the most important services, both as a personal friend and in his capacity of Governor General of Western Greece, it is unnecessary to say that he could not have received a severer blow. His first measure was to issue the following decree.

" PROVISIONAL GOVERNMENT OF WESTERN GREECE.

" The present day of festivity and rejoicing is turned into one of sorrow and mourning.

" The Lord Noel Byron has departed this life, after an illness of ten days : his death being caused by an inflammatory fever. Such was the effect of his Lordship's illness on the public mind, that all classes had forgotten their usual recreations of Easter, even before its afflicting end was apprehended.

" The loss of this illustrious individual is undoubtedly to

be deplored by all Greece, but it must be more especially a subject of lamentation at Messolunghi, where his generosity has been so conspicuously displayed, and of which he had even become a citizen, with the ulterior determination of participating in all the dangers of the war.

"All are acquainted with the beneficent acts of his Lordship, and none can cease to hail his name as that of a real benefactor.

"Until, therefore, the final determination of the national Government be known, and by virtue of the powers with which it has been pleased to invest me, I hereby decree.—

"First, 'To morrow morning at daylight, thirty-seven minute guns will be fired from the grand battery, being the number which corresponds with the age of the illustrious deceased.'

"Second, 'All the public offices, even to the Tribunals, are to remain closed for three successive days.'

"Third, 'All the shops, except those in which provisions or medicines are sold, will also be shut; and it is strictly enjoined, that every species of public amusement, and other demonstrations of festivity at Easter, may be suspended.'

"Fourth, 'A general mourning will be observed for twenty-one days.'

"Fifth, 'Prayers and a funeral service are to be offered up in all the churches.'

"Given at Messolunghi this 19th day of April, 1824.

(Signed) "MAVROCORDATO.

"GEORGIUS PRIADES, Secretary."

Whilst Messolunghi was deploring a loss which all those who were within its walls felt could never be repaired, the necessary preparations were made to embalm the body, and an account of the process has appeared in the Greek Telegraph. The most remarkable facts stated in this report, relates to the quantity of brains, which are described as being at least one fourth greater than those of ordinary persons; they were saturated with blood. The heart was also very large, but its fibres were extremely relaxed, so that it must have performed its functions very feebly. The liver is represented as small. In other respects, the body was found to be perfectly sound and healthy. Dr. Bruno, who drew up the report, concludes by stating, that had his illustrious patient consented to be bled when first attacked, there is no doubt but he would be still alive; arguing, however, from the exhausted state in which he found the vessels of the heart, smallness of the liver, and the peculiar structure of the cranium, added to a want of more precaution with regard to his health, not to mention his excessive literary occupation, the doctor adds, that his Lordship could only have survived a few years.

There being no possibility of procuring sheet lead at Messolunghi, the body was placed in a strong tin case, and elevated on a bier covered with black cloth. The arms of the Byron family were represented at one end of the coffin, while the sword and cap which his Lordship had intended to wear at the siege of Lepanto, were placed on the top.

The necessary arrangements being made for conveying the body to the principal church in the town, this ceremony was omitted in consequence of a suggestion that the rugged state of the pavement might lead to some accident happening to the coffin; it was therefore determined that instead of the corpse every object would be answered by merely conducting the heart in procession. A separate case having been made for this, it was accordingly substituted for the body. The procession took place on the 24th, and was attended by the clergy, civil and military authorities, as well as the whole population. On reaching the church, the case was placed on an elevated pedestal prepared for the occasion, upon which a solemn service was pronounced by the Bishop of Arta Porfirius; this was followed by the chaunting of a requiem. The mournful ceremony concluded with a funeral oration from the pen of my friend Spiridion Tricoupi. This composition, so creditable to the talent of the writer, contains a very eloquent and affecting tribute to the memory of his Lordship.

It being necessary to wait for the vessels sent over by Mr. Barff, the body was not embarked until the 30th, when another procession took place. The coffin was carried down to the sea side, on the shoulders of four military Chiefs, and attended in the same order as before; minute guns continued to be discharged till the moment of embarkation; these were followed by a salute of thirty-seven cannon.

The vessel which bore the body, appeared off this Island about two o'clock, on the 4th instant, and was recognized at a considerable distance, owing to her colours being lowered. She entered the Mole towards sunset. The corpse was accompanied by the whole of his Lordship's attendants, who conveyed it to the Lazaretto, on the following morning.

When the melancholy event was first communicated to Mr. Barff, he lost no time in dispatching an express to Lord Sydney Osborne, who holds a high official situation at Corfu, and is said to be a distant relation of Lord Byron. His Lordship came here in a gun boat some days after, in order, it is said, to confer with the Resident, as to the best mode of disposing of the body, for there had been an intention of interring it in this island, until an answer could be obtained from the executors, ascertaining their wishes on the subject.

I need not say with what sort of feelings the notion of hesitating to send home the body was met here; there could indeed be but one opinion on the subject; and much to his credit, the Resident no sooner heard what this was, than he at once acquiesced. Some circumstances have been also disclosed, by Fletcher, relative to conversations held with his late master, that left no doubt as to the course most proper to be pursued. The first sentiment expressed by those who heard of the above intention, was that, if it should be thought expedient to inter the remains of his Lordship in a foreign soil, they ought to be transferred once more to Greece. In this case, the Parthenon was pointed out as by far the most eligible spot for the ashes of one, who died while labouring in the sublime work of Grecian regeneration. The former plan has, however, been fixed upon, as more consonant with the wishes of his Lordship's family, and the universal feelings in England, and the Florida has, in consequence, been taken up to convey the body home. I should inform you that the whole of his Lordship's papers found at Messolunghi, were sealed up immediately after his death, some others left in the hands of Mr. Hancock, at Cephalonia, have been forwarded to Mr. Barff, and will be sent home in the Florida.

I am told the literary remains found at Messolunghi, are very scanty; they consist of fourteen Stanzas, of the seventeenth Canto, of his inimitable Satire, a song to the Suliotes. Some prose remarks on Mr. Moore's "Loves of the Angels," and Stanzas written on the 22nd January, his Lordship's thirty-sixth birth-day, together with a few other fragments.* I have been favoured with two stanzas of this, repeated from memory: these will afford you some notion of the feelings which then animated the lamented author.

> If thou regret'st thy youth, *why live?*
> The land of honourable death
> Is here,—Up to the field and give
> Away thy breath!†

* The report circulated previous to my departure from England, stating that his Lordship had composed a poem entitled the "Triumph of Hellas," has been formally contradicted in the Greek Telegraph.

† I was subsequently indebted to Lord Charles Murray, for a copy of

Seek out—less often sought than found,
A soldier grave, for thee the best;
Then look around and choose thy ground,
And take thy rest!

It is devoutly to be hoped, that the remains of Lord Byron's muse, however limited, will ere long be incorporated with a correct edition of his works, as the introduction of many spurious pieces, and a great deal of mutilation, which has occurred both in London and Paris, render this task particularly due to his memory and fame.

With respect to the faults of Lord Byron, faults which have furnished such a fertile source of occupation to calumny and slander, for the last six years, and which some may be found to dwell on after his death; this is not the place to point them out, much less to refute many charges known to be the offspring of envy and malevolence. Where the virtues of charity and benevolence, emanating from genuine goodness of heart, united to an unconquerable love of freedom, formed the ruling passion and predominant characteristic; surely one may be excused from noticing blemishes that arose rather from the inevitable infirmity of our nature, than any predilection for evil. Without alluding to the merit of the various productions which confer immortality on the name of his Lordship, it may be said without fear of contradiction, that his services to Greece, were most eminent and conspicuous. It should also be observed, that their value was greatly enhanced by the circumstances of privation and distress, under which they were rendered to that suffering country. When I saw his Lordship at

the whole of these Stanzas, perhaps the most pathetic and beautiful of Lord Byron's fugitive poetry, they appeared in a morning paper, soon after my arrival in England. They are indeed full of pathos, and have not been unaptly compared to the notes of the Cygnet, for they were the last lines ever written by his Lordship, and but too plainly point to his premature and early fate.

Genoa, last year, I well remember with what enthusiasm he spoke of his intended visit, and how much he regretted not having joined the standard of freedom long before.*

When once in Greece, both his actions and private letters, bear ample testimony to the zeal, with which he espoused her most sacred cause. His Lordship had not advanced less than fifty thousand dollars, up to the time of his being taken ill, and there is no doubt but he intended to devote the whole of his private income to the service of the confederation.

From all I have been able to collect, and my information has been communicated by individuals who were about the person of his Lordship for many years, I should not hesitate to say, that he was pre-eminently brave, possessing a fearlessness of death approaching to contempt. He has indeed been frequently heard to say, he was sure he should not live to the age of forty.

Among his Lordship's numerous acts of benevolence while at Messolunghi, he had taken under his protection a little Turkish child, who was, together with her mother, in the town when captured by the patriots. A letter to his

* Having on the morning of my arrival, written to inform his Lordship, that I had come by Genoa, for the express purpose of seeing him, the messenger brought me back the following answer :—

Dear Sir,

I shall be delighted to see you and your Greek friend, and the sooner the better. I have been expecting you for some time, you will find me at home. I cannot express to you how much I feel interested in the cause, and nothing but the hopes I entertained of witnessing the liberation of Italy itself, prevented me long ago from returning to do what little I could as an individual, in that land which it is an honour even to have visited.

Ever yours truly,

Noel Byron.

Albaro, April 5th, 1823.

Lordship's sister, written some time before his death, gives an account of the object and nature of this adoption. It appears that he wished the child to be respectably educated, and expressed a desire that if her character and abilities fitted her for the situation, she might become the attendant and companion of his daughter. It is somewhat a singular coincidence, that this should have been a poetical creation in the first instance, as may be seen by a reference to the eighth Canto of Don Juan. The child, whom I have frequently seen in the Lazaretto, is extremely interesting, and about eight years of age. She came over with the body, under her mother's care. They had not been here many days, before an application reached this from Usouff Pacha, to give them up. It being customary, whenever claims of this kind are made, to consult the parties themselves, both the mother and her child were questioned as to their wishes on the subject ; upon this, the latter with tears in her eyes, said, that had his Lordship lived, she would always have considered him as a father, but as he was no more, she preferred going back to her own country ; the mother having expressed the same wish, they were sent to Patrass.

Having thus given you all the facts I could obtain from those who were about the person of his Lordship ; I am sure you will not be displeased with another extract, from the details furnished by the first authority alluded to. These relate to the habitual benevolence of his master, and like those already given, are transcribed nearly in his own words. "I could, if you require it, fill fifty pages with traits of his Lordship's generosity, which have occurred during the time I have served with him, but will now only trouble you with a few. So long back as December, 1807, a poor man came to Newstead Abbey, where we then resided, and asked alms of a youth, son to one of the farmers. Perceiving that he sent the beggar away without giving him even a morsel of bread, my master called to the lad, who was his favourite servant, and said, "I insist on your going after that poor man, and serving him the whole of this day with every thing he wants, and in case you act in such a way again, I will make you provide a good dinner for him: and recollect if you ever insult or ill use any other person in distress, you shall be made to wait behind their chair, till they have dined, this will teach you how to behave yourself in future."

"Indeed there is no part of Europe in which we lived that I have not witnessed numerous proofs of his Lordship's kindness of heart. While we were one day walking in the woods near Ravenna, my master saw an old woman decrepid with age, gathering sticks, he inquired into her circumstances, and immediately granted her a pension for her future maintenance. It was customary to dress a dinner daily for his Lordship while at the above place, as the servants were all on board wages, and my master scarcely every dined at home, I had orders to find out twelve of the most helpless poor of the city, to whom the victuals were always given.

"One of the dogs happening to get into a mill dam, a man, who saw that he was likely to be carried into the wheel, leaned over the brink so far, that he fell in, and was unfortunately drowned. My master seemed to suffer very much from this accident, and not only defrayed the expences of the funeral, but settled fifteen shillings a week on his children, till they should grow up, and be otherwise provided for. These are, indeed, only a few instances of his Lordship's goodness; but should you require any more, I could furnish you with a thousand."

Every letter of his Lordship's, in which any allusion was made to the Greek cause, proved how judiciously he viewed that great question, while it displayed a thorough knowledge of the people he had come to assist. This latter circumstance, which made him more cautious in avoiding every interference calculated to wound the self-love of the Greeks, who, though fallen, are still remarkable for their pride, accounts for the great popularity he had acquired.

Indeed it may be truly said, that no foreigner who has hitherto espoused the cause, made greater allowance for the errors inseparable from it than did Lord Byron.

With respect to his opinion, as to the best mode of bringing the contest to a triumphant close, and healing those differences which have been created by party spirit or faction; there is reason to believe, that the subject occupied the particular attention of his Lordship, and he was even more than once heard to say that "no person had as yet hit upon the right plan for securing the independence of Greece."

While sedulously employed in reconciling jarring interests, and promoting a spirit of union, the grand maxim which he laboured to instil into the Greeks, was that of making every other object secondary and subservient, to the paramount one of driving out the Turks. It is needless to say that every hour tends to confirm the wisdom of the above doctrine.

May 24th, 6 o'clock, P. M.

POSTSCRIPT.—I have this instant returned on shore, after having performed the melancholy duty of towing the remains of Lord Byron, alongside the Florida, on board which vessel they are embarked to be conveyed to England.

I should add, that in consequence of there being no means of procuring a lead coffin at Zante, it was determined that the tin case prepared at Messolunghi, should be put into a large recipient of wood; so that there is now no fear of the body reaching London in perfect preservation. The only mark of respect shown to-day, was displayed by the merchant vessels, in the Bay and Mole; the whole of these, whether

English or Foreign, had their colours lowered, and many fired guns. Minute guns were discharged from the Florida, from the time of our quitting the Lazaretto, until we got alongside, when the recipient was taken on board, and placed in a space prepared for the purpose. The whole is painted black, and thanks to the foresight of my friend Robinson, an escutcheon very well executed, designates the mournful receptacle.

Although no honours have been paid to the manes of our immortal bard here, we look forward with a melancholy satisfaction to those which await him in the land of his birth; and however bitterly his pen may have lashed the vices and follies of the day, it is not the least honourable trait in our national character, that neither personal dislike, nor those prejudices which arise from literary jealousy and political animosity, prevent us from duly appreciating departed worth, and even forgetting those aberrations to which all are more or less liable in this state of imperfection and fallibility.

FUNERAL ORATION ON LORD NOEL BYRON,

COMPOSED AND DELIVERED BY MR. SPIRIDION TRICOUPI, OF MESSOLUNGHI.*

Printed by Order of Government.

Messolunghi, 10th April,
Thursday in Easter Week, 1824.

"UNLOOKED-FOR event! deplorable misfortune! But a short time has elapsed since the people of this deeply-

* Although this eloquent tribute has been already before the public, I could not do less than give it a place, since I received it from my friend, the author, for this purpose, and was indeed the first who sent it to England.—E. B.

suffering country welcomed, with unfeigned joy and open arms, this celebrated individual to their bosoms; to-day, overwhelmed with grief and despair, they bathe his funeral couch with tears of bitterness, and mourn over it with inconsolable affliction. On Easter Sunday the happy salutation of the day, 'Christ is risen,' remained but half pronounced on the lips of every Greek; and as they met, before even congratulating each other on the return of that joyous day, the universal demand was, 'How is Lord Byron?' Thousands, assembled in the spacious plain outside of the city to commemorate the sacred day, appeared as if they had assembled for the sole purpose of imploring the Saviour of the world to restore health to him, who was a partaker with us in our present struggle for the deliverance of our native land.

"And how is it possible that any heart could remain unmoved, any lip closed, upon the present occasion? Was ever Greece in greater want of assistance than when the ever-to-be-lamented Lord Byron, at the peril of his life, crossed over to Messolunghi? Then, and ever since he has been with us, his liberal hand has been opened to our necessities — necessities which our own poverty would have otherwise rendered irremediable. How many and much greater benefits did we not expect from him; and to-day, alas! to-day, the unrelenting grave closes over him and our hopes!

"Residing out of Greece, and enjoying all the pleasures and luxuries of Europe, he might have contributed materially to the success of our cause, without coming personally amongst us; and this would have been sufficient for us, for the well-proved ability and profound judgment of our Governor, the President of the Senate, would have ensured our safety with the means so supplied. But if this was sufficient for us, it was not so for Lord Byron. Destined by nature to uphold the rights of man wherever he saw them trampled upon; born in a free and enlightened country; early taught, by reading the works of our ancestors (which indeed teach all who can read them,) not only what man is, but what he ought to be, and what he may be —he saw the persecuted and enslaved Greek determine to break the heavy chains with which he was bound, and to convert the iron into sharp-edged swords, that he might regain by force what force had torn from him!—His Lordship saw this, and leaving all the pleasures of Europe, he came to share our sufferings and our hardships; assisting us, not only with his wealth, of which he was profuse; not only with his judgment, of which he has given us so many salutary examples;—but with his sword, which he was preparing to unsheathe against our barbarous and tyrannical oppressors. He came, in a word, according to the testimony of those who were intimate with him, with the determination to die in Greece and for Greece! How, therefore, can we do otherwise than lament, with heartfelt sorrow, the loss of such a man! How can we do otherwise than bewail it as the loss of the whole Greek nation.

"Thus far, my friends, you have seen him liberal, generous, courageous—a true Philellenist; and you have seen him as your benefactor. This is, indeed, a sufficient cause for your tears, but it is not sufficient for his honour; it is not sufficient for the greatness of the undertaking in which he had engaged. He, whose death we are now so deeply deploring, was a man who, in one great branch of literature, gave his name to the age in which we live; the vastness of his genius and the richness of his fancy did not permit him to follow the splendid, though beaten, track of the literary fame of the ancients; he chose a new road—a road which ancient prejudice had endeavoured, and was still endeavouring, to shut against the learned of Europe: but as long as his writings live, and they must live as long as the world exists, this road will remain always open; for it is, as well as the other, a sure road to tue knowledge. I will not detain you at the present time, by expressing all the respect and enthusiasm with which the perusal of his writings has always inspired me, and which indeed I feel much more powerfully now than at any other period. The learned men of all Europe celebrate him, and have celebrated him; and all ages will celebrate the poet of our age, for he was born for all Europe and for all ages.

"One consideration occurs to me, as striking and true as it is applicable to the present state of our country; listen to it, my friends, with attention, that you may make it your own, and that it may become a generally acknowledged truth.

"There have been many great and splendid nations in the world, but few have been the epochs of their true glory: one phenomenon, I am inclined to believe, is wanting in the history of these nations, and one, the possibility of the appearance of which the all-considering mind of the philosopher has much doubted. Almost all the nations of the world have fallen from the hands of one master into those of another; some have been benefited, others have been injured by the change; but the eye of the historian has not yet seen a nation enslaved by barbarians, and more particularly by barbarians rooted for ages in their soil—has not yet seen, I say, such a people throw off their slavery unassisted and alone. This is the phenomenon; and now, for the first time in the history of the world, we witness it in Greece, yes, in Greece alone! The philosopher beholds it from afar, and his doubts are dissipated; the historian sees it, and prepares his citation of it as a new event in the fortunes of nations; the statesman sees it, and becomes more observant and more on his guard. Such is the extraordinary time in which we live. My friends, the insurrection of Greece is not an epoch of our nation alone; it is an epoch of all nations: for, as I before observed, it is a phenomenon which stands alone in the political history of nations.

"The great mind of the highly-gifted and much-lamented Byron observed this phenomenon, and he wished to unite his name with our glory. Other revolutions have happened in his time, but he did not enter into any of them—he did not assist any of them; for their character and nature were totally different; the cause of Greece alone was a cause worthy of him whom all the learned of Europe celebrate. Consider, then, my friends, consider the time in which you live—in what a struggle you are engaged; consider that the glory of past ages admits not of comparison with yours; the friends of liberty, the philanthropists, the philosophers of all nations, and especially of the enlightened and generous English nation, congratulate you, and from afar rejoice with you; all animate you: and the poet of our age, already crowned with immortality, emulous of your glory, came personally to your shores, that he might, together with yourselves, wash out with his blood the marks of tyranny from our polluted soil.

"Born in the great capital of England, his descent noble, on the side of both his father and his mother, what unfeigned joy did his philellenic heart feel, when our poor city, in token of our gratitude, inscribed his name among the number of her citizens. In the agonies of death; yes, at the moment when eternity appeared before him; as he was ingering on the brink of mortal and immortal life; when all the material world appeared but as a speck in the great works of Divine Omnipotence;—in that awful hour, but two names dwelt upon the lips of this illustrious individual, leaving all the world besides—the names of his only and much beloved daughter and of Greece: these two names, deeply engraven on his heart, even the moment of death could not efface. 'My daughter!' he said; 'Greece!' he exclaimed; and his spirit passed away. What Grecian heart will not be deeply affected as often as it recalls to mind this moment!

"Our tears, my friends, will be grateful, very grateful to his shade, for they are the tears of sincere affection; but much more grateful will be our deeds in the cause of our country, which, though removed from us, he will observe from the heavens, of which his virtues have doubtless opened to him the gates. This return alone does he require from us for all his munificence; this reward for his love towards us; this consolation for his sufferings in our cause; and this inheritance for the loss of his invaluable life. When your exertions, my friends, shall have liberated us from the hands which have so long held us down in chains; from the hands which have torn from our arms our property, our brothers, our children;—then will his spirit rejoice, then will his shade be satisfied!—Yes, in that blessed hour of our freedom, the Archbishop will extend his sacred and free hand, and pronounce a blessing over his venerated tomb; the young warrior, sheathing his sword, red with the blood of his tyrannical oppressors, will strew it with laurel; the statesman will consecrate it with his oratory; and the poet, resting upon the marble, will become doubly inspired; the virgins of Greece, (whose beauty our illustrious fellow-citizen Byron has celebrated in many of his poems,) without any longer fearing contamination from the rapacious hands of our oppressors, crowning their heads with garlands, will dance round it, and sing of the beauty of our land, which the poet of our age has already commemorated with such grace and truth. But what sorrowful thought now presses upon my mind! My fancy has carried me away; I had pictured to myself all that my heart could have desired; I had imagined the blessings of our bishops, the hymns, and laurel crowns, and the dance of the virgins of Greece, round the tomb of the benefactor of Greece;—but this tomb will not contain his precious remains; the tomb will remain void; but a few days more will his body remain on the face of our land—of his new chosen country; it cannot be given over to our arms; it must be borne to his own native land, which is honoured by his birth.

"Oh Daughter! most dearly beloved by him; your arms will receive him; your tears will bathe the tomb which contains his body; and the tears of the orphans of Greece will be shed over the urn containing his precious heart, and over all the land of Greece, for all the land of Greece is his tomb. As in the last moment of his life you and Greece were alone in his heart and upon his lips, it was but just that she (Greece) should retain a share of the precious remains. Messolunghi, his country, will ever watch over and protect with all her strength the urn containing his venerated heart, as a symbol of his love towards us. All Greece, clothed in mourning, and inconsolable, accompanies the procession in which it is borne; all ecclesiastical, civil, and military honours attend it; all his fellow-citizens of Messolunghi, and fellow-countrymen of Greece, follow it, crowning it with their gratitude, and bedewing it with their tears; it is blessed by the pious benedictions and prayers of our archbishop, bishop, and all our clergy. Learn, noble Lady, learn that chieftains bore it on their shoulders, and carried it to the church; thousands of Greek soldiers lined the way through which it passed, with the muzzles of their muskets, which had destroyed so many tyrants, pointed towards the ground, as though they would war against that earth which was to deprive them for ever of the sight of their benefactor; —all this crowd of soldiers, ready at a moment to march against the implacable enemy of Christ and man, surrounded the funeral coach, and swore never to forget the sacrifices made by your Father for us, and never to allow the spot where his heart is placed, to be trampled upon by barbarous and tyrannical feet. Thousands of Christian voices were in a moment heard, and the temple of the Almighty resounded with supplications and prayers that his venerated remains might be safely conveyed to his native land, and that his soul might rest where the righteous alone find rest!"

Account of the Author's Visit to Anatolico, in company with Lord Charles Murray, and which is alluded to in the Text.

"Messolunghi, June 5th, 1824.

I have just returned from Anatolico, where I accompanied a mission, sent there by Prince Mavrocordato, to confer with Constantine Botzaris, and the Souliotes generally, relative to the delays which have taken place in the payment of their arrears, and which have alone prevented them from taking the field. It is, in fact, impossible to describe what the Prince has suffered on account of his inability to satisfy the claims of those brave men, who have experienced the greatest privations ever since the loss of their celebrated fortress, in 1822. Subsequent to that period they were reduced to the necessity of wandering about the Ionian Islands, with their wives and families, without any adequate means of existence. Called upon, however, to aid in the defence of this place last year, nearly the whole body came over, and as usual, greatly distinguished themselves, both in the memorable exploit at Carpenissa, where Marco Botzaris fell, and in various other parts of Acarnania. When the campaign terminated, they collected, within the walls of this place, but removed to Anatolico soon after the death of Lord Byron, under whose banners they were enrolled, and destined to march against Lepanto. You will have already heard into what a state of chaos and confusion his Lordship's lamented fate has thrown the affairs of all Greece, and of this neighbourhood in particular. The natural consequence of being thus left in a state of destitution and misery, has been the cause of great discontent and frequent remonstrance. No sooner, however, had they heard of the arrival of the money at Zante, than their impatience increased, and another most pressing application having reached the Prince two days ago, he determined to send M. Melas, of Yanina, and M. Inian, formerly a professor in one of the Greek colleges, to explain by what an unforseen combination of circumstances it has been hitherto impossible for the Government to avail itself of a loan upon which it calculated with such anxious solicitude, even before the negociation was completed in England.

Anatolico is about ten miles to the north-west from this, owing to the shallowness of the water between both places, extending five or six miles into the sea, and on which a most valuable fishery is established, as also very productive salt works; the water communication is kept up by means of small canoes, not unlike the gondolas of Venice; these are impelled along by a single boatman, who is provided with a pole, and placing himself at the stern, is enabled to manage his little skiff with uncommon dexterity. We embarked at eight yesterday morning, and were landed by half-past ten at the house of the Eparch, at Anatolico. The novelty of this mode of navigating, added to the ever varied scenery presented by the mountains of the Morea, Acarnania, and the Ionian Islands in the distance, was still more heightened by the numerous fishing boats and trading vessels passing us in all directions. Although the approach to Anatolico is so shallow and difficult, the gulph, which extends for some miles beyond it towards the north, is both deep and spacious. The town itself, consisting of about five hundred houses, is built on a small round islet, almost level with the lake, and washed by it on every side. In whatever direction you look, the eye rests on beautiful and fertile plains, covered with gardens and olive groves, which ascend gradually from the water's edge up to the base of lofty hills, that bound the prospect. On our approaching the town, I could not help calling to mind the small islands so profusely scattered about Venice, to which it bears an exact resemblance. As if there had been some notion of our visit, we had scarcely rounded a point of land that had hitherto concealed the little gondola, when several guns were fired from different parts of the town; and on our getting nearer, we perceived the beach and houses covered with people of both sexes, whose greetings were manifested either by the usual salutation, of Kalosorisite! "You are welcome!" or the waving of handkerchiefs. What with the long robes, flowing locks, and many coloured hues in the dress of the women, and warlike appearance of the Souliotes, who formed groups wherever they found an elevated spot, I had forgotten the nineteenth century for a few moments, and fancied myself transported to a much remoter period.

On landing at the northern extremity of the town, we almost stepped from the boat into the house of Kitso Sotiriote, who had prepared it for our reception. On ascending two stories, we were ushered into a spacious room, commanding a charming view of the Gulph, which now assumed the appearance of a Lake, quite unconnected with the sea, as well as the surrounding scenery. The customary refreshments of pipes, coffee, and sweetmeats, had hardly been served, when a crowd of visitors arrived; the first persons who presented themselves were Porfirius, the Bishop of Arta, Primates, and their attendants. Like those whom I had seen on my arrival here, they asked a hundred questions about the state of Europe, more especially as to what was said of Greece, and ended by expressing the most heartfelt gratitude to England, for affording them the means of achieving their independence. Our next visitor was the Souliote General Javella, attended by not less than fifty officers and soldiers. Having embraced me in the most friendly manner, he began by welcoming our arrival, inquired after several of his friends in the Ionian Islands, and concluded some other remarks on various subjects, by expressing the sorrow felt by himself and all his nation, at the irreparable loss sustained by the death of Lord Byron, whom he designated as the "Father of the Souliotes." On asking for Costa Botzaris, as he is called by the soldiery, I was sorry to hear he had been suffering from a severe attack of fever, brought on by the fatigues and privations of the late campaign. Javella is a very fine young man, and one of those who served in the brigade organized by General Church. When the number of our visitors had somewhat diminished, Sutzo, the Eparch, apologised for the dinner being so late, adding, that it arose from his anxiety to indulge us with a dish of fish peculiar to the Gulph, and which he had sent the divers to procure! You will not be surprised to hear that my curiosity was excited in an extraordinary degree by this singular intimation, the first I had ever heard of divers being employed to bring any thing but pearls from the deep; on further inquiry, I found that several families derived a very profitable livelihood from this novel mode of fishing. A servant came in soon after, and brought a large earthen bowl of the very fish of which we had been speaking; it greatly resembles the John Dory, in form and flavour, the latter being really exquisite. Determined to inform myself of the particulars of a practice which no traveller seems to have hitherto noticed, our host, Sotiriote, told me, that if I waited at his house another day, he would be happy to shew me the process used in taking the fish in question; he then proceeded to state, that nothing could be more simple; the divers being provided with a rope made of a species of long grass, and which floats near the surface, has only to moor his canoe where he knows there is a rocky bottom; this done, he throws the rope out so as to form a tolerably large circle, and such is the timid nature of the fish, that instead of rushing out, it never attempts to pass this imaginary barrier, which acts as a talisman, but instantly descends, and endeavours to conceal itself under the rocks. Having waited a few moments, till the charm has taken effect, the diver plunges downwards, and not unfrequently returns with four or five fish, weighing from two to six pounds each. As they seldom find more than the heads concealed, there is the less difficulty in bringing forth their rich prizes; and when the harvest is good, the divers are so dexterous, that they have a method of securing three or four fish under each arm, besides what they can take in their hands. My informant added, as a very curious fact, that only one accident had happened within his remembrance, to those who pursued this apparently perilous mode of fishing, and it only arose from the diver's arm being entangled under some of the apertures of the rocks. I shall probably be enabled to give you some further particulars relative to this subject in a future letter; meanwhile, it may be as well to tell our friends that, if they want to see and taste the rival of the John Dory, they must come to Anatolico! Besides the fish, of which there was some boiled and fried, we were treated with pilaf, roast and boiled fowls, stews, and vegetables in great abundance.

As toasts, patriotic and otherwise, have now become quite the rage in Greece, there was no paucity of them at this repast, wherein "the feast of reason and flow of soul" may be said to have followed a most excellent dinner. Having closed with coffee and pipes as usual, after which each *convive* threw himself on the ottoman that surrounded the room, and indulged in a *siesta* for nearly an hour. When the heat had somewhat subsided, we sallied forth to return the visits of our friends; when about half way to the residence of Costa Botzaris, Melas stopped and asked me, whether I felt disposed to enter the church of St. Michael, which had been the scene of a miracle, during the famous defence of Anatolico, during the last campaign; when four hundred men, principally armed with swords and pistols, and four small guns, resisted the Pacha of Scutari and Omer Vrione, at the head of twenty thousand Turks, for two months, and finally forced them to retreat, with the loss of their guns and baggage.

You have probably heard something of this singular event, but the most extraordinary part of it remains to be told. Indeed, nothing but a thorough conviction, that the fact I am about to relate actually occurred, and my having ascertained its exact truth from eye witnesses, would have induced me to notice such an incident, at a time when there are so many attempts to impose on public credulity. Being aware that there was neither water nor cisterns in the town, one of the first measures of the Turks was to possess themselves of the fountain on Terra Firma, at a distance of nearly two miles, where the inhabitants had always drawn their supplies, so that the blockade had not continued many days, before those who remained were in the greatest distress, and would have been forced to surrender, had not a small supply been occasionally sent from this place during the night. But every farther hope was destroyed, by the enemy placing a strong post and battery close to the narrow channel through which the boats had to pass, so that the garrison looked forward to their immediate destruction as inevitable, for the town was hemmed in on every side, and had been without any communication with Messolunghi for several days, when a shell from a ten-inch mortar, entering the front of the above named church, and penetrating the flagged pavement, lighted on a source of excellent water! What adds to the singularity of the circumstances is, that a few women and children who continued in the town, for the greatest part had been sent here, took up their abode in the church, as the most secure asylum, and were in it when the shell entered, without receiving the least injury. With respect to the water thus miraculously discovered, it was not only most abundant, but fully equal in quality to that of the fountain, of which the enemy had taken possession. It is needless to say that this fortunate coincidence was regarded as a miracle in every sense of the word ; that it saved Anatolico there is no doubt.

New vigour being thus given to the brave defenders, they made several sallies afterwards, by means of their boats, and destroyed numbers of the infidels, who were at length forced to make a precipitate retreat, after having thrown no less than three thousand nine hundred shot and shells, into the town, without doing any more injury than knocking down two or three old houses, while the loss of the Turks in killed, and through a contagious malady by which they were attacked, is estimated at three thousand men ; that of the Greeks did not exceed seventeen in killed and wounded. In order to prove the state of the Turkish artillery, our host informed us, that one hundred and seven, eighteen pound shot, had been fired at his house without one taking effect ! with respect to the miraculous Well, it continued to be very well supplied until the end of April, and has still more than a foot of water.

The circumstance of his being a brother to the hero of Carpenissa, and no less a brave and meritorious officer himself, made me very anxious to become personally acquainted with Costa Botzaris. Proceeding to his quarters from the church, we were most cordially received, but I was sorry to find he had suffered so much from his late illness, which has left him in a state of extreme debility. The General is thirty-four years of age, of the middle size, and has remarkably fine features. We had a long conversation, in which he expressed the deepest regret at the obstacles that have hitherto prevented the Souliotes from taking the field ; adding, that all they wanted was an asylum, and the means of existence for their families, whom they could not think of leaving destitute. When Inian and Melas told him that the government had already determined to allot a fertile district in Acarnania to them, and that every possible effort was making, to procure them the amount of their arrears, he seemed perfectly satisfied, and, turning to myself, said, that he would be content to leave his own fate, as well as that of all his countrymen, in my hands. In thanking him for his unmerited proof of confidence, I assured him, that while the fate which befel his lamented brother, however heroic, was considered as the greatest loss Greece could sustain, both himself and his brave companions in arms were held in the highest estimation in England; and that so far as the removal of those obstacles which prevented the Souliotes from taking the field before the season advanced too far, depended on me, every possible exertion should be made to enable Prince Mavrocordato, to furnish them with those pecuniary means of which they stood so much in need. The last topic of our conversation related to the invitation he had received a few days before from Mr. Bentham, to send his nephew, the eldest son of Marco, to England, for the purpose of being educated at the philosopher's expence, and under his immediate auspices. This liberal offer has been accepted with the utmost gratitude, and letters were already sent to the hero's widow, at Ancona, directing that young Marco, who is about eleven years old, and full of natural talent, may be sent to London without loss of time.*

* Young Marco has not yet arrived in England, but steps have been taken to have him brought without loss of time. Madame Botzaris, is at Zante, where she has experienced every attention from the inhabitants. I also understand, that the Provisional Government has settled a pension on the widow of the departed hero.

Having taken a cordial farewell of the General, we next paid a visit to the Bishop Javilla, and Primates, all of whom vied with each other in civilities and expressions of kindness. The object of the mission being thus happily attained, we returned to our quarters, where supper had been prepared, and having gone through the usual round of toasts and sentiments, once more stretched ourselves on the ottomans. Rising at day-light, coffee was served, after which we re-embarked, and arrived here in time to breakfast with the Prince, to whom we recapitulated all that had happened.

Extracts from the Correspondence which took place relative to the Instalments of the Greek Loan, sent to Zante, and detained in that Island, &c.

No. I.

FROM E. BLAQUIERE TO JOHN BOWRING, ESQ.

AS HON. SECRETARY OF THE GREEK COMMITTEE.

Zante, April 27th, 1824.

" The friends of Greece will be gratified to hear that the Florida has had the unusually quick passage of nineteen days from Portsmouth, having arrived here on the evening of the 24th instant. I cannot describe to you the anxiety with which this most seasonable supply has been looked for throughout the confederation. Polysoides, whom the deputies sent out, has already proceeded to Argos, where I have also sent the copy of the Contract, and other communications addressed to Col. Stanhope, together with a letter from myself, announcing the arrival of the money and suggesting such means of facilitating its transfer as appeared most likely to effect that object.

"As there is some uncertainty about the Colonel being at the seat of Government, for no letters have been received from him during the last three weeks, when he was at Athens, actively occupied in pursuing the object of his philanthropic mission there, Barff and myself thought it advisable to send an express to Messolunghi, to be sent on by Prince Mavrocordato without delay. The messenger was charged with duplicates of the letters sent by Polysoides, informing the Colonel, that if not already there, he had only to repair to the seat of Government, where he would find communications of the highest importance from the Committee.

" With respect to the state of affairs in Greece, I am as yet unable to furnish all the data I could wish, but I can assure you that the loan is likely to produce all the effects which were anticipated from it, both here and in England. Forced to abandon every hope of subduing his late vassals, the sultan has resorted to the desperate expedient of transferring the future government of the revolted provinces to Mehemet Ali, the Pacha, or rather sovereign of Egypt. It is not, however, as yet ascertained, whether the latter has accepted the offer, and thus entered into a contest of which the issue cannot be doubtful. Although the Greeks have not been able to avail themselves of the loan, it would appear that so far from being daunted by the reported preparations of the enemy, the general cry is, 'Let the Infidels come, we are ready to receive them!' I understand the legislature and executive bodies, are busily employed in allaying the dissensions which have been excited by Colocotroni and Mavromichalis, spurred on by Metaxa, an adventurer from Cephalonia, who has been the prime mover of these senseless quarrels. I will, however, send you more ample details in the course of a few days; meanwhile, it is devoutly to be hoped, that the friends of the cause in England are not relaxing in any of their endeavours to ensure the triumph of freedom and humanity in the east of Europe.

"E. BLAQUIERE.

"P.S. I enclose the copy of a letter addressed to Hastings, who is, I am informed, at Argos, and will, I am sure, do his utmost to promote the wishes of the Committee."

No. II.

Copy of the letter alluded to above, and addressed to F. A. Hastings, Esq., at Argos.

"Zante, Monday, April 25th, 1824.

"You will no doubt be somewhat surprised to hear of my return to Greece. I arrived here yesterday, or rather late on Saturday night, on board the brig Florida, in twenty-five days from London, but only nineteen from the Mother Bank, to which we were driven by a strong north-wester. We have brought out £40,000 in sovereigns and dollars, being the first instalment of the loan. As, however, no part of it can be handed over to the Provisional Government, without the previous consent of three commissioners named by the Greek Committee and deputies in town, and only two of these are forthcoming, viz. Col. Stanhope and Lazzaro Conduriotti, I fear much time will be lost. I am, however, doing every thing to obviate difficulties, and trust that matters will go on well so far as the money is concerned. M. Polysoides, who has come out with me, starts to-night for Navarin, and will take this. I sincerely hope you are at the seat of Government, and that you will remain there till I have the pleasure of seeing you. I am somewhat puzzled how to act: though most anxious to get to the Morea as soon as possible. I do not like to go over empty-handed, but it is more than probable that a line, which I expect to-morrow or next day from Mavrocordato, to whom I wrote yesterday, will at once decide the course I shall take. You will readily conceive what an effect the news of poor Lord Byron's death has had on my spirits, and how much it has deranged all my plans. There is, however, no time to dwell on this sad event now. What I am most anxious about is, that we should knock our heads together, and urge the Government to act with redoubled energy, now that they possess the means of doing so. Your first question will be, 'What use can I be?' My answer is prepared. If not already near the Government, hasten there on receipt of this, and in conjunction with Colonel S., who is, I trust, there, insist on their ratifying the loan, and sending it back post haste.

"I shall say no more about the above point, and am sure you will feel its all-importance as much as myself. The next point to be managed is, to prevail on the leading men of the islands, &c. to advance money for the immediate wants of the government, on an engagement that they will be repaid *with interest* out of the very sum brought here.

"This strikes Mr. Barff and myself as the best, if not the only way, of obviating every objection and preventing delay. I am in great hopes that Mr. Gordon, of Cairness, will be out as one of the commissioners, in the course of three weeks or a month. His arrival has now become an object of infinite importance.

"With respect to your co-operation with myself, I look to it as absolutely essential to success. I therefore trust that the report of your being about to return home may not be true, and that you will, at all events, remain out a little longer.

"Hoping to find you perfectly restored to health, and that we may yet be enabled to realize some of our good wishes for the Greeks, believe me to be, &c.,

"E. BLAQUIERE."

No. III.

Extract of a Letter from Prince Mavrocordato to E. Blaquiere.

"Messalunghi, le 16-28th Avril, 1824.

"C'est avec le plus grand plaisir que je viens d'apprendre par votre lettre, votre arriveé à Zante à bord de la Florida. Jamais notre pays ne s'est trouvé dans des circonstances plus difficiles, faute des moyens pecuniaires. J'ai tout de suite expedié votre lettre au Gouvernement qui se trouve actuellement à Argos.

"Vous êtes déjà informé de ce qui se passe en Moreé ; mais vous devez apprendre avec plaisir, que la grande majorité de la nation a soutenu le Gouvernement dans ses efforts patriotiques, et que la bonne cause triomphe. J'ai la douce espérance, je suis même persuadé, que l'arrivée de l' emprunt, servira à l'extinction des troubles, et à la pacification générale.

"Je comprends bien la necessité de vous rendre le plutot possible près du Gouvernement, et mon opinion en cele ne peut pas être different de la votre. Je desire avoir le plutot, les informations que vous me promettez et de vous avoir surtout en Grèce ; vous qui avez si essentiellement contribué à sa cause.

"Votre lettre à M. le Colonel Stanhope, sera immediatement expediée á Salona, où il se trouve actuellement.

'A. MAVROCORDATO."

TRANSLATION.

"Messolunghi, April 16-28th, 1824.

"It is with the greatest pleasure that I have just learnt by your letter your arrival at Zante, on board the Florida.

Never did our country find itself in more difficult circumstances, owing to the want of pecuniary means. I sent your letter off immediately to the Government, which is now at Argos.

" You are already informed of what is passing in the Morea; but you must hear with pleasure that the great majority of the nation has supported the Government in its patriotic efforts, and that the good cause triumphs. I entertain the pleasing hope, nay I am convinced, that the arrival of the loan will lead to the extinction of our troubles, and to a general pacification.

" I can easily conceive the necessity of your proceeding to the seat of Government as soon as possible, and my opinion in this respect cannot be different from your own. I am very anxious to receive the details you promise, and, above all, to have you in Greece; you who have so essentially contributed to her cause.

" Your letter to Colonel Stanhope will be despatched immediately to Salona, where he is at present.

" A. MAVROCORDATO."

No. IV.

From E. Blaquiere to the Contractors for the Greek Loan, Messrs. Loughnan and Co.

" Zante, Saturday, May 1st, 1824.

" Sirs,

" As the letter which Mr. Barff has forwarded to you, *via* Otranto, will announce the arrival of the Florida, as well as the arrangements decided on between himself and M. Logotheti, it only remains for me to inform you, that my whole attention is directed to fulfilling your wishes relative to the ratification of the contract. Having dispatched M. Polysoides to the seat of the Provisional Government the day after our arrival here, viz. on Monday last, I feel confident that there will be no time lost there; so that in the event of the Florida's being taken up to convey the body of Lord Byron to England, I look forward to the satisfaction of sending back the contract in her; and as our passage out was so prosperous, it is to be hoped she will make an equally good voyage homewards.

"You will readily conceive into what an awkward dilemma the death of Lord Byron has thrown us all. Such, however, is the urgency of the wants, on the part of the Greek Government, that there was really no course left for Messrs. Barff and Logotheti, except that which they have stated in their joint letter.* Now that the campaign is on the eve of commencing, upon what principle of equity could we ask the Government to ratify the contract, while the equivalent was retained in the hands of the opposite party? We are, therefore, waiting, most anxiously, a reply from Colonel Stanhope; and trust that he will not lose a moment in putting himself in communication with M. Conduriotti, the other Commissioner, in order that no time may be lost in enabling the Provisional Government to avail itself of the succours which I have brought out.

"As I have written fully to Mr. Bowring on all those points in which the holders of Greek scrip are likely to feel any interest, I beg to refer you to him for more ample details, and remain, &c.

"E. BLAQUIERE."

* This alludes to the determination which they had formed, to give up the money on the requisition of Col. Stanhope and Lazaro Conduriotti, the only two Commissioners in Greece.

No. V.

From E. Blaquiere to John Bowring, Esq.

"Zante, Saturday, May 1st, 1824.

"As Salona is three days journey from Messolunghi, I do not expect to hear from Stanhope for three or four days longer; meanwhile Lord Sidney Osborne has come here from Corfu to determine about what is to be done with the body of poor Lord Byron. I hope to be able to remove your doubts on this subject before my letter is closed. My plan will, of course, be to wait for S.'s answer, and occupy myself till then in persuading the people here to send the Body to England, in which I shall be cordially aided by Mr. Barff. It would have been most advantageous had the Lion been here at this moment: as it is, I can only pray that you have lost no time in sending her out. Mr. Gordon's arrival is also most devoutly to be wished for.

"As I am persuaded the immediate application of the money can alone save the cause, do not be surprised if all my efforts are directed towards this object, (see my letter to Messrs. Loughnan and Co.) With respect to the enemy, he is making very formidable preparations, and will no doubt be powerfully aided by Mahemet Pacha.

"E. BLAQUIERE."

No. VI.

Extract of a Letter from E. Blaquiere to John Bowring, Esq.

"Zante, May 11th, 1824.

"I AM sure you will all be highly gratified to learn, that every difficulty with regard to sending poor Lord Byron's remains home are removed. Mr. Barff has engaged the Florida to sail about the 1st of June; she is to take the body and four attendants. The delay is indispensible, on account of the latter having to work out their quarantine, which will continue above a fortnight longer.

" With respect to my plans, they are simply as follows: —Having duly reflected on the ill-fated result of Parry's expedition, and the total disorder in which every thing is thrown, I have determined to do my best to restore some degree of regularity, convinced that I shall best meet the wishes of the committee by this course. Taking it for granted, therefore, that Colonel S. will do what is right with respect to sending the contract back, I shall, in the event of not hearing from him, leave this in three or four days, and having touched at Chiarenza, for the purpose of seeing Sessini, the primate and ruler of that district, who is desirous of quitting Colocotroni's party, and adhering to the government, go on to Messolunghi, and make whatever arrangements I can relative to the stores and park of artillery, every thing connected with these being in a state of the greatest confusion.

" In the mean time, I ought not to omit informing you, for the information of the Committee, that every thing in the shape of *matériel* is most sadly wanted. The heavy guns for Messolunghi, about which I spoke so often and so earnestly, would be a treasure; indeed every thing you can send out in the way of cannon, small arms, and ammunition, will be truly acceptable. Leaving the Committee to provide for existing and probable contingencies, I am

" Yours ever truly,

" E. BLAQUIERE."

No. VII.

From Prince Mavrocordato to E. Blaquiere.

"Anatolico, le 9 Mai, 1824.

"A mon retour de Vrachori, où je me suis rendu pour contribuer à la pacification de quelques différents survenus entre plusieurs capitaines, et que j'ai eu la satisfaction de voir terminés sans aucun accident facheux, j'ai été extrêmement affligé de ne trouver aucune lettre de votre part; ne sachant pas à quoi attribuer votre silence, je m'empresse de vous écrire et j'attendrai votre réponse avec la plus grande impatience. Par des lettres que je viens de recevoir de Malte par Corfou, j'apprends que l'expédition de l'Egypte était déjà prête pour partir; on dit même que le Pacha devoit la commander en personne, et qu'elle est destinée directement pour le Péloponnèse. Je me suis empressé de donner ces nouvelles au gouvernement, pour le décider de hâter aussi le départ de notre flotte.

"A. MAVROCORDATO."

TRANSLATION.

"Anatolico, May 9th, 1824.

"On my return from Vrachori, where I went to contribute to the removal of some differences which arose between several captains, and which I had the satisfaction of seeing terminated without any unpleasant accident, I have been extremely sorry not to find a letter from you. Not knowing to what I am to impute your silence, I hasten to write, and shall await your answer with the utmost impatience. By letters which I have just received from

Malta, through Corfu, I understand the Egyptian expedition is ready to sail; it is even said that the Pacha is to command it in person, and that it is destined direct for the Peloponnesus. I lost no time in sending this news to the government, in order that it should also hasten the sailing of our fleet.

"A. MAVROCORDATO."

No. VIII.

From E. Blaquiere to John Bowring, Esq.

"Zante, May 12th, 1824.

"I MUST hasten to tell you the result of a very short interview I had with Colonel Stanhope, before the Lazaretto barrier was cleared at noon. He had received the letters I sent to Salona, and immediately wrote to Argos, requesting the government to dispatch five commissioners *here* with all possible dispatch, to confer and arrange on the appropriation of the money. Having settled this all-important point, he intends proceeding to England *via* Ancona. The Colonel's account of the state of affairs in Greece, is very favourable indeed. The dissensions are at an end, and there is an universal belief that the money, so providentially sent, will heal every wound. Barff, and Logetheti, are to see us this evening, when, a preliminary conference will take place, so that every thing may be ready by the time the five deputies arrive. With regard to myself, I shall now prepare for my departure, and as stated in my letter of yesterday, cross over to Messolunghi. I am however in a state of infinite perplexity. Such is the state of that place, and the position of poor Mavrocordato, that he writes to say his life will be endangered if money be not instantly sent over to pay the troops, especially the Souliotes, who have become quite ungovernable. It would, of course, be a most awkward thing to make my appearance there, without any means of alleviating existing miseries. I shall therefore do my utmost to procure a supply to take with me, and however small it may be, they will not be able to say I came empty handed. I should hope that every thing will be ready for my starting in three days. My motive for not dwelling on the news of the day, is that I do not like to trust to hearsay; when once on the spot, I trust my details may not be without interest, they will be at least as correct as I can procure them. What I shall now feel most anxious about, is the arrival of Mr. Gordon.

"I have already told you that *matériel* of every kind is dreadfully wanted throughout the confederation.

"E. BLAQUIERE.

"P.S. Surely the Deputies are aware of the wants of their country; if they do not act, the consequences may be most fatal!"

No. IX.

From E. Blaquiere to the Hon. Colonel Leicester Stanhope, at the Lazaretto of Zante.

"Barff's Villa, Sunday, May 16th, 1824.

"MY DEAR COLONEL,

"I HAVE already written in every direction relative to renewing the commissioners. Our first letters on that most important point, left this on Thursday fortnight, so that they ought to be well on their way to England ere now.

"I am very glad to hear your letters have come; my mind is still agitated more than I can describe, from apprehensions of the consequences which may arise from any delay in transferring the money. Would to God, my dear Colonel, there were any means of furnishing the temporary relief of which we spoke; without this, we shall surely be doing a manifest injustice to the people we have come to assist, and whose cause we have espoused. After having again and again weighed the matter with all the little intellect I possess, I solemnly declare it, as my final opinion, that Barff and Logetheti, would be fully justified, nay, are bound, by the crying exigency of the case, to give up a *part* of the instalment on *your single* requisition.

"With respect to the effects of bringing out the money and retaining it here, they are developing themselves fast and fatally for the cause. You, of course, know that the Capitoni have a number of partisans at Zante; these have already spread a report that the money is to be sent back to England! On the other hand, many persons who had promised to supply corn, &c. for Messolunghi, will no longer act, and refuse to fulfil their recent promises. Should this state of things proceed, will not the enemies of the cause, internal and external, take advantage of it?

"The last consideration which I am anxious to submit, is that there ought not to be a moment lost in strengthening the *good party:* and how can this be done, if they are left to struggle with their difficulties?

"*Au reste*, I am confident that the whole of our friends in England will calculate on your doing that which would have been done, had not poor Lord B. died so unexpectedly.

"You have, perhaps, heard that the Turkish fleet has landed a body of troops at Negropont, and relieved Carysto, we may, therefore, expect to see them here every day; add this to the loss of Candia, surely the dangers are most imminent! I confess to you, that I cannot contemplate them without the greatest alarm. God grant, however, that my fears may be groundless!

"I have begged Mr. Robinson, who presents this, to explain why I have not gone down to-day. If you wish to see me, I will certainly obey the first summons. Yours most truly and sincerely.

"E. BLAQUIERE."

No. X.

E. Blaquiere to the same.

"Zante, May 24th, 1824.

"MY DEAR COLONEL,

"HAVING read your memorandums with great attention, I beg to assure you that every possible effort shall be made on my part to carry your suggestions into effect; I hope it is needless to say more to prove how highly I estimate their value. I shall now proceed to offer you a few of my own crude opinions, and trust they may not be altogether useless in the course of your communications with the Committee. The hurry in which these remarks are drawn up, will, I trust, be a sufficient excuse for their desultory and unconnected character. I shall, however, make no apology for the undisguised expression of my sentiments, being assured that you will prefer candour to every thing that savours of duplicity.

"To begin with the loan: if you had not already seen the fatal consequences of sending any part of it to Zante, without the special permission of ministers, Mr. Barff's letter of the 22nd, and which he was kind enough to show me, will place the matter in its true light, and cannot fail to prove a highly important document for the Committee. With respect to my own opinions on the subject, they have been expressed in several letters to Bowring; and as I feel very anxious on this point, I shall be much obliged by your laying the note I addressed to you on the 16th instant before the Committee. All that has occurred since, more especially the certainty that the enemy is making very formidable preparations by sea and land, has only tended to increase my conviction that the most serious injury may accrue to the Greek cause by the delay that is likely to take place in transferring the money brought out in the Florida; as to its effects in diminishing our popularity and influence in Greece, there can, I think, be no doubt whatever. Nothing, indeed, but timely measures of precaution in England, or the arrival of Mr. Gordon, whose large fortune and liberal views will enable him to assist the struggling Greeks at once, affords me any hope of averting impending calamities.

"Should the Greek loan proceed, of which there is now surely some reason to doubt, Mr. Barff's letter contains all the suggestions required for its future transmission; if, on the other hand, the wished for precautionary measures have not been taken in London, it will be an immense aggravation of present evils. Should Messrs. Barff and Logotheti persist in conceiving themselves bound, by the late intimation of Sir Frederick Adam, to retain the money in their hands until an order is sent from the contractors to deliver it up, I hold it to be almost impossible to get such an order before the expiration of ten weeks or three months. Here I should observe, that the various obstacles proceeding from other causes, are very much increased by the nomination of Logotheti; and pray inform the Deputies of this circumstance. Though a good man in other respects, he is so timid and punctilious, that there is no chance of his ever departing from the letter of the recent intimation, if Mr. Barff were even inclined to do so.

"While in London, and when the arrangements were making, I took the liberty of more than once expressing my fears, that infinite difficulties might ensue from the mode unhappily adopted. The event has proved that these fears were not altogether devoid of foundation; even had Lord Byron's life been prolonged, the circumstance of your being so peremptorily ordered home, would have suspended the transfer, while it must be known to the deputies in England that several weeks would unavoidably elapse before any understanding could be established between the two remaining commissioners. You are aware of the difficulties of communication, and I have heard since my arrival here, that there is very little probability of Lazaro Conduriotti being able to quit Hydra: so that it will be necessary for whatever new commissioner that is named, to proceed there. When once united, they must enter into a correspondence with the Government, and we know that a week or ten days have often elapsed before an answer could be procured from Hydra, at Tripolitza, to which place there is every reason to believe the Executive and Legislative Body are about to remove. Upon the whole, I cannot now help expressing my apprehensions that, unless some important modification be made in the mode of delivering the loan, the campaign may close, or, at least, all the anticipated danger arrive, before a farthing is received by the borrowers. It is scarcely necessary to say, that such a circumstance would give rise to several important questions, not less injurious to the lenders than to the Greeks themselves. In my last letter to Bowring, sent *via* Otranto, a few days ago, I ventured to suggest, that a great deal of altercation and time would be saved, by sending one or two persons in the confidence of the contractors and committee with all future remittances, and leaving it to them, in concert with an equal number in Greece, to decide whether matters were in such a state as to justify the money's being handed over to the Executive. As to the propriety of transferring the first instalment, I am humbly of opinion that it ought to be done the moment those appointed to deliver it are satisfied a government conformable to that provided for by the constitution is established. That this is the case, even now, there seems to be no doubt. With respect to the dissensions, all the recent accounts concur in stating that they are at an end; that the two refractory chiefs, Colocotroni and Mavromichalis, have proceeded to the seat of Government to confirm their adhesion, as well as to aid in carrying the projected plan of campaign into effect. Admitting, however, that differences did exist, how is it possible to put an end to them without the friends of Greece afford the Government some means of making itself respected? *

"You have already given your opinion on the state of par-

* It will thus be seen, that the point upon which Colonel Stanhope and myself were principally at issue, related to the transfer of the money. I need scarcely say, that I anticipated some dreadful calamity, if not the ruin of the cause, by the delay which unhappily occurred at Zante. The gallant Colonel's sentiments will be best seen by the following extract from a letter he addressed to Mr. Bowring, and published in his work, on the 22nd of May, six days after my note of the 16th, and which seems to have been written just as we had conferred together on the subject:—

"Blaquiere has been with me this morning; he is dreadfully alarmed; he has had a moving letter from Mavrocordato. The Turkish fleet is out; the fortresses in Negropont are relieved; the Egyptians and Ottomans are coming on, and the loan is all in Barff's counting-house. My opinion is known to you; the Turkish fleet, when collected, is always master at sea; their fortresses will, therefore, be relieved, their troops will effect their landings, and succeed in their first efforts; but with the winter comes the ebb: then is the time for the Greeks to commence their blockades and sieges, and to march. Judge from experience which is right."

Would to God that experience had proved that the apprehensions of the Government, my own fears, as well as those of Prince Mavrocordato and so many others, were not destined to be realised! In less than ten

ties in Greece; permit me to give mine. I have never been able to discover more than two: the people, and the captains and primates. If you ask me what is the best remedy possessed by the people, who have a constitution, my answer is, a good mode of election and the nomination of the most virtuous representatives they can find. I really believe the actual members of the Legislative Body are the very best that can be found in Greece: and it is to their prudence, aided by the co-operation of the people, as they have always been, that I look for its present safety and ultimate triumph.

"Although efforts may have been made by the agents of the Holy Alliance, to form a kingly faction, I am convinced nothing deserving the name of such a party exists in Greece. I have many reasons for making this assertion, and I trust I shall be very soon able to prove it by uncontrovertible facts. It is with unfeigned regret, that I have heard you repeat your belief that Prince Mavrocordato is in favour of a foreign King; nay, more, that he has been intriguing in concert with the metropolitan Ignatius, for the purpose of introducing one into the confederation. Owing to various circumstances, which it would now be superfluous to relate, I am confident there is no truth whatever in the above report. With respect to the numerous other stories spread in this country and written to England, which represent a man who honourse m with his personal friendship, and for whom I entertain the warmest esteem, as the partisan of faction and intrigue, I am bound by every tie of honour and honesty, to regard them as gratuitous and malignant calum-

days after the above was penned, Ipsara was destroyed, and more than four thousand men, women, and children, were put to the sword!

Prince Mavrocordato's letter of the 30th of August, forwarded to me from Zante, since my arrival in England, and of which a copy will be found in another page, shows what his opinions are on this important, but melancholy subject.

nies, until the proofs are brought home to my illustrious friend in a somewhat more tangible shape than the assertion contained in certain letters which I have seen handed about the table of the Greek Committee, and heard of since my arrival in Zante. In the mean time, I do most particularly entreat, that you will cause the Prince's last letter, of which I subjoin a verbatim copy, as well as a literal translation of that which he has just addressed to the Greek Chronicle, to be read to as full a Committee as can be formed when you reach London. Those who have heard the charges in question will not deny him the right of making a defence. I want no better explanation for the motives which actuate Mavrocordato, until my arrival in Greece, when it shall be my very first care to call upon the Prince himself for a refutation of all that has gone abroad to blast his character, and lower him in the eyes, not only of Europe, but of that people for whom he has sacrificed his all.

"I cannot close this matter without informing you, that although I have no more veneration for the title of Prince than I ought to have, it does not belong to me to strip Mavrocordato of an appendage which, though it can be of no earthly use to him, has been conferred by some of the most liberal and enlightened Englishmen who have espoused the Greek cause, not to mention the best patriots of Greece. Admitting that this title is one of mere courtesy, has any individual among his own countrymen, much less a foreigner, the smallest right to deprive him of it, or call its legality into question, until the Government under which he lives takes the subject into consideration? Mavrocordato is the lineal descendant of the family which has furnished several Hospadars to Walachia and Moldavia, a post that has always been honoured with the title of Prince. I am, therefore, of opinion, that my illustrious friend is, so far as courtesy goes, as much entitled to the appellation as if it had been registered in all the Herald's Colleges of Europe. In making the foregoing observations on a subject of great insignificance, I ought to add my conviction, that Mavrocordato does not attach the smallest importance to his title, and that he has never either signed his name or called himself a Prince; it is a matter of perfect indifference to him whether others call him so or not.

"I expressed myself very warmly on Saturday last, on the gross impropriety of those foreigners, and more especially Englishmen, who come to aid Greece, interfering in its internal dissensions, or abusing its public functionaries. In again deprecating this conduct, I will put to yourself, my dear Colonel, whether it be fair or honorable in those who write and repeat such serious charges against Mavrocordato, and others holding the highest situations under the Government, to do so without affording the accused party any means of defending or exculpating themselves; yet that this has been the case in a hundred instances, and above all in that of the Prince, who can deny? I will not disguise from you that I hold it to be not only greatly injurious to the Greek cause, both here and in England, but mean and vindictive, to put such passages to paper as an individual, professing to advocate the cause, read to you and myself on Saturday. I repeat, therefore, that the sooner such auxiliaries either leave or are turned out of Greece the better.

"With reference to the Prince's letter, convinced, as I am, that his situation is precisely as he describes it, and moreover, that it is of infinite importance to secure Messolunghi against the meditated attack of the enemy, there is no alternative left for me but to hasten over with all the pecuniary aid I possess myself, or can procure. In other respects, as friendship is not a name with me, I am fully prepared to fulfil all the duties it imposes. Having done whatever I can to alleviate the sufferings of the Prince, I shall hasten to the seat of Government, there to pursue the great object of the friends of Greece as diligently as I can.

"Being decidedly of the lamented Lord Byron's opinion, that the grand consideration for the Greeks themselves, and their foreign friends, is to drive out the Turks, I need not add, that every suggestion I venture to offer will have an immediate reference to this all-important and paramount desideratum. Nor will I conceal from you my apprehensions, that very little progress can be made in the scarcely less important objects of legislation and public instruction, before the above grand triumph be attained; much, however, may be done in the way of preparation, and I will do all that depends on me in this way.

"In allusion to the importance of publicity, and the general freedom of the press, those corner stones of the edifice of liberty in every country, and which you have laboured so successfully to establish, the only limit I would place before them is clearly pointed out in the letter of Mavrocordato to the Greek Chronicle. I also think that the Greeks may become as free as any people on earth, without the repetition of certain words, or the insertion of articles, which only tend to awaken the attention and excite the hatred of those who would gladly see them once more subjected to the infidel yoke. The inevitable effect of discussing abstract principles of government, or political theories, in the present state of Greece, will be that of rousing the Holy Alliance to resistance, without enlightening the Greeks, who must be taught the first rudiments of knowledge, before they can ascend to the higher walks of politics and legislation. From what I have here said, do not be surprised if nearly the whole of my attention be directed towards urging the most prompt and vigorous measures of naval and military organization. You are so well prepared to inform the Committee of what is wanted to promote these great objects, and for increasing the means of defence possessed by the confederation, that I deem it unnecessary to add any thing on the subject. Equally needless is it for me to dwell on the disastrous result of Parry's expedition.

"Wishing you a prosperous passage, and all the applause your meritorious exertions in the cause of freedom so justly merit, believe me to be, my dear Colonel,

"Your's very faithfully and truly,

(Signed) "EDWARD BLAQUIERE.

"P.S. In pursuance of my determination to succour Messolunghi, I have given my personal guarantee for the payment of eighty barrels of gunpowder, consigned to a chant of this place, and am doing all I can to procure some lead, of which article the Prince stands in the greatest need.—E. B."

No. XI.

From Prince Mavrocordato, to E. Blaquiere, and which is alluded to in the preceding.

"Messolunghi, le 9 21, Mai, 1824.

"Je ne suis pas moins affligé, déconcerté même, lorsque je pense à l'impossibilité de faire agir notre flotte, et au decouragement genéral qu, ameneront toutes ces difficultés, de l'emploi de l'argent venu. L'ennemi sera tout-à fait libre dans ses operations, sa flotte arrivée dèja depuis quelque tems à Negrepont, ne manquera pas de parcourir impunément l'Archipel, et celle qui vient de partir d'ici pour l'Egypte, unie à celle qui s'y trouvait dèjà, retournera bièntôt pour mettre en execution ses projets dèsastreux.

Dieu, le seul Dieu protecteur de la Grèce fasse, que l'arrivée de Mr. Gordon, mêt un fin à cet etat d'incertitude, et de perplexité !

"Quant à vous, cher ami, je n'ai qu'à vous remercier de vos sentimens, de vos peines, de votre zéle pour la plus belle des causes: faites le mieux que vous pouvez. Vos actes ont mérité et mériteront toujours la plus vive reconnaissance de la Grèce. Je ne puis qu'approuver les raisons qui vous font rester à Zante: j'adresserai votre lettre ainsi que celle de notre bon et digne ami Mr. C***, à Mr. Rodius; mais que voulez vous qu'il fasse ainsi lui ou le Gouvernement? je prevois mille choses sinistres . . . . !

(Signé) "A. MAVROCORDATO."

TRANSLATION.

"Messolunghi, May 9-21st, 1824.

"I am not less afflicted, and even disconcerted, when I think on the impossibility of making our fleet act, and on the general discouragement to which all these difficulties in employing the money will lead. The enemy will be completely free in his operations. His fleet, which has arrived within these few days, at Negropont, will not fail to scour the Archipelago with impunity, and that which has just quitted this for Egypt,* united to the one already there, will shortly return to carry its disastrous projects into execution. God, the only protector of Greece, grant that the arrival of Mr. Gordon may put an end to this state of

* This alludes to the recent departure of the Turkish squadron of two frigates, and eight or ten smaller vessels of war, stationed at Patrass, for Alexandria, where they were to take on board a part of the troops, composing Mehemet Ali's expedition.—E. B.

uncertainty and perplexity. As to you, my dear friend, I have only to thank you for your sentiments, your sufferings, and your zeal for the best of causes, do as well as you can. Your actions have merited and will always merit the most lively gratitude of Greece. I cannot but approve the motives which induce you to remain at Zante. I will send your letter, as well as that of our good and worthy friend M. C * * *, to M. Rodius. But what can you expect him or the government to do either? I foresee a thousand sinister circumstances . . . . !

"A. MAVROCORDATO."

Extract of a Letter from the Secretary of Government, to Prince Mavrocordato, dated from the Mills of Argos, May 9th, 1824, and enclosed in the foregoing.

"THE Honourable Colonel Stanhope has not yet made his appearance; we hope he will not be long in arriving, convinced as he is, that his delay will lead to the greatest obstacles being opposed to our military operations, and very unfortunate consequences for this campaign. Our ships are already prepared, but it is impossible to embark a single man, until their wages are paid. The Turkish fleet, composed of fifty sail, has unexpectedly arrived at Negropont, upon which the blockade of that place, by land, was immediately raised. No news from Salona. Odysseus has just addressed letters to the Government, Colocotroni, Nikitas and Colliopulo, in all of which it is easy to trace the obscure and malignant style of * * * *."

No. XII.

From E. Blaquiere to Colonel Stanhope.

"Zante, May 26th, 1824.

"My Dear Colonel,

"I had scarcely closed my long letter of yesterday's date, when one, of which the enclosed is a verbatim copy, reached me from Messolunghi; by comparing its contents with all I have already said and written, you will perceive that I am not alone in the apprehensions of the consequences which are resulting, and may in future arise from the detention of this money. It pains me more than I can describe, to find that our opinions are so completely at variance upon the wants of Greece, and while I feel convinced that you exercise your best judgment with the very best intentions, I owe it to the cause we are engaged in to say, that my fears are the fears of every person for whose opinion I entertain any value. I entreat, therefore, that this letter of Mavrocordato may be also laid before the Committee as soon after your landing as possible.

"Allow me to correct a misunderstanding into which you have fallen. Barff told me distinctly, last night, that although he should be inclined to give up the money on a requisition from three new commissioners, he is convinced old Logotheti would not do so, without he is exonerated from the effects of the re-published proclamation, by the contractors.

"I had intended to refer to other points, but my mind is too much agitated; nor can I describe to you my deep regret at having come out to witness such a state of things. With respect to my plan; painful as it will be to suffer all the feelings which must attend my presence at the seat of government, I shall go there and do what I can to remove the impressions which have been created even already. Would to God, my dear Colonel, you had gone to Argos, instead of coming here!

"Most truly and sincerely your's,

"E. BLAQUIERE."

No. XIII.

From Prince Mavrocordato to E. Blaquiere, and to which allusion is made in the preceding letter.

"Anatolico, le 3-15 Mai, 1824.

"Nous connaissons ici depuis plusieurs jours l'arrivé de M. Polysoides près du gouvernement, qui ma adressé une lettre pour vous, laquelle je me suis empressé de vous expedier par une occasion sure, et qui doit être déjà entre vos mains. Je n'attribue le retard de la ratification qu'à ce qu'on attendait M. le Colonel pour qui on avoit immediatement expedié un courrier à Salona. Il parait cependant, que M. le Colonel etait parti de cette ville avant l'arrivé du courrier du gouvernement. Quoiqu'il en soit, il eut êté beaucoup plus avantageux que M. Stanhope se fut rendu à Argos avant de partir pour Zante: mais je ne désespére pas, lorsque je pense que vous êtes là pour tout arranger.

"Vous connaissez très bien mon caractére, pour me croire incapable de conserver le moindre inimitié contre qui que ce soit; et a plus forte raison contre des personnes que j'estime et que j'estimerai se fussent ils même declarés mes ennemis, ce que je ne crois pas. Voila en quoi il peut consister une difference d'opinion entre ces Messieurs et moi: ils croient peut être que M. Negris a changé, et qu'il ne sera plus dorénevant *l'ancien Negris*.

"C'est ne pas que j'ai de l'inimitié personnelle contre M.

Negris ; je fut le premier à prendre publiquement sa defence, lorsque je l'ai vu attaqué dans les Chroniques, ainsi qu'il paraîtra dans le numero prochain ; mais je dirai toujours qu'un *chat* est un *chat*. Ces Messieurs croient, ou pour mieux dire, on leur a fait croire aussi, que les divisions existantes sont l'effet des principes oligarchiques, qui se sont trouvés en opposition avec le parti militaire : je crois au contraire, que le chef du parti oligarchique, en union avec celui du parti militaire, ont voulu opprimer le parti national, que ce dernier a eu le dessus, parcequ'il avoit l'avantage de l'opinion publique, et parceque la grande masse du peuple, c'est de suite declaré contre leurs oppresseurs. L'opinion du Colonel Stanhope est que, l'introduction du General Ulysse dans le corps executif amenera des avantages immenses. Cette introduction appartient exclusivement aux representans du peuple qui vont bientot se rassembler à Argos, pour renouveller la periode du gouvernement ; mais je crois qu'en deplaçant le Général Ulysse de la tête des armées, on commit une faute. J'espere, du reste, que l'example de Colocotroni, ne permettra a aucun homme d'honneur de marcher sur ses traces : et si Ulysse à résolu de l'être, il saura se conduire de maniere à meriter l'estime publique. C'est sur des pareilles choses qu'il peut y'avoir une divergence d'opinion entre ces Messieurs et moi, et je desirerais avant tout, qu'ils ne s'empressent pas à se former un opinion sur les personnes et les affaires de la Grèce, chose si difficile pour ceux méme qui s'y trouvent depuis longtemps. Leur bonne foi pouvàit être très facilement surprise et le mal serait quelques fois irrémédiable.

" Me voila en possession d'une autre lettre de vous en date du 11, que M. Vitali arrivé cet instant, vient de me remettre. Je crois par tout ce que vous m'ecrivez, ainsi que notre commun ami M. C * * * *, qu'il y'a très peu d'espoir d'avoir le numéraire necessaire pour le payement de la solde des

Souliotes. Je vous assuré, mon cher ami, que je ne me suis jamais trouvé dans une circonstance plus difficile que celle où je me trouve actuellement; il m'est impossible d'abord de pourvoir aux depenses journalieres que leur sejour dans ces deux villes occasionne.

"Je me suis très utilement servi de la lettre ostensible que M. C * * *, m'a adressée pour les tranquilliser de nouveau; mais quel sera mon sort, si nos émissaires retournent ici ayant les mains vides! Je ne le sais pas; mais je vous assure que je me crois incapable de souffrir que des malheureux citoyens soient pillés sous mes yeux, la catastrophe la plus horrible finira ici mes jours et mes peines, je vois bien que c'est ce que mes ennemis veulent et ce qu'ils ont taché de preparer de loin, mais j'aurais encore assez de courage pour mourir un homme d'honneur.

"Je ne sais pas si ma lettre vous trouvera à Zante, vous supposez bien que je suis impatient de vous voir, cher ami, ce serait un soulagement pour mon ame accablée d'amertume depuis si long tems.

"Je n'ecris que très peu de mots à notre commun ami M. C * * * *, car je ne vois rien de plus pressant que de reexpedier la barque, pour donner l'ordre aux deputés de ne pas retourner sitot: s'ils n'obtiennent pas l'object de leur mission; retarder le mal, est encore un bien. Mon Dieu! chaque jour en augmentant la somme de nos dettes, nous conduit à l'impossibilité de nous voir délivrés d'un fardeau qui est déjà devenu insupportable!

"A. MAVROCORDATO."

TRANSLATION.

"Anatolico, May 3-15th, 1824.

"We have for some days past known the arrival of M. Polysoides at the seat of government. He has sent me a letter for you, which I hastened to forward by a safe opportunity, and which ought to be ere this in your hands. I can only attribute the delay in the ratification, to their expecting the Colonel, for whom a courier was immediately dispatched to Salona. It appears, however, that the Colonel had left that place before the arrival of the courier sent by government. At all events, it would have been much more advantageous had M. Stanhope gone to Argos before going to Zante; but I do not despair, when I reflect that you are there to arrange every thing.

"You know my character too well to believe me capable of retaining the smallest enmity towards any person, much less against those whom I esteem, and shall ever esteem, though they had even declared themselves my enemies, which I do not think is the case. It is here that there may be a difference of opinion between those gentlemen and myself:—They believe that M. Negris has changed, and that he will no longer be the former Negris. It is not that I entertain any personal enmity against M. Negris. I was the first to defend him publicly, when I saw him attacked in the Chronicles, as will appear in the next number; but I will always say, a *cat* is a *cat*. Those gentlemen think, or rather they have been made to believe, that the existing differences are the effects of Oligarchical principles, which are in opposition to the military party. I think, on the contrary, that the head of the Oligarchical party united with that of the military party, wished to oppress the National party; that the latter had the upper hand, because it had the advantage of public opinion in its favour, and because the great mass of the people immediately declared against their oppressors. The opinion of Colonel Stanhope is, that the introduction of General Odysseus into the executive body would lead to immense advantages. This introduction belongs exclusively to the representatives of the people, who will shortly be assembled at Argos for the purpose of renewing the period of government; but I think that to displace General Odysseus from the head of the armies, would be to commit an error. At all events, I hope the example of Colocotroni will not allow any man of honour to walk in his steps; and if Odysseus has resolved to enter the government, he will know how to conduct himself so as to merit the esteem of the public. It is on such matters that there may be a difference of opinion between these gentlemen and myself; and I desire, above all things, that they do not be in too great a hurry to form an opinion on the individuals and affairs of Greece,—a thing of much difficulty, even for those who have been a long time in the country. Their good faith may be very often surprised, and the evil would be sometimes irreparable.

"I am in possession of another of your letters, dated the 11th instant, and which M. Vitali, arrived at this moment, has handed to me. I imagine, from all you tell me, as well as our common friend M. C * * *, that there is very little hope of obtaining the money required for paying the Souliotes. I assure you, my dear friend, that I never found myself in a more difficult situation than that in which I now am. It is impossible for me, in the first place, to meet the daily expenses which their stay in these two places occasions. I have availed myself very usefully of the ostensible letter M. C * * * has addressed to me, in order to tranquillize them; but what will be my fate if our emissaries return here with empty hands? I do not know; but I assure you, that I think myself incapable of suffering these unfortunate citizens to be pillaged before my eyes. A horrible catastrophe will terminate my days and my sufferings here. It is what my enemies want, and what they have long since tried to prepare; but I shall still have the courage to die as a man of honour.

"I only write a few words to our common friend, M. C * * *,

for I see nothing more urgent than to re-expedite the boat, to order the two deputies not to come back so soon. If they do not obtain the object of their mission, to defer the evil is still an advantage. My God! every day, in augmenting the amount of our debts, leads us to the impossibility of seeing ourselves delivercd from a weight that has already become insupportable.

"A. MAVROCORDATO."

No. XIV.

From Col. Stanhope to Prince Mavrocordato.

"Zante, May 18th, 1824.

"MY DEAR SIR,

"MY cordial thanks are due to you for your kind letter. I request your sanction for the delivery of three three-pounders, and one howitzer, with the necessary ammunition to General Odysseus; likewise of a map of Greece. Captain Trelawny will take charge of these articles.

"I am anxious to see your letter, which appeared in the Greek Chronicle, and was alluded to in your last communication. My political opinions may be expressed in two words--I am for *your* constitition. Every man and measure that leads to that object I embrace; every man and measure that has a tendency either directly and manfully, or indirectly and by intrigue, to counteract the constitution, I condemn, and endeavour, by all possible means, to thwart. Among these bad men, the most odious and black-hearted are those who are intriguing in the dark to saddle on the Greek people a foreign king.

"I am, &c.

"L. STANHOPE."

No XV.

From Prince Mavrocordato to E. Blaquiere.

"Messolunghi, le 10-22, Mai, 1824.

"Mon très cher ami,

"Vous trouverez ci-inclus les extraits d'une lettre de Yousouf Pacha, interceptée, et d'une autre que le Général Scaltza vient de m'adresser. Vous y verrez l'imminence du danger si le plan de l'ennemi n'est pas paralysé et je ne vois pas d'autre expédient que celui de faire sortir le plutôt possible notre flotte à la rencontre de celle qui vient de l'Egypte : celle-ci pourra être d'autant plus facilement attaquée avec avantage, qu'elle aura à protéger plus de deux cents transports. L'expedition maritime une fois paralysé, il n'y a plus rien à craindre des expéditions du côté de terre, et tout le plan de campagne de l'ennemi est renversé ; mais pour faire sortir notre flotte, il faudra de l'argent : le donnera-t-on ? Qu'on le garde pour une meilleure occasion. Le Général Scaltza demande du secours ; comment les lui envoyer ? Puis-je décider les Souliotes ? Ah ! si je l'avais pu, ils ne seraient pas dans ces deux malheureuses villes à exiger ce que nous ne pouvons pas leur procurer, et à menacer d'une destruction totale le peu qui reste de la Grèce Occidentale ; mais que m'importe que ces deux villes, qui ont deja deux fois servi de boulevard au Péloponése, à toute la Grèce même, tombent plutôt sous les coups des Souliotes que sous ceux du Pacha de Scoudra ? C'est tout à fait la même chose.

"On demande de tout côté des munitions, et je n'ai pas même mille livres de plomb. Nous vous devons une reconnaissance infinie de la poudre que vous nous avez procurée moyennant votre garantie ; sans cela, nous en aurions également manqué. Je ne sais quelles difficultés à-t-on voulu élever encore aujourd'hui sur l'emploi de l'argent destinó à la réparation des fortifications, et remis par M. le Comte Gamba aux soins d'une commission. Cet argent est, dit-on, du Comité, et d'après un ordre de M. le Colonel Stanhope, ne devrait pas été employé jusqu'à l'arrivé de M. Gordon. Je n'ai pas encore eu le tems de me bien informer ; mais ce serait bien extraordinaire, puisque je crois être sur que cet argent appartient à Milord, et que c'est de lui même qu'il fut destiné à cet effet. Du reste, M. le Colonel ne m'en dit rien dans sa lettre, dont je vous envoye copie, et sur laquelle vous me permettrez sans doute de vous faire quelques observations, que je me reserve de lui faire aussi dans une response, que lui sera addressée à Londres, puisque on m'a assuré, qu'il a du quitter Zante depuis avant hier.

" M. le Colonel m'invite à remettre à M. Trelawny trois canons et un obus, le seul existant ici, avec les munitions necessaires, pour le Général Ulysse. Je prevois bien des difficultés que je rencontrerai de la part du peuple ; qui voyant cette ville menacée par terre et par mer, et connaissant le grand besoin qu'il y a des canons, et surtout, le manque presque total de munitions, ne verra pas sans doute avec indifference, tous ces objets emportés d'ici, tandis qu'on avait déjà pensé de placer ces mêmes canons, en cas de besoin, à Procopanistos, et sur les batteries des ailes. Je ferai cependant tout ce que je pourrai pour prevenir une tumulte de sa part, mais M. Trelawny a voulu aussi emporter d'abord toute la brigade de l'artillerie, en y engageant les officiers et soldats à mon insçu, ce qui m'ayant obligé à rappeler ces braves à leur devoir : il est venu alors me demander la permission de prendre avec lui une partie de la brigade. Ce serait diviser inutilement un corps, qui, au lieu d'être ainsi affoibli devait être au contraire augmenté, afin de servir au but pour lequel il fut créé.

"Je passe au dernier paragraphe, principal objet, à ce que je crois, de la lettre de M. le Colonel. Je n'ai rien à m'approprier de tout ce qu'il écrit. S'il est attaché à notre constitution, je crois que celui qui se glorifie d'avoir contribué à sa confection, doit l'être beaucoup plus que tout autre. Je sais, (et j'ai même tous les documens entre mes mains) que M. Negris avait addressé, il y a plus de 18 mois, des circulaires en faveur d'un gouvernement monarchique, dont l'ex-roi de Vestphalie Jerome, devait être le chef, et je sais aussi, que je fus le premier à combattre son opinion. Serait-ce M. Negris le *bad man* de M. le Colonel Stanhope? Je sais positivement aussi, que sous l'ombre de la constitution, plusieurs Capitaines font tout ce que les plus grands despotes du monde ne feraient peut être pas: qu'ils cassent les bras et les jambes, et laissent dans cet état des plus affreuses douleurs, mourir des innocens; qu'ils tuent, qu'ils pendent, qu'ils font perir des hommes sans jugement préalable, qu'ils se permettent des vexations de toute sorte, qu'ils se revoltent, qu'ils trahissent même la Patrie. Seraient-ils les *good men* de M. le Colonel? C'est à ces derniers que je me suis toujours opposé au peril méme de ma vie; mais j'ai toujours respecté et soutenu la constitution, la constitution forte et agissante, et M. le Colonel ne parait courir qu'après son ombre. Tout ce que je vous dis, cher ami, je n'hesiterai de le dire devant tout le monde.

"M. Trelawny croit necessaire que vous alliez à Hydra, et je crois plus necessaire d'y envoyer de l'argent pour que la flotte sorte immédiatement. Mon opinion est, que vous devrez ou rester à Zante jusqu'à l'arrivé de M. Gordon, ou passer ici et vous rendre près du gouvernement. Je viens d'apprendre que M. Trelawny est tout en rage contre moi, peut être à cause de la brigade. Je me moque bien de sa rage; cette conduite de ces messieurs, est vraiment digne de l'amour de la liberté dont ils veulent se glorifier. Ya t-il de despotisme plus cruel que celui d'un étranger qui, sans aucun droit, veut commander sans avoir aucun égard aux loix existantes? Mais, mon Dieu! le premier venu croit-il donc qu'il peut nous fouler aux pieds, ou nous croit-on capables de nous laisser mener par le nez par le premier intriguant? Avons nous sécoué le joug Ottoman, pour succomber à celui d'un autre? Ah que non! On a dit que j'ai vendu la Grèce à l'Angleterre. La Grèce existe, et ceux qui on été porteurs de mes lettres en Angleterre, sauront dire ce qu'elles contenaient, et si j'ai vendu ma patrie. Je crois lui avoir rendu des services; c'etait mon devoir. On dit à present, que je veux un despote; non, c'est justement parceque je n'en veux aucun, que l'on m'accuse. Je veux que les loix règnent et qu'elles ne soient pas à la discretion d'une centaine de despotes qui les foulent aux pieds. J'ai toujours donné, et je suis encore le premier à donner, l'exemple de l'obeissance; mais s'il est destiné que la Grèce tombe aux pieds d'un despotisme militaire, d'un Hydra, pas à sept, mais à cent têtes, je ne serai ni l'instrument aveugle, ni le serviteur très humble de ces nouveaux tyrans. Adieu, cher ami, j'espere vous voir bientôt, faites tout ce que vous pouvez pour secourir ma malheureuse patrie dans ces momens critiques; faites sortir la flotte, et utilisez, s'il est possible, le corps des Souliotes, qui non seulement sont inutiles ici, mais nous menacent encore d'une guerre intestine. Agréez l'assurance de mon devouement. Vous pourrez faire l'usage que vous croyez à propos de ma lettre.

"A. MAVROCORDATO."

TRANSLATION.

"Messolunghi, May 10-22, 1824.

"My very Dear Friend,

"You will find enclosed extracts from an intercepted

letter of Yousouf Pacha, and from another, which General Scaltza has just addressed to me. You will there see the imminence of the danger if the plan of the enemy is not paralyzed, and I see no other expedient than the sending out our fleet as speedily as possible to meet that of Egypt, which may be attacked with so much more advantage, as it will have to protect more than two hundred transports. The naval expedition once paralyzed, there will be no longer any thing to fear from the land expeditions, and the whole of the enemy's plan for the campaign will be overthrown. But to fit out the fleet money will be wanting: will it be granted? Let it be reserved for a better occasion. General Scaltza asks assistance: how is to be sent to him? Can I determine the Suliotes? Ah! could I have done so, they should not now have been in these unfortunate towns, exacting what we cannot procure them, and threatening the little that remains of Western Greece with total destruction. But what matters it to me whether these two towns, which have already twice served as bulwarks to the Peloponnesus, and even to the whole of Greece, fall under the vengeance of the Suliotes or of the Pacha of Scutari? It is all one.

"Ammunition is demanded on all sides, and I have not even a thousand pounds of lead. We owe you an infinite deal of gratitude for the powder which you have procured for us by means of your guarantee. Without that, we should have been equally in want of it also. I know not what difficulties it has been wished even now to raise, with respect to the employment of the money destined for the repairs of the fortifications, and placed by Count Gamba in the charge of a commission. This money, they say, belongs to the Committee, and, in pursuance of an order of Col. Stanhope, cannot be made use of until the arrival of Mr. Gordon. I have not yet had time to inform myself well upon the subject; but this would be very extraordinary, as I think I am sure that this money belongs to his Lordship, and that it was by himself that it was destined to that purpose. Moreover, the Colonel says nothing to me about it in his letter, of which I send you a copy, and on which you will undoubtedly permit me to make some observations to you, which I reserve to myself to make also to him, in an answer which will be addressed to him in London, as I am assured that he was to quit Zante the day before yesterday.

"The Colonel desires me to deliver to Mr. Trelawny three field pieces and a howitzer, the only one in the place, together with the necessary ammunition, for General Ulysses. I foresee that I shall meet with many difficulties on the part of the people, who seeing this town threatened by land and sea, and knowing the great need that there is of cannon, and the almost total want of ammunition, will not undoubtedly see with indifference all these objects carried away from hence, while it was already in agitation to place these pieces at Procopanistos, and on the batteries of the wings. I will, nevertheless, do all in my power to prevent a tumult on their part; but Mr. Trelawny has also wished to carry off, in the first place, the whole brigade of artillery, by engaging the officers and soldiers of it unknown to me; this having obliged me to recall these brave men to their duty, he has since come to ask my permission to take with him a part of the brigade. This would be uselessly to divide a corps which, instead of being thus weakened, ought, on the contrary, to be increased, in order to fulfil the object for which it was created.

"I pass on to the last paragraph, the principal object, as I believe, of the letter of the Colonel; I have nothing to appropriate to myself of all that he writes. If he is attached to our constitution, I think that he whose boast it is to have contributed to its formation, ought to be much more so than any other. I know (and I have even all the documents in my hands) that M. Negris addressed, more than eighteen months ago, circulars in favour of a monarchical government, of which the ex-King of Westphalia, Jerome, was to be the head, and I also know that I was the first to combat his opinion. Can this M. Negris be the *bad man* of Colonel Stanhope? I know positively also, that under the shadow of the constitution, several captains do that which the greatest despots in the world would not, perhaps, do: that they break legs and arms, and leave in this state of the most dreadful torture, innocent men to perish; that they kill, that they hang, that they destroy men without previous trial; that they allow themselves all sorts of vexations; that they revolt; that they even betray their country. Can these be the Colonel's *good men?* These latter I have always opposed, even at the peril of my life; but I have always respected and maintained the constitution, the constitution in its strength and activity, and the Colonel appears only to be running after its shadow. All that I say to you, my dear friend, I will not hesitate to say before the whole world.

"Mr. Trelawny thinks it necessary that you should go to Hydra, and I think it more necessary to send money thither, that the fleet may be immediately fitted out. My opinion is, that you should either remain at Zante until the arrival of Mr. Gordon, or come hither and proceed to the seat of government. I have just learned that Mr. Trelawny is quite enraged against me, perhaps on account of the brigade. I laugh at his rage. This conduct, on the part of these gentlemen, is well worthy of the love of liberty of which they wish to make their boast. Can there be a more cruel despotism than that of a foreigner, who, without any right whatever, wishes to command, without the least regard to the existing laws? My God! does the first comer think then that he can tread us under his feet, or are we thought capable of being led by the nose by the first intriguer? Have we shaken off the Ottoman yoke only to fall beneath another? Oh, no! It has been said, that I have sold Greece to England Greece still exists, and those who were the bearers of my letters to England know well what they contained, and whether I have sold my country. I believe that I have been of service to her: it was my duty. It is now said that I wish for a despot; no, it is just because I do not want one that I am accused. I wish that the laws may reign, and that they may not be at the discretion of a hundred despots who trample them under foot. I have always given, and I am still the first to give, an example of obedience; but if Greece is fated to fall at the feet of a military despotism, of a hydra, not with seven, but with a hundred heads, I will neither be the blind instrument, nor the very humble servant of these new tyrants. Adieu, my dear friend: I hope soon to see you; do all that you can to assist my unhappy country in this critical moment; provide for the fitting out of the fleet, and, if possible, make the corps of Suliotes useful, who are not only useless here, but who even menace us with an intestine war. Accept the assurance of my devotedness. You may make whatever use you may think proper of my letter.

"A. MAVROCORDATO."

Translation of a Letter addressed to Prince Mavrocordato, by General Scaltza, and subjoined to the foregoing.

"Lidoriki, 8-20th May, 1824.

"I hasten to inform you of all the plans and operations of the enemy, and which we have received from our correspondent at Zeitouni.

"The troops assembled in that city, under the orders of Yousouf Pacha of Bercoftzelo, and of the Kihaja, Lieutenant of the Visir Generalissimo, amount to nearly 12,000 men. They have resolved to march against Salona and Lidoriki. The Greeks have sworn in the name of God and their country, either to die gloriously on its soil, or put down the enemy. The day of battle will prove whether our plans of attack are good. We place our whole confidence, first, in DIVINE PROVIDENCE; secondly, in the known courage and patriotism of the Hellenists; thirdly, in you who have always sought the welfare and happiness of your country. We therefore entreat, that you will, if possible, cause the corps of Souliotes under Constantine Botzaris to March to our succour without delay, and if the enemy appears in greater force at some other point, we will all hasten where the danger is most imminent.

"P. S. Odysseus, after being informed of the enemy's movements, proceeded to the government. He has set at liberty Yousouf-Bey Lefsista for the sum of 215 purses, 105,000 Turkish piastres, as the price of his ransom. All the positions from Livadia to Athens are left without any defence. The project of the enemy is to possess himself of Salona, and occupy the northern coast of the Gulph of Lepanto, open his communicatious with the fortress of that name, and then wait with his eyes steadily fixed on the Peloponnesus, until the arrival of the fleet. If, therefore, we are left without succours from you, as well as the Morea, we are lost. Do not also fail to reinforce the corps of General Andro-iskos.

The following note was added to this letter by Giorgio Valtinos, Eparch of Lidoriki.

"Take the necessary steps with regard to other quarters, and send General Macri to Carpenisi, where Andro-iskos impatiently waits his arrival. Let him be well supplied with every thing, so as that the above important post may not fall into the enemy's hands.

No. XVI.

Extract of a Letter from Yousouf Pacha, addressed to the Cadi, Moufti, military commandant of all the beys, agas, officers, and the inhabitants generally of Coron; intercepted on board an Ionian boat, on her way from Patrass to that place.

"Patrass, the 19th of the month of Ramazan.

"I HAVE received the letter which you have sent me in common with the inhabitants of Modon, relative to the victory which you lately gained over the Infidels, who had by an assault possessed themselves of a house and battery in your fortress,—and whom you at last dislodged from these positions, after killing numbers and forcing the rest to make a shameful retreat. I have also seen the fears you say you entertain of another assemblage of the same Infidels at Calamata, and of their preparations to return to the attack with Morters, and experienced officers, also with combustible missiles, and that to oppose these new forces, you require that I should send with the ships of war here, a reinforcement of 3 or 4,000 men, and a supply of provisions, of which you say you are in great want, with the exception of bread, which you have still in abundance.

"To send succours, demanded by such brave men as you, is without doubt a sacred duty for every Mussulman—a duty equal to that of saying his prayers five times a day I should not therefore have hesitated doing so, if the fleet which was here, had not sailed two days ago, to meet that which is coming from Egypt. But do not be alarmed, the Infidels, far from being in a state to do you any injury, will soon have only to think of providing for their own safety. You will yourselves be convinced of this, when you hear that Ibrahaim, son of the Pacha of Egypt, named Commander-in-chief of the Egyptian expedition, and Governor-general of the Morea, has just embarked with fifty thousand select troops and an immense quantity of ammunition and provisions, on board more than two hundred transports—that the Pacha's fleet, reinforced by twelve ships of war sent from Constantinople, are to accompany them to the Morea; that the Generalissimo Dervish Pacha, having Beker Pacha, Omer Pacha, and several other distinguished chiefs under his orders, are to march on Salona and Lidoriki; and that the famous Pacha of Scutari, will employ the whole of his forces in taking possession of Messolunghi and Anatolico. All these combined movements are to be carried into execution in ten or fifteen days, so that you will be able to judge, whether the infidels are likely to be able to attack Coron, and lose their time before its walls, while their very existence is at stake. Be therefore firm and resolute.*

No. XVII.

Translation of a Letter from Prince Mavrocordato to his Secretary G. Praides, inserted in No. 36 of the Greek Chronicle, and referred to in the two preceding letters.

"MY DEAR SIGNOR PRAIDES.

"Anatolica, May, 2-14th 1824.

"I AM exceedingly sorry to perceive in No. 31 of the *Greek Chronicle*, which fell under my eyes yesterday, a

* The above letter was accompanied by another for the Pacha of Modon, and a third for the inhabitants of that place—both were couched nearly in the same terms.

long and abusive article against M. Theodore Negris. It has never entered my thoughts to limit the freedom of the press, thus opposing the existing laws on the subject; but I am of opinion that the editor has exceeded the limits allowed by those laws, and fallen into the indulgence of personal injuries, by the above-named article. I do not know whether I may not be mistaken in this opinion, but it will be for the tribunals to decide, since the matter will, no doubt, be brought before them. In the following remark, however, I feel satisfied that I do not deceive myself;—it is, that in publishing similar attacks, the Editor of the Greek Chronicle not only irritates the passions, but causes great injury to the public internally, and externally by the insertion of various articles, which, though they may be sometimes copied from foreign journals, are altogether useless to the Greeks, and imprudent under existing circumstances. They are also contrary to the positive promise made by the Editor, whose prospectus declared, that he would limit his columns to the concerns of Greece, without meddling in those of other countries.

"The responsibility of the abusive article against M. Negris falls exclusively on the Editor, since it has appeared without any signature. It is not my intention to make any apology for M. Negris, as he is capable of doing so himself, and the Editor cannot refuse its insertion. I am, however, very anxious to see such articles as the one alluded to, omitted, since I feel satisfied they will do no good to the cause of our country. In the meantime, I beg you will send a copy of this to the Editor of the Greek Chronicle, to be inserted in his next number.

(Signed) "A. MAVROCORDATO."

No. XVIII.

*Translation from the Greek, and addressed to Demetrius Ipsilanti.**

"Prince,

"The frequency of my letters, and the too great force of my observations, are, perhaps, displeasing to you, but my duty to my country, and my respect for your family, oblige me to it, and I shall not desist until I receive your commands to that effect. The relations in which our friends here have, for some months past, placed themselves with Mavrocordato, had, for their sole object, the discovery of his designs and the prevention of all the mischief which his intrigues might entail upon the nation. The object which they proposed to themselves, and which they still principally have in view, is to deprive Mavrocordato of all the means which might be recommended to his direction, a thing of

* The above letter has also appeared in Colonel Stanhope's volume, with the following note, to which the gallant Colonel's initials are subjoined:—

"I solicited the government and the editor of the Greek Chronicle to publish it, for the purpose of confounding the intriguers."

After such an allusion to Prince Mavrocordato, and associating his name with that of a person whom the Colonel does not, I am sure, consider as worthy of such a high honour; it is due to the Prince's character to say, that he never attached the smallest importance to the letter of Sophianpulos, much less made it the subject of any declamation against the gallant Colonel. It will indeed appear evident, from the Prince's letters, that he has confined himself exclusively to noticing the charges which were made against his own character, without resorting to personalities of any kind, except in one solitary instance, when it became altogether unavoidable.

With respect to Sophianpulos, the copy of his letter, from which the above is a transcript, was forwarded to me while at Zante, by a mem-

which your highness would by no means hear, but contented yourself with writing and speaking against him.

"Now, having persuaded the English to quit Messolunghi, and to come hither, having secretly raised and excited against Mavrocordato his own organs, and having cast him down into that abyss into which he wished to precipitate our country and its defenders, we communicate the circumstance to you. Finally, this is what Ulysses and Goura write against Mavrocordato's friends at Cranidi; this is what Ulysses writes against Mavrocordato himself, with his habitual sarcasm: at some future time, I shall communicate to you all that the English have said, and are going to write, against Mavrocordato.

"According to the testimony of Colonel Stanhope, Envoy of the Greek Committee of London, the English took the part of the Cranidi people, in the first instance, only because they were deceived by Mavrocordato; but, having been since persuaded that Mavrocordato and those of Cranidi, instead of seeking the independence of Greece, are endeavouring, without the consent of the people, to invite kings, and to demand the protection of foreign powers, they have quitted the party of Mavrocordato and those of Cranidi,

ber of the Legislative Assembly, then at Argos, who accompanied it by the following remarks:—

"I beg to observe, that what Sophianpulos calls the *government*, is that which the people would not obey; and his *Legislative Body*, an association composed of ten or twelve obscure individuals without wealth or talents; several of these were, however, forced to join the anti-patriot faction, to save their families who happened to be in its power. By way of keeping up the farce, the names of several persons, who never joined those who thus pretended to represent the nation, were added, to make up the number required by law. Flaviano, whose name has been already mentioned, was first secretary to the *soi-disant* Legislative Body. This person is, as you must know, now at Zante, for the express purpose of persuading Barff and Logotheti, as well as all others concerned, not to give up the money."—E B.

and now panegyrize the conduct of the Tripolitza people, with whom they are desirous of entering into correspondence, seeing that they desire only a national assembly, union, and a cessation of faction. Mavrocordato had so prejudiced the English against Ulysses, Nikitas, and Colocotroni, that they could not listen to their names with patience: but the conferences of Colonel Stanhope with Ulysses, although very brief, and his acquaintance with Goura, and other persons of good sentiments, have compelled him to declare that the fall of Mavrocordato, the introduction of D. Ipsilanti into the national government, and the reinforcement of the government with Colliopulo and Goura, are the only means of securing the independence of Greece and the consolidation of her laws, by putting a stop to the civil war and intestine disturbances.

"At present, it has been considered necessary to cause proclamations to be issued by the Legislative Body, to invite Lord Byron to Tripolitza, to excommunicate the Cranidi people, to call Goura and Colliopulo to seats in the government, to compose its executive force, and to dispatch a thousand men from the Peloponnesus, with ammunition and provisions, to occupy the position of Amphorite; all these dispositions will replace affairs on their proper footing. It is useless to dilate upon this subject; while continental Greece is occupied in defending itself against the enemy, and while the Peloponnesians think only of sharing the revenues among themselves, we hope to succeed in our designs.

"I am, &c.

"PANAJOTES SOPHIANPULOS.

"Athens, 25th February, N. S. 1824.

"*To His Highness Prince D. Ipsilanti, at Napoli di Romania.*"

No. XIX.

From Prince Mavrocordato to Colonel Stanhope.

" Messolunghi, le 6 Juin, 1824.

" MONSIEUR LE COLONEL,

" Je dois la reponse à votre lettre du 18 du mois passé dateé du Lazaret de Zante.

" Les munitions et les 4 pieces fureut remises a M. le Capitaine Trelawny pour être transportées à Athenes. Le depart de ces objets essentiels dans un moment critique, a un peu aigri le peuple, j'ai eu toutes les peines du monde pour preveuir un tumulte qui aurait pu avoir de suites fâcheuses.

" Je ne puis que louer vas sentimens pour la constitution : mais puisque je le crois, je n'hesiterai pas de vous le dire franchement M. le Colonel, que trompé par des apparances, vous avez manqué de porter un coup mortel à cette constitution, même, en erigeant sur ses débris, le despotisme militaire. Ce n'etait pas sans doute votre intention, vous avez cru voir des protecteurs de nos loix dans les personnes de ceux qui n'en desirent que l'ombre ; et celá encore dans le but d'agir plus à leur aise ; vous avez cru contribuer à un rapprochement des partis, et vous avez manqué d'amener le plus grand des malheurs, le massacre des representans de la nation, et la dissolution de ce corps qui a vraiment merité de la nation par sa fermeté et par son courage. Voilà de nouveau, les factieux obligés de reconnaitre ce que peut que la volonté de la nation ; mais devrait on les encourager tacitement en se montrant defavorable au parti du Corps Representatif? Cela n'a jamais été votre intention sans doute ; mais les faits n'en sont pas moins lá, ne devrait on pas Soutenir le Gouvernement, dans un moment que ses énnemis s étaient vûs obligés de reculer devant l'influence de l'opinion publique ! Il est vrai que les vœux de la nation ont de nouveau remporté une victoire éclatante, et peut étre triompheront enfin pour toujours : mais le sang versé de nouveau n'aurait on pas du l'epargner ? Quant à ce que vous dites relativement à la Monarchie, je n'ai rien à vous répondre, puisque je n y trouve rien que m'appartient ; tout ce que je puis vous dire, c'est, que l'oppression seule et le regne du despotisme militaire, peuvent engager le peuple a un pareil choix ; sans cela, que des traitres intriguent, ils ne feront rien. Voila une raison de plus pour appuyer le corps legislatif et les representans de la nation ; tous ceux qui s'ecartent de ce seul chemin de salut, sont des traitres, puisque ils preparent par une voie indirecte, le chemin au despotisme et à la tyranie.

" Veuillez bien agréer l'assurance de la plus haute estime, et de la consideration la plus distinguée avec lesquelles jái l'honneur d'etre.

" Monsieur le Colonel,

" Votre devoué Serviteur,

(Signé) " A. MAVROCORDATO."

" A l'Honorable Colonel Stanhope,

" &c. &c. &c.

" à Londres."

TRANSLATION.

" Messolunghi, June 6th, 1824.

" I owe an answer to your letter of the 18th ultimo, dated from the Lazaretto of Zante.

" The ammunition and four field pieces were consigned to Captain Trelawny to be transferred to Athens. The departure of these essential objects at this critical moment, has rather soured the people; I had the greatest difficulty in preventing a tumult which might have had unpleasant consequences.

" I cannot but applaud your sentiments in favour of the constitution; but since it is my belief, I will not hesitate to tell you, Colonel, that, deceived by appearances, you have been on the point of giving a mortal blow to that constitution, by erecting on its ruins a military despotism. This was not, doubtless, your intention; you thought you saw protectors of our laws, in the persons of those who only desire the shadow ; and this only with a view of acting more at their ease.—You wished to contribute to a junction of parties, and you might have brought about the greatest misfortune—the massacre of the representatives of the people, and the dissolution of that body, which has really merited well of its country, by its firmness and courage. Here is another instance to prove, that the factious are forced to recognise what the national will can effect; but ought any one tacitly to encourage them, in showing himself unfavorable to the party of the representative body ? This was, doubtless, never your intention, but the facts are not less conclusive. Was it not necessary to support the government at a moment when its enemies saw themselves obliged to retreat before public opinion ?—It is true, that the wishes of the nation have again achieved a glorious victory, and will perhaps triumph for the future; but would it not have been as well to spare spilling of blood anew ?

" As to what you say relative to the monarchy, I have nothing to answer, as there is nothing in it which belongs to me—all that I can say is, that oppression and the reign of military despotism, can alone engage the people to make such a choice ; without that, let the traitors intrigue, they will do nothing. This is an additional motive for supporting the legislative body and the representatives of the nation.

All those who stray from this sole path of safety are traitors, since they prepare, by an indirect channel, the way to despotism and tyranny.

"Accept the assurance of the high esteem and distinguished consideration, with which I have the honour to be,

"Colonel,

"Your devoted servant,

(Signed.) "A. MAVROCORDATO."

No. XX.

From M. Rodius, Secretary General ad interim of the Provisional Government, to E. Blaquiere.

"Mills of Argos, June 6th, 1824.

"Sir,

"The unexpected arrival of our common friend, M. Polysoides, has put me in possession of your letter, which I hasten to answer, *via* Messolunghi. I am rejoiced to hear of your quick and happy voyage, for the good of Greece, and I look forward soon to have the pleasure of seeing you. I doubt not but you will hasten your wished-for presence at the seat of government. When you come, I would recommend you to pass over by the way of Vastitza.

"On receiving your letter, I did not fail to write to Colonel Stanhope, inviting him to come here without a moment's delay.

"A translation of the contract relative to the loan is preparing this day; when finished, it will be ratified, and sent back to London forthwith. Our affairs are proceeding better every day. The internal disasters which lately arose in the Peloponnesus have nearly ceased, and our fleet to the number of fifty-one ships and fifteen fire vessels, are preparing with all speed, so that we hope the fourth year of our struggle will be the most glorious of all.

"Accept the assurance of that real esteem and high consideration, with which I have the honour to be, &c.

"P. I. RODIUS."

No. XXI.

Lord Charles Murray, to E. Blaquiere.

"Messolunghi, Sunday Evening.

"Sir,

"I am happy to state that we are now in a more tranquil state than we have been since you left us; your presence here is absolutely requisite, in fact, as the people know you so well, and you know them, I believe, better.

"The fever is, I am in hopes, abating: Dr. Millingen is almost entirely recovered, and Mr. Hodges in a progressive state of amendment; I hope your own valuable health has not suffered.

"Since writing the above, I have just received your kind letter. I have reason to believe you have not received a long letter I wrote by Captain de Botte; however, it comes to nearly the same, as you have anticipated my wishes.

"Allow me to recommend, that the rest of the money should arrive secretly, and if possible in the night, for, as you may suppose, we have so many hungry mouths here, that the simple idea of the arrival of money sets us all agog.

"How much bloodshed have we not unwillingly occasioned!—how much disorder and how much distress to the government! However, a little money goes so great a way, that I have reason to hope we are set on our legs again for another month at least, for as Horace says,

'*Aurum per medios ire satellites,*' *&c.*

Four days ago I placed at the Prince's disposition all the little *disponible* money I had, and he immediately sent 150 dollars to the Suliotes, who have been most *turbulent and vindictive*. I went to Anatolico, and wrote a Greek letter to the chiefs, of which I transcribed the copy in a letter to you which, with others, Captain de Botte was to have delivered. I have little to add, but best wishes, and remain,

"Your faithful and obedient servant,

(Signed.) "CHARLES MURRAY."

No. XXII.

From E. Blaquiere to Messrs. Barff and Logotheti.

"Lazaretto of Zante, June 10th, 1824.

"GENTLEMEN,

"HAVING, agreeably to the promise I made to you yesterday afternoon, fully explained to Messrs. Xenos and Kalergi, the difficulties which have arisen with regard to the first instalment of the Greek loan deposited in your hands, those gentlemen have written to you on the subject, and as it is of such vital importance to the interests of the lenders, on whose behalf, as well as that of the Greek Committee, I accompanied the money to this island, that the Provisional Government should have no plea for omitting to fulfil its engagements in England, I confidently trust that some means may be devised of removing existing obstacles, and preventing those consequences which are inseparable from any farther delay in its transfer. I have already so frequently offered my opinion on the certainty of any steps taken by you with regard to the disposal of the money, being fully approved and confirmed by the lenders, that it is almost needless for me to repeat that opinion; I will, however, now add my thorough conviction, that the very extraordinary situation in which the lamented death of Lord Byron, the sudden departure of Colonel Stanhope, and non-arrival of Mr. Gordon, has placed you, not only justifies, but renders it necessary for you to adopt such measures as you may deem best calculated to secure the interests of those who have committed the money to your care.

"So deeply impressed am I, Gentlemen, with the necessity of doing something to prevent the apparent want of good faith, that cannot fail to follow a refusal of the money at this most critical juncture, that in the event of your considering it impossible to comply with the request of the deputies sent here at the particular desire of Colonel Stanhope, I still feel myself bound to make a proposition, by which the immediate wants of the Provisional Government may be supplied, without exposing those who may be disposed to facilitate its execution, to any of the pains and penalties attendant on a breach of the neutrality established by the Ionian Government.

"I am, &c.

(Signed) "E. BLAQUIERE."

"P.S. It may not be irrelevant to inform you, that I have this day done myself the honour of addressing a letter to his Excellency the Lord High Commissioner of these islands, on the subject of the Greek loan, and explanatory of the motives which led to the first instalment being sent to Zante."—E. B.

No. XXIII.

Reply to the foregoing.

"Zante, June 15th, 1824.

"Sir,

"We beg leave to acknowledge the receipt of your much esteemed communication of the 10th inst., which served to accompany another letter from the deputies, Messrs. Xeno and Kalergi, of the same tenor, and to which letter we have very particularly replied, as well as at subsequent meetings at the Lazaretto. We deem it superfluous our giving you a detäil of the various obstacles which present themselves for the payment of any part of the money deposited in our hands by Messrs. Loughnan, Son, and O'Brien to the said deputies, without further instructions from London.

"We have the honour to be, &c.

(Signed) "SAMUEL BARFF,

"CESARE LOGOTHETI."

No. XXIV.

From Prince Mavrocordato to E. Blaquiere.

"Monastère de St. Geneon près de Messolunghi,
le 1-13 Juin, 1824.

J'ai recu votre lettre du 9. vous avez dèjà beaucoup fait en faisant recevoir nos deputés au Lazeret, je ne désespére pas du reste. Les nouvelles de Prévésa ne sont que trop vrais. Notre expedition contre Arta est déja effectuée, et nos troupes doivent avoir franchit les frontieres dupuis hier. J'espere que cette expedition aura les suites les plus brillantes, et ce sera une réponse de fait á nos ennemis qui ne font que crier, tandis que nous agissons, malgré notre miserè. Mr. * * * vous communiquera ma lettre; ainsi que la copie d'une lettre de M. Zaimis: vous y verrez que le gouvernement a enfin triomphé, et que tout va se tranquilliser, j'en envoye une autre copie aux commissaires du gouvernement. Cet état de choses contribuera beaucoup à faciliter vos operations.

(Signé) "A. MAVROCORDATO.

"P.S. L'affaire des Souliotes m'a obligé de venir en ville, Lord Charles Murray est arrivé à mon secours, il m'a prêté 300 tallaris, avec lesquels je pourrais les tranquilliser pendant une semaine encore. En arrivant ici j'ai trouvé votre lettre du 10, voila des nouveaux secours arrivés, qui ne peuvent pas cependant être utilisés, patience! Je suis persuadé que vous ferez tout ce que vous pouvez pour arriver au secours de la Grèce."

TRANSLATION.

"Convent of St. Geneon, near Messolunghi,
June 1-13th, 1824.

"I HAVE received your letter of the 9th instant. You have already done much in causing our deputies to be received at the Lazaretto; I do not despair of the rest. The news from Prevesa is but too true. Our expedition against Arta is already effected, and our troops must have crossed the frontiers since yesterday. I hope this expedition will have the most brilliant results, and these will be the best answer to our enemies, who do nothing but complain, whilst we act, notwithstanding our poverty. M. * * *, will communicate the contents of my letter, as also a copy of one from Zaimis, you will see by it that the government has at length triumphed; and that every thing is about to be tranquillized. I have sent another copy to the commissioners of the government. This state of things will greatly contribute to faciliate your operations.

"A. MAVROCORDATO.'

"Messolunghi, June, 2-14th, 1824.

"P.S. The affair of the Souliotes has obliged me to come into town. Lord Charles Murray has come to my assistance; he has lent me three hundred dollars, with which I shall be able to tranquillise them for another week. On arriving here, I found your letter of the 10th. Here are new succours arrived, which cannot, however be turned to any account. Patience! I am convinced you will do all you can, to come to the relief of Greece.

"A. M."

No. XXV

Extract of a Letter from Mr. Rodius, Secretary of the Provincial Government, ad interim, to E. Blaquiere.

"How afflicting has not all this delay been to Greece, more particularly under the critical circumstances in which she now finds herself placed! The greater part of the hopes she had formed of warding off the perils of the present year, were founded on the arrival of the loan from London; but the same being now retarded, the affairs of Greece cannot but become doubly critical in their position.

Much do we hope, that the philellenic and indefatigable exertions of Mr. Blaquiere, the unwearied champion of the best interests of Greece, much do we hope, that through his means, the obstacles that present themselves may be overcome, and the money finally remitted to our deputies to serve the purpose, for which the most Philellenic Committee of London raised and transacted the loan; that is, for the salvation of Greece. It is not unreasonable to fear that the delay in the remission of the money should, in the meantime, occasion the most frightful evils, and perhaps incalculable dangers to Greece. By how much the more we are grieved that the money has not been consigned up to the present moment, by so much the more we rejoice on the perfect cessation of the afflictions which have disturbed our internal peace. The few individuals who have opposed themselves to the establishment of social order, have already sunk into oblivion. Theodore Colocotroni has at length demanded the mercy of the law, Panos Colocotroni quits Nauplion this very day.

"The Greek Government has nominated a commission composed of six members, and among them three of our counsellors, consisting of the secretary-general of the executive body, the Admiral Miaoulis, and the minister of war, to receive the keys of the fortress; these commissioners have under their command more than two thousand soldiers, for its protection and defence. The government will make their public entry in two days.

"The enemy's fleet from Constantinople, feeble in the extreme, and infected by sickness, is still within the gulph of Thessalonica. Up to the present hour, the enemy has not effected any considerable movement of the land forces. It appears that the Sultan reposes his entire hopes in the Pacha of Egypt. On all sides, it is repeated to us, that this last, is making great preparations. He will probably arrive in Greece towards the end of the present month.—

Should he effect a landing in the Peloponnesus, Greece must then run the very greatest danger, because the enemy will then have it in their power to direct their operations with equal activity both by sea and land. It is on this account, that, on the commencement of the present month, orders were expedited both to Hydra and Spezzia, to send with all possible speed, two of the swiftest sailing ships, to observe the motions of the enemy, and to give us notice of the moment the Turkish fleet shall quit the shores of Egypt. The Greek ships are ready to sail, and are no longer delayed, but by our utter want of money. God grant that through your co-operation the money may be remitted to our deputies as soon as possible, and that the first of your next letters to us, may contain that intelligence.

"P. G. RODIUS,"
"Sec. General, ad interim."

"Mylos of Nauplion, this
5th of June, 1824."

No. XXVI.

From Lord Charles Murray, to E. Blaquiere.

"Messolunghi, June 14, 1824.

"Sir,

"It is impossible to imagine more embarrassing circumstances than those under which we are both placed; and I am sorry to observe by your letter, that you overrate both my abilities and my importance.

"In case of necessity, and in the absence of all the other friends of the committee, I should certainly not shrink from undertaking a *provisional* charge here, up to a certain extent; that is to say, with your sanction, and under your guidance, but I trust your absence will not be long, as I feel terrified when I think, that, owing to the illness of Dr. Millingen, and Mr. Hodges, I am left for the moment, the sole depositary, both of the honour of great Britain, and of the responsibility attached to a situation like mine.

"My views in coming to Greece were entirely of a private nature, and to my astonishment I find myself at once called upon to take part in what is passing around me, without military experience, or adequate resources; however, once embarked in the cause, I shall certainly nail my colours to the mast, as we say in England.

"The Prince's kindness to me has been so great, and I have conceived so great an interest in his behalf, that I never should wish to abandon him; I am already aware that his reputation is at its height throughout Europe, and I only hope, that the merchants of London will make amends for their extraordinary and still unaccountable delay of the promised loan, by more active and energetic measures for the future. His Highness is, however, endowed with equanimity sufficient to meet more arduous circumstances, and, as Mr. Bowring says, the moment we can see a regular force both by sea and land, at the disposition of the lawful Provisional Government, Messolunghi, from its near neighbourhood to the south of Italy, and the Ionian Isles, will, I hope, be the first to set an example of social order, and good government, which will at least stimulate the emulation of the rest of Greece. Colonel Gordon's delayed arrival is most extraordinary, and inexplicable, but the more I think of the present state of affairs, the more I am lost in a labyrinth of conjecture and disappointment.

"As long as the Germans remain in Messolunghi, I am without immediate fear of any internal troubles in the Prince's province, but should any more of them be sent from this, together with any more guns, as took place on Mr. Trelawney's departure, it will then be necessary to send an immediate and large supply of money, in order to provide for the security of this place.

" I fear you are most uncomfortable in the Lazaretto of Zante, besides the anxiety of mind you must also feel; but the time of probation will not I hope be long, and if your health does not suffer, I hope you will be enabled to return here the moment you receive final instructions from England. The instructions hitherto resemble, I think, the ultimatums of Russia and the Porte. I have the honor to remain,

" Sir,

" Your most obedient and faithful servant,

(Signed) " CHARLES MURRAY."

No. XXVII.

From Lord Charles Murray, to E. Blaquiere.

" Messolunghi, 18th June, 1824.

" Sir,

" I wrote you a letter in answer to your most kind communication; I also wrote a long letter by the hands of Captain de Botte, who, instead of going to Zante as he told me, has gone off at a tangent for Chiarenza.

" For God's sake hasten the period of the end of all miseries, doubts, and difficulties! The Souliotes are for the moment tranquillized, but their bad humours are no sooner off than they are on.—Last night we heard a heavy cannonade and this morning in came an Ionian boat, (falsely ycleped English) which was on its return from Patras. Yousouf Pasha behaves most shamefully, forgetful of all Lord Byron's magnanimous demeanour towards him.—The master of the boat had the insolence to present himself before me this morning. This is the second time he has been taken, and he seems to glory in his perversity: I was very anxious to have him imprisoned, as fair reprisal; however, his Highness, who is patience and moderation personified, overruled all my arguments. He told me, "These fellows, Sir, have taken me in the night, what am I to do?" I replied, "This have you to do, serve your God, your King, and your Country, as you ought to serve them, and not bring disgrace upon all three by your present most shameful conduct. I am happy to see you a prisoner, you richly deserve chastisement; but with all that, I blame your employers more than you." With best wishes, ever believe me,

"Your's most truly,

(Signed) "CHARLES MURRAY."

No. XXVIII.

From Lord Charles Murray, to E. Blaquiere.

"Messolunghi, June 21st, 1824.

"Dear Sir,

"Understanding from Captain Hesketh, that there are some cannon on sale at Zante, and amongst them two twelve pounders, which Hesketh supposes may be got at a reasonable rate, I am willing to offer as far as from fifteen to twenty pounds a piece; and, if those cannot be got, I shall have no objection to two of the nine-pounders, although his Highness says they are of too small a calibre for him, as his artillery is already rather too Liliputian.

"The Souliotes are behaving most abominably ill; I quite give them up, and am only sorry I wasted my time and my patience to convince them of their wilful and flagitious conduct: for those who betray their country in the days of its prosperity are still traitors of the blackest dye, much more than those who forget their duty to Greece in adversity.

"Ever your's most truly,

(Signed) "CHARLES MURRAY."

No. XXIX.

From Prince Mavrocordato, to E. Blaquiere.

"Messolunghi, le 10-22 Juin, 1824.

"Je viens de voir à l'instant même le General Costa Botzaris, qui a montré toute la bonne disposition de se conformer aux ordres du gouvernement et passer à Gastouni à la téte de 500 hommes, mas il demande une partie de l'arriéré de sa solde, les soldats qui le suiveront, devant laisser quelques petites sommes à leurs familles ici, sa demande est des plus justes, mais pour y satisfaire il nous faudra 3000 tallaris, le moutant de la solde du Corps de Javella qui'il faudra egalement payer, est de 8000: vous voyez par conséquent, qu'il nous faudra 11000 tallaris en tout: faites, cher ami, tout ce qui est possible pour completer cette somme. J'attends ce soir, l'autre barque avec le reste de l'argent que vous m'avez promis dans votre derniere, et j'éspere que vous ne tarderez pas de nous munir de ce qui nous manquera encore. J'ai prié Mr. Hesketh de venir vous rejoindre pour vous persuader de tout cela, ce qu'il a accepté avec son zèle, et son dévouement ordinaires.

(Signé) "A. MAVROCORDATO."

TRANSLATION.

"Messolunghi, June 10—22d, 1824.

"I have this moment seen General Costa Botzaris, who has shown every disposition to conform to the orders of the government and cross over to Gastouni at the head of 500 men: but he claims a portion of the arrears, as the soldiers who accompany him must leave something with their families here; this demand is most just, but to satisfy it, 3000 dollars are required. The amount of pay due to Javella's corps, which must also be paid, is 8000 dollars; you see, therefore, that we want 11,000 dollars in all. Do, dear friend, your utmost to complete this sum. I expect the other boat to-night, with the rest of the money which you promised in your last. And I hope you will not delay in providing us with what we still require. I have begged Mr. Hesketh to rejoin you, to convince you of all this, and he has consented to do so with his accustomed zeal and devotedness.

"A. MAVROCORDATO."

No. XXX.

From Lord Charles Murray, to His Excellency Sir Frederick Adam, Lord High Commissioner of the Ionian Islands.

"Messolunghi, June 28th, 1824.

"Sir,

"I have now been some days at Messolunghi, in which time I have had good opportunity of judging both of the present state of affairs, and of the future and necessary consequences of all that has been taking place. One great source of exultation to me, is, the knowledge I have, that the characteristic goodness of heart, and long experience which your Excellency possesses of the inhabitants of this quarter of Greece, will put it into your power to render as much service to the cause of Christianity and humanity throughout Greece generally, as within your own extensive government.

" Prince Mavrocordato has received me with so much kindness and hospitality, that I shall ever retain a lasting sense of his Highness's liberal principles, and moderate and upright conduct. When I add, that he unites to all the first-rate qualities of a statesman, the most critical and accurate knowledge of his own language, as well as of the Arabic, Persian, Turkish, Wallachian, French, and Italian languages, and that he reads English with the utmost facility and the most correct pronunciation, I feel I am only describing a patriot, a scholar, and a philosopher, worthy in every respect of your Excellency's good opinion.

" Nothing can exceed his Highness's deep regret on the issuing of the Proclamation by the Greek Government, which caused the last necessary and unavoidable measures taken by your Excellency. I have good reason to suspect that a project for a new law has already been devised by the Prince, which will entirely remove all existing difficulties.

" I am about to accompany Mr. Blaquiere to the seat of Government, whence I hope to address to your Excellency many interesting details—that is to say, if I have your permission so to do.

" At all events, with most respectful and grateful compliments to Lady Adam, I have the honour to remain,

" Your Excellency's

" Most obedient and humble Servant,

(Signed) " CHARLES MURRAY."

No. XXX.

[Although the date of the following correspondence is anterior to my arrival in Greece, I am induced to give it place, from its being so strongly illustrative of the nature of the Greek contest.—E. B.]

Correspondence between the Pacha of Romelia and General Panouria, Primate and Governor of Salona.

"THE Visir Mohamed Emir Pacha, Vali of Romelia, Naseri of Dervent, Commander-in-Chief, Plenipotentiary, &c. to the honorable Captain Panouria, Primate of Salona, and to all the other Rajahs.

"After our health, we notify to you, that it grieves the heart to see, contrary to all our hopes, those evils and continued misfortunes which have, for the space of three years, fallen upon you, and continue to occur, have not induced you to abandon your revolutionary projects, and invoke pardon of our magnanimous and powerful sovereign, in order, henceforward, to lead a steady life, in repose, under his protection, like all other well governed nations. It would appear that two objects excite your foolish propensities, keeping you back from this salutary resolution: first, the expectation of weakening the power of our master, and thus realising your vain and imbecile hopes; but this will never happen; on the contrary, the more you persevere in your present iniquitous pursuits, the more will his choler and power increase, until he has subdued your insolence and pride. In the second place, the circumstance of your having so unadvisedly given way to such excesses, may render his ire against you implacable. Yet, do not think so: because his generous magnanimity is boundless, more especially towards his rajahs, and the people confided to him by God. On this account, I call upon you to return to your duty : frankly demand the pardon of our generous sovereign : do not doubt, since I assure you that you will be paternally received, and all your past errors forgotten. Do not delay giving me an answer, and may heaven inspire your thoughts. If you persevere in crime, let the blood of every innocent be on your own heads !

"Neopatra, the first day of the Moon Zamaran."

No. XXXII.

Reply of General Panouria to the above.

"General Panouria to Mohamet Emir Pacha, &c. health !

"I have, together, with all the Salonites, heard with pleasure of your health ; I was, until now, glad to have you near us, because I thought you entertained generous sentiments, and not like those of a Turk ; but your letter has undeceived me. If you feel for the evils and misfortunes occasioned by this war, the Greeks know how to support them with cheerfulness, when they reflect on those endless miseries which they suffered under your sovereign.

"The Greeks have not risen so unadvisedly as you assert ; but after having patiently supported innumerable oppressions for centuries, they have irrevocably resolved to raise the standard of the cross, and to liberate their country from an insupportable tyranny. This, their magnanimous resolution, has been approved of by every civilized nation.

"You deceive yourself in calling the Greeks rebels, as those alone who are under a regular government deserve that name, when they take arms against their lawful king. Your master was never our legitimate sovereign, and yet he had four centuries to change his oppressive system of rule. The Greeks have now established a national government, and they are contented to enjoy freedom under it, so that they are totally indifferent to any proposal you can make. They will no longer be called rajahs, nor ask pardon: and the infinite magnanimity of him of whom they were so heartily tired, may be reserved for others. The Greeks have not stained their hands in innocent blood; whereas the Ottomans have shed it in torrents. The ire of your sovereign is therefore unjust; but whatever it may be, it will only excite our courage. What we have done, is nothing in comparison with what we shall still perform. Our duties are great; and since our ancestors communicated knowledge to all other nations, we cannot consent to be slaves any longer. Make all this known to your master, and if you have any thing more to communicate, address it to our Government. I shall take great care of your letters, as I would those of a friend, and they shall be duly forwarded.

"Salona, February 7th, 1824."

No. XXXIII.

From E. Blaquiere to John Bowring, Esq.

"Napoli di Romania, July 19th, 1824.

"My Dear Bowring,

"Lord Charles Murray and myself* have just returned from the church of St. Georgio, where we accom-

* We were also accompanied by Mr. Gower Winter, who has, I regret to hear, also fallen a victim to his zeal in the Greek cause. Mr. Winter belonged to a highly respectable family of Dublin, and had relinquished very advantageous prospects in the legal profession, to join the standard of the cross.

Having proceeded to Messolunghi, Mr. W. was named aid-de-camp to Lord Byron, and accompanied the body to Zante. The object of his proceeding to the seat of government, was to offer his services wherever they might be required; and I had the satisfaction of obtaining an appointment for him in the corps of Dimo Scaltza at Salona, where he died in the early part of November, deeply regretted by his friends and companions in arms.

panied the members of the executive, the whole of the Legislative Body, and an immense concourse of military, citizens, &c. to hear *Te Deum* sung for the deliverance of Ipsara from the presence of the Turks. This event was announced in a despatch of the brave Miaoulis, dated on board his own ship off Ipsara, the 4-16th, on the morning of which day he had attacked and dispersed the whole of the Turkish vessels, left behind for the purpose of carrying off the plunder and prisoners. A party of Greeks having landed, the Turks took refuge in several houses of the town, where they were closely invested, and not likely to hold out more than a few hours. With respect to the Capitan Pacha's squadron, it has separated: one half having gone to Smyrna and the other to Mytelene. In the attack made on the morning of the 16th, a number of transports and armed vessels were either taken or destroyed. Miaoulis describes the ardour and bravery of his men to have been above all praise, indeed all classes of the islanders only seem to be animated by one sentiment,—that of revenge for the recent cruelties of the enemy. The best consequences are expected to result from the successes of the fleet; other ships are preparing, so that an additional reinforcement will sail in a few days. The whole will then be formed into two divisions, of which one is destined to watch the Capitan Pacha, while the other cruises off Alexandria, there to await the expedition projected by Mehemet Ali. From all the latest accounts received here, it is reported that although the Pacha of Egypt has collected about 15,000 men and some transports, it is doubtful whether he intends carrying his threat into execution or not; upon the whole, I do not think there is any thing whatever to be apprehended from that quarter. You will receive a most spirited proclamation of the government, on the subject of foreigners allowing their vessels to be taken up as transports by the infidel chief. This has been received by the consuls a Alexandria and produced the desired effect. Although the money has not yet arrived from Zante, we are in hopes of seeing it very soon, as all the necessary steps have been taken, and there is no doubt of Mr. Barff doing his utmost to facilitate its transfer to the seat of government.

"From the church, I proceeded to the legislative, also accompanied by Lord Charles, where Tricuoupi read a long paper of mine, stating the objects of my visit to Greece, and calling on them to take immediate steps for raising the loan, &c. I was received in the most flattering manner, and promised that immediate attention should be paid to all my propositions. A law will be passed forthwith, empowering the executive to send home produce for the payment of the interest, and I shall most probably sail in about ten days in a national vessel for the Thames. I hope to be the bearer of some highly important documents, which shall satisfy the creditors, and all others interested in the march of the Greek cause. It is also intended, that a part of the youth intended for education in England shall accompany me. I am to present a letter to the executive this evening, containing divers proposals, to all of which I anticipate a favourable reply, having already sounded the parties. But as I ask for nothing but that which is easy of execution, and for their own good, there is no reason to expect that difficulties will be thrown in the way.—It was when I gave up all hopes of hearing from you, that your letter of the 15th of June reached me, about four days after my arrival here. I need not tell you how concerned we all are to hear of the dreadful fall in the loan,—the more so, as we are at a loss to what it is to be attributed. Besides the arrangements with the government, I am concerting with the Candiotes, as to the best means of forwarding the needful there. A dreadful calamity has occurred to that terrestrial Paradise, but the deputies assure me the mountaineers are in arms, and even fighting daily. I was so ill for several days after my arrival on the 8th, that I could only address a few hasty lines to Mr. Barff with a request that he would send you the substance of them. I had a most violent attack of fever, but am now, thank God, quite well, except that the usual symptoms of debility and loss of appetite remain. I fully intended to have written a long account of our journey from Messolunghi, but my illness prevented it. You can have no conception of any thing half so interesting as the country through which we passed,—the whole plain of Vostitza is covered with passolini and olive-trees, the crops of both most abundant; but this beautiful plain is only a small part of the wealth we saw. Lord Charles Murray, who has been of the greatest use, returns to Messolunghi, where his lordship is to write to you regularly once a month detailing every thing. Orders have been sent home by this conveyance to the deputies, directing them to see that the bills I drew from Zante are duly paid by the contractors. Believe me, &c.

(Signed) "EDWARD BLAQUIERE."

No. XXXIV.

Address of E. Blaquiere to the Legislative Body of Greece, and of which a Romaic translation by M. Tricoupi was read to the Assembly on the day of its date.

"Napoli di Romania, July 4—16, 1824.

"Fathers of your Country!

"Athough I had the honour of being presented to you on the first day of my arrival at the seat of government, I regret that the illness with which I was attacked immediately after, should have prevented me from again appearing before you, to express the gratification I experienced in once more seeing the representatives of the Greek people assembled, and discharging those great duties which have been confided to their vigilance and care by the nation.

"Having already heard through the medium of the

worthy M. Contumas, that my humble efforts to promote the Greek cause among my countrymen, had happily met with your approbation, I now beg to repeat, that while that approbation is the highest honor I could desire, it is an ample reward for the trifling service I may have been ab to render.

"Enthusiastically favourable to Grecian freedom, not less from a sense of religion than of gratitude to your ancestors, I only waited for the information obtained during my visit to Tripolitiza last year, for the mode in which I could most effectually do so. Finding on my return to England, that a number of prejudices, arising solely from an ignorance of the real state of Greece, existed in several parts of Europe, it became my first duty to dissipate them. To effect this object, my report to the Greek committee was read and circulated. In a visit which I paid to the principal cities of the kingdom on behalf of the committee, for the purpose of raising subscriptions and exciting sympathy in favour of the suffering people of Greece, I found all classes strongly disposed to second its views. The general enthusiasm was manifested in a number of public meetings, and the formation of sub-Greek committees in the large cities of Bristol, Manchester, and Liverpool; also at the University of Cambridge, one of the most distinguished seats of learning in Europe. A female society had also been formed at Bristol, for the purpose of disseminating the blessings of education among the women of Greece. Upon the whole, it will no doubt be gratifying to the representatives of the nation, to hear, that on my leaving England, it was impossible for the feelings of my countrymen to be more decidedly favourable to the cause of Greece, and that there was no longer any difference of opinion as to the justice and necessity of the contest in which you are engaged.

"Having thus alluded to the state of public opinion among the people, I should be omitting a most pleasing duty, were I not to add my own conviction and that of the friends for whom I am acting, that the favourable sentiments of the British nation are very warmly participated in by the Government, and that although it is the interest of Greece herself, that England should not interfere too directly in the pending struggle, there is no longer any doubt but that her ministers have recognized the justice, as well as importance, of admitting Greece into the great European family. The British cabinet had done much towards proving the above assertion, when it acknowledged the right of blockade; if any thing were wanting to prove it now, the recent negociation of the loan, by which truly important operation the independence of Greece is virtually acknowledged, decides the question beyond contradiction.

"Convinced as the friends of Greece in England have been from the first, that her deliverance from the enemy and final independence as a nation, must depend on the establishment of her credit in the great commercial cities of Europe, your august Body will not be surprised, if their whole attention has been almost exclusively devoted to the best means of effecting the loan in the first instance, and of devising such means, in the second place, as shall most effectually realize the object of their wishes.

"Although contracted for under circumstances which might have proved very injurious, had public opinion been less favourably pronounced, it may be truly said, that the Greek loan was one of the most popular which had appeared for some time on the London Exchange; while the terms were regarded as highly favourable by all parties. Yet, no wonder if the recent occurrences, by which the internal peace of Greece has been disturbed, should have produced some alarm among the lenders; the result of this has been a considerable fall in the stock. Here it may be of importance to apprize your body, that owing to the whole of the payments of the loan not having been yet made when the late fall took place, it is of the very highest importance to Greece, that every possible measure should be adopted to renew confidence among the lenders, and re-establish her credit on its former footing; for without this, there is reason to apprehend that many individuals might be found to say, they would defer paying up the remainder of their quotas, until they knew what steps the Provisional Government had taken. It is needless for me to point out, that such a determination on the part of the lenders, would have the most fatal tendency, in not only suspending the present operation, but totally preventing any other which the government may have in contemplation.

"With respect to the best mode of removing the ill effects produced on the loan, by the intelligence which may have been recently communicated from this country, I am humbly of opinion, that the immediate establishment of a commission of public credit, chosen from among your own Body, to be followed up by a law authorizing the executive to provide for the payment of the interest with the produce of the soil, is the most effectual that could be devised. I beg leave furthermore to add, that if the executive did me the honour of making me the bearer of such a law to England in a national vessel, no matter how small, I have no hesitation in assuring you, that the Greek loan would thereby recover its former footing in the money market.*

"Although I am most anxious to see the above plan carried into prompt execution, so far as my own feelings are concerned, it is on behalf of all the best friends of Greece in England, and especially of the Greek Committee, that I have been induced to dwell on it with so much anxiety and earnestness. It is indeed my bounden duty to add that,

* This hope was in a great measure realized, for the Amphitrite had not been ten days in the Thames before the loan, which was at a discount of 15 per cent. on her arrival, rose to 58. E. B.

without such a measure, there is no reasonable hope of their being able to re-establish the credit of the loan.

"In addition to the proposals I was charged by the committee to make to the executive, and which relate to the facilities it may obtain in England for promoting the establishment of a regular army and national marine, I should also state, that the Society of Friends who have shown such indefatigable zeal in the cause of Greece, have lately signified their wish to educate twenty Greek youths, who may be thus enabled to communicate the fruits of their information to their countrymen.

"I beg very particularly to recommend the last named subject to the consideration of your august Body, feeling, as I do, that there is no better mode of promoting a friendly understanding with the people of England, than by encouraging the youth of Greece to pursue their studies among them. With respect to the system of education in England, and the progress made by those Greeks who have already studied in that country, I need only refer your august Body, to those young patriots who have been brought up under the auspices of that distinguished patron of modern Greek learning, Lord Guilford.

(Signed) "E. BLAQUIERE."

No XXXV.

From E. Blaquiere to M. Rodius, Secretary General, ad interim, of the Provisional Government, and referred to in the preceding.

"Napoli di Romania, July 7—19th, 1824.

"Sir and Friend,

"Being at length sufficiently recovered from the effects of my late indisposition, to pursue the objects which led to my visiting the seat of government, I lose no time in apprizing you of the circumstance.

"With respect to the motives which led to my second visit to Greece, it is scarcely necessary to say, that the first object was to have the satisfaction of presenting the money, which the lamented death of Lord Byron unhappily prevented from being consigned to the Government in time to prevent the sad consequences which have followed; and the second, to suggest such measures, on the part of the Greek committee, as are best calculated to secure the credit of the loan,—on the success of which the committee considers the future prosperity and independence of Greece chiefly to depend.

"Having, in a written paper, recently addressed to the legislative body, pointed out the most effectual measure to be adopted for the moment, and which I had already detailed to a member of the executive, M. Coletti, it remains for me to express a hope, that the Government will be pleased to take the notes which I presented to Prince Mavrocordato, while at Messolunghi, into its earliest consideration.

"Should government decide on the necessity of commencing a national marine, by the purchase of a few frigates, it would, I presume, be advisable to begin by appropriating a small portion, say ten thousand pounds sterling of the present loan, to the above purpose. In this case, it is more than probable the Greek committee will be able to find a ship owner, who would give two years' credit for the remainder. In the event of the Provisional Government's deciding on this important point, and that its wishes are communicated to the committee, on my return to London, I have no hesitation in promising that a frigate of forty guns, fitted up in the English style, and which would thus serve as a model for the rising navy of Greece, shall be at Napoli di Romania or any other point of the confederacy, by the month of March next.

"With regard to the purchase of a steam boat, as Mr. Hastings has already stated all that is necessary on the subject, it merely remains for me to recommend, in the most earnest manner, the immediate adoption of his plan, which has been fully approved of by all the friends of Greece in England. This gallant young officer, who is so highly respected in his own country, has given every necessary guarantee for his zeal and sincerity in the Greek cause, and will, I am convinced, render highly important services, in the event of his being encouraged. As to the effect of steam vessels in destroying the infidel fleet, I have the most confident opinion of its efficacy.

"Knowing how anxious the Provisional Government is to observe the strictest economy, I beg it to be clearly understood, that nothing is farther from the wishes of the committee, than to encourage the smallest departure from such a system; convinced, however, that neither pains nor expence should be spared to establish a plan of naval and military organization, that shall enable the executive to drive the enemy from the territory of Greece, without farther delay, the committee conceives that nothing which tends to promote this grand object ought to be regarded as being in any way extravagant or improvident.

"Although I have not alluded to the subject, it is proper to add, that the ordering a frigate and steam boat to be prepared during the ensuing winter, will have a most excellent effect on the British public, as it will prove that the Provisional Government has begun the long wished for system of naval organization and a national marine.—I should imagine that the utmost expence of the frigate and steam vessel will not exceed fifty thousand pounds sterling.

"Presuming that the government is already sufficiently impressed with the importance of putting the fortresses of the confederation into a better state of defence, as well as procuring arms and cloathing for a small body of cavalry and infantry, I have only to suggest, that it shall issue orders for the number of cannon and various calibres that may be required, together with such besieging materials as are likely to be wanted for the reduction of Patrass and other points still in the enemy's hands. Should I be the bearer of the instructions of government on the subject, I think there will be no difficulty in transmitting a proportion of heavy artillery and besieging materials, complete in all their parts, with shot, &c. by the month of December, a period at which there will be ample leisure for mounting the guns and making arrangements for using the besieging materials with effect. Should the above proposition meet the wishes of government, I would further suggest the propriety of sending out two or three experienced sergeants of artillery, to superintend the landing of the new guns, and placing them in the batteries, &c.

"I have, in the notes sent through Prince Mavrocordato, suggested the facilities which would attend the payment of the heavy artillery, by giving up a portion of the useless brass cannon: I shall here add, that it might be adviseable for the government to contract for the construction of some light field-pieces out of those which may be given in exchange. Indeed from the specimens I have already seen of these guns, I consider them to be in general totally unfit for any purpose of real service or utility in their actual worn and neglected state. It is needless to say, that the greatest care should be taken that their value is exactly estimated; this would be best effected by the appointment of a commission to see them weighed and examined, previous to their removal from the batteries.

"With regard to ammunition, small arms and military cloathing, as there happens to be various individuals in London, who are willing to supply these articles to the

Provisional Government on credit, or by merely receiving a third part of the amount furnished, in cash, it would, I presume, be more advantageous to accept their offers, than have recourse to the uncertain mode of collecting supplies here.

"In the event of a determination on the part of government to order the supplies in question, I beg leave further to suggest the propriety of its deciding on some distinguishing mark and appropriate mottos to be placed on the cannon, &c. which will of course be cast for the occasion. These marks and mottos will serve for such naval and military stores as may be ordered at any future period.

"The last observation with which I shall trouble you, relates to the policy of appropriating a portion of all loans raised in England for the service of Greece, to the purchase of naval and military stores. The effect of this plan is two-fold—it shews a disposition on the part of the government to encourage British trade, while it also interests a much larger number of individuals in the success of the cause; there is, in fact, no instance on record of any of the new governments that have contracted for loans in England, having withdrawn the whole of the money from the country, without making some purchases.

"Upon the whole, however inconvenient it may be to alienate any part of the present loan for the purposes I have pointed out, still is it so much for the interest of Greece, that some should be appropriated in the way I have named, that I could not help recommending the matter to the serious attention of the executive.

"Being convinced that in addition to sending some produce to England, to pay the interest of the loan, nothing would have a greater tendency to raise the credit of Greece on our stock exchange, than the appearance of the national flag in the Thames, I trust and hope that no obstacle may intervene to prevent this part of my proposal from being carried into effect. Indeed I am so impressed with its necessity, that I do not think any other means now present themselves, for removing the dangerous effects produced by recent events—and as those effects will be greatly increased by the catastrophe of Ipsara, it is of infinite importance that some strong and decisive measures should be adopted without loss of time.

"My motive for urging the executive to decide on the propriety of dispatching a national vessel before the 5th of August is, that there may be sufficient time for its return to Greece before the winter commences.

"Having thus stated the principal points by which I am led to believe the interests of Greece may be most effectually promoted in England, it is, I trust, needless to say that it will afford me the greatest satisfaction, if any personal exertion of mine can in the smallest degree contribute to their speedy accomplishment.

"I am, &c.

(Signed) "EDWARD BLAQUIERE."

No. XXXVI.

From Lord Charles Murray to His Excellency Sir Frederick Adam, &c. &c. &c.

"Napoli di Romania, July 11th, 1824.

"Sir,

"On my way to this place, in company with Mr. Blaquiere, I remained two days in the Acropolis of Corinth, where we were received with great hospitality and kindness by the Commandant Georgio Kitzos, general of the district, a very excellent and worthy man. Your Excellency is probably aware of the detention of his sister, Madame

Vasilica, at Constantinople, and who was forcibly seized by Ali Pacha, and whom that tyrant, unworthy of the name of a human being, afterwards married. Painful as it must be to a brother to be unable to procure the enlargement of a favourite sister, a lady of the greatest beauty, and whose munificent charities and extensive benevolence are to this day a theme of admiration and of gratitude to all Albania, still more painful trials have fallen to the lot of this amiable and excellent man himself.

"I am invited by the Greek government to direct this communication to your Excellency, to intreat your mediation as to effecting the exchange of Mogafoot Pacha, now prisoner, together with the persons of his suite in Napoli di Romania, with the family of the aforesaid General Kitzos—who are now detained in slavery at Valona, by Ismael Bey. The family consists of the following persons :—

"1. The wife of the General.

"2. His son, Christodylos Kitzos, aged eight years.

"3 and 4. Two daughters, name unknown.

"5. A lady, the relative of General Kitzos, named Vasilica Zakootzi, who was before seized on by Mouctar Pascha.

"6. A female attendant named Maria.

"7. A young man attached to the family.

"8 and 9. Two domestics.

"Together with this letter, I have written to Mr. Canning, to whom I have the honour to be known, enclosing a copy of the communication I have now the honour to make to your Excellency.—I think it right that your Excellency should be informed forthwith, that during the massacre of Ipsara, a French man-of-war carried several Tchaoases, and other Turkish officers, to Naxos, in order to reduce that island again under the ignominious and brutal yoke of the Porte. The Eparch, remaining faithful to his God, his country, and his government, is said to have been forcibly depostęd from Naxos.—Your Excellency is perhaps aware likewise, that a few days back, a French man-of-war came to treat for the ransom of the two Pascha's here,—one of them that perfidious wretch who refused to fulfil the articles of the capitulation of Napoli.—Mr. Secretary Rodius addressed, by the order of the government, a very spirited letter, ordering them to quit the port, as the Turkish agents offered 200,000 francs to corrupt the executive, and 40,000 for M. Coletti, third member of that body. The answer made was, "the Greeks are poor, but they are not to be bribed."—With respectful compliments to Lady Adam, to whom I enclose a few lines, I have the honour to remain, with great respect,

"Your Excellency's
"Most obliged and faithful,
"And obedient and humble Servant,
(Signed) "CHARLES MURRAY."

No. XXXVII.

TRANSLATION FROM THE ROMAIC.

From Mavromichalis to E. Blaquiere.

"Calamata, 10-22d July, 1824.

"Dear Sir,

"I acknowledge the receipt of your letter dated the 9th of this month, which reached me ten days ago. You tell me that this is the second you have written to me: I regret, however, to say, that I have not received your first.

"With respect to your kindness, in saying that you believe me to be a patriot and a friend to my country, I can assure you that I have given proofs of this from the beginning of the sacred struggle for our religion and soil, to the present time; and such I shall continue to be until the last moment of my existence,—sacrificing readily even my own life, as I have sacrificed that of my son, my brother, and my all.

"I regard and esteem you for your humane and friendly sentiments towards Greece, and I am desirous to cultivate your valuable acquaintance. You advise me to be united with the government, and to forget the past. I assure you that this depends on the government itself, when it shall think proper to cure the deadly wound it has inflicted on my political existence. The true prosperity of every one, individually, as well as that of a whole nation, depends on obeying the laws, provided those laws are properly executed.

"I do not doubt that your sensible and humane heart laments the present state of my country; unanimity for the general good, and sincerity of conduct, are the foundations of every state; but those virtues cannot exist where self-interest and the passions unhappily prevail.

"I leave to your sound judgment all that regards myself as an individual, and whatever you think proper to be done, I shall accede to without opposition.

"I hope you will continue to think me worthy of your friendship, and believe me,

"Your most sincere Friend,

(Signed) "PETROBEY MAVROMICHALIS."

No. XXXVIII.

TRANSLATION.

From Andreas Miaoulis, Admiral of the Greek Fleet, to E. Blaquiere.

"At Anchor off Cape Sunium, July 15-27th, 1824.

"Sir,

"I have this moment received a letter from the Primates of Athens, by which they inform me of your arrival there, and that you had immediately set out to join the Greek fleet.

"Unhappily for me, who am so anxious to become acquainted with a person that takes such a deep interest in the affairs of my country, I received orders at five o'clock yesterday evening, from the Government and Primates of Hydra, to proceed to the north-east of the Egean; and having ordered the fleet to put to sea, I was on the point of weighing anchor myself the moment the letter from Athens reached me.

"I regret exceedingly being thus deprived of the opportunity of becoming acquainted with one from whose counsels I could derive so much benefit for the good of my country; but I hope another may present itself ere long. I have the honour to be, with great respect, &c.

(Signed) "ANDREAS MIAOULIS."

No. XXXIX.

From the same to the same.

"Hydra, August 1-13th, 1824.

"Sir,

"I have this day been favoured with your friendly letter of yesterday, and by which you pay me the undeserved compliment of saying I have more than once been the saviour of my country; if our country has been saved till now, it is because the Almighty acts in her favour by ways unknown to his creatures. While I am grateful for the flattering opinion you entertain, I feel that I have not done more than my duty.

"I have not terms sufficiently strong to express the gratification I experienced on hearing, from your friend M. Chiappa, the good intentions you have conceived for the interests of Greece, hitherto so unfortunate in being deprived of that co-operation of which she stands in so much need. And I trust, that on carrying your project with regard to the navy, into effect, our country will not fail to give a public proof of gratitude towards those who have come forward to serve her in this manner, under such critical circumstances. I have the honour to remain, with the greatest respect and esteem, &c.

(Signed) "ANDREAS MIAOULIS."

No. XL.

From J. Tombasi to E. Blaquiere.

"Hydra, July 21st, 1824.

"Sir,

"I am very sorry that the absence of my brother, and my own illness, have deprived me of the pleasure which Mr. Hastings had provided for me, of becoming acquainted with you. This disappointment, however, I reconcile myself to, by seeing in your letter a promise to visit our island again, by which I hope soon to obtain the object of my wishes.

"Mr Hastings, besides the above, has provided for me another pleasure, that of inserting, through your means, the names of my sons among those boys who are to be educated in England, and to return to serve their country. Scarcely did I propose this to my sons, before they leaped for joy, and immediately expressed their willingness to go any where for the acquirement of knowledge. I told them that I should not allow more than one of them to go; but as they were very fond of each other, they wished to be always together; I have, therefore, sent both to Mr. Hastings, and I hope that you will decide for them agreeably to your praiseworthy views for our country, and as we all desire. I have not sufficient terms to express my gratitude towards a person to whom Greece owes so many acknowledgments, but with the deepest respect, I sign myself,

"Your most devoted Servant,

(Signed) "GIACOMAKI TOMBASI."*

No. XLI.

TRANSLATION OF THE FAC-SIMILE.

From the Ephors of the Philomusæ Society to E. Blaquiere.

"Salamis, July 21st, 1824, O. S.

"Esteemed Sir,

"According to your request, the Philomusæ Society have chosen the three Athenian youths who are to be instructed in England, and whom they now send to Napoli di Romania.

"The Athenians and the Philomusæ Society feel sensi-

* Circumstances which have been already explained, prevented me from taking charge of more than one of M. Tombasi's sons. Georgius, whom I brought to England, is a remarkably amiable and intelligent lad, and has made a very satisfactory progress in his studies.—E. B.

ble of the kindness of the Greek Committee in London; and they beg you to represent to them personally the deep respect and gratitude which they feel for that distinguished association.

"Your noble and philellenic sentiments, which are now well known to all Greece, give us good grounds of hope that you will co-operate in every thing else that can promote the interests of our beloved country. With due respect, we sign ourselves the Ephors of the Philomusæ Society,

"S. PATUSSAS.
(Signed) "GEORGIUS PSYLLAS.
"ANARGYRUS PETRAKIS.

"P.S. The names of the boys are—Panagis Scapessus, Michael Chaliocondylis, Demetrius Callifornas."*

No. XLII.

Address to the Ladies of England, by Madalena Mavrojenes of Myconos.

"Ladies!

"Since the war, into which we have entered, involves not merely our freedom, but our very existence, it becomes

* Of these, I regret to say that only one, Demetrius Callifornas, accompanied me to England. The other two were taken ill soon after their arrival at Napoli di Romania, so that I was very reluctantly obliged to leave them behind. It is worthy of remark, that when informed of the impossibility of bringing them with me, they burst into tears, and were quite inconsolable for some days. Demetrius is a very amiable boy, and continues to make a rapid progress in his studies. When one day asked, what he would do on his return to Greece, he replied, "I will establish a school at my native place, Athens!"—E. B.

necessary to consider what may be the issue of the conflict. On our part the crisis is aweful, and leaves no alternative but victory or death;—either Greece, regenerated shall arise fresh and lovely from the long night of bondage, and once more rejoicing in the morning star of liberty,—either the land so long alienated and contemned, shall reclaim the rights of brotherhood with Christian communities, or her despairing sons shall fall prostrate before the altar of glory, and perish on the ashes of their fathers: there can be no other alternative than this. In a situation thus desperate, it is natural they should appeal to the sympathy of all noble minded and benevolent Christians throughout the world; and by what civilized nation, what class of humanized men, shall this plea be rejected? Surely not by the philosopher, who must with gratitude remember that land in which philosophers were born to enlighten mankind;—nor is it for the hero to regard with indifference the indignities offered to the posterity of the race of Mars. Where is the artist, the poet, or even the citizen, who can contemplate without emotion the degradation of a people to whom belonged a Plato, a Miltiades, a Socrates, an Agesilaus, an Apelles, a Phidias. If such men exist, there is at least no woman so insensible to honour and humanity. Be it the exclusive prerogative of the stronger sex to remain unmoved by the agonizing struggles of the Greek nation:—for you, Ladies, no arguments are necessary to awaken pity and benevolence. In whatever view the female character may be contemplated, it is impossible but that the women of all Christian communities should be eager to extend protection to the insulted maids and matrons of Greece. In compassion, or generosity, when did women yield the palm to their masculine compeers—most of all in Britain, whose fair daughters are eminently distinguished by the virtues that belong exclusively to noble souls,—charity, beneficence, and philanthropy. It is not, Ladies, sufficient for my nation that it defends a just cause, and devotes itself with intense enthusiasm to the standard of liberty—it suffices not, since alas! ages of tyranny and oppression have dried up its natural resources; not energy is wanting, but that physical force, which even energy cannot create—arms, ammunition, good clothing—of these our heroes are often destitute. It is to solicit pecuniary aid, without which these aliments of war and life cannot be procured, that I presume, Ladies, to appear before you,—not without the encouragement of Mr. Blaquiere, to whose humanity and sympathy my nation already owes a debt never to be repaid. The object of my application is to secure a safe asylum for the women and children during this eventful crisis. Such an asylum might be supplied by the island of Eubœa, could we but procure by your beneficence the means to conquer it—to be ever dedicated to the memory of the British Ladies. I leave to Mr. Blaquiere the task of affording circumstantial information; by him I shall hope to be assured that my petition is not rejected.*

I avail myself of this occasion to render you the homage of my most profound respect.

"I remain, Ladies,

"Your devoted and respectful Servant,

(Signed) "MADALENA MAVROJENES."

"Napoli, August 12th, 1824."

* Pursuant to the promise I made to the heroine of Myconos, previous to my departure from Napoli di Romania, her letter was laid before the Greek Committee immediately after my arrival. And I should not have deferred giving it still greater publicity, had there been any hope of its producing the desired effect. The very praiseworthy example recently set by the ladies of Edinburgh, has been already communicated to Madalena, and I trust it may be ere long in my power, to transmit information of a similar nature, with regard to other points of the Empire.—E. B.

No. XLIII.

From E. Blaquiere to John Bowring, Esq.

Napoli de Romania, August 1, 1824.

"My dear Bowring,

"The necessity for changing the air, and my anxiety to see Athens, induced me to set out from this a few days after the date of my last. I only returned to the seat of government two days ago, having, in the course of little more than ten days, visited the ruins of Epidaurus, Egina, Salamis, and the first named city. I reached Athens on the 24th, and had a long conference with General Goura, who had just returned from the plain of Marathon, where, in concert with Morfopulos of Cefalonia, he greatly distinguished himself on the 14th instant, at the head of three hundred men against three thousand, whom he forced to retreat, with the loss of four hundred killed and wounded, and several standards. From Athens, the most interesting spot on earth, I returned to Ambelachi, the ancient Salamis, to confer with the members of the philomusæ, and thence proceeded to Hydra, where I saw the Primates, who received me in the most friendly manner, giving me letters to the Central Government, expressing their anxiety that all the propositions I had previously made to the legislative and executive bodies should be acceded to. The whole population of this truly astonishing rock were busily occupied in fitting out a large division of the fleet, which has sailed ere this, and is destined to join the division intended to act against Mehemet Ali, also in adding to the defences of the island, which are already of the most formidable description. From Hydra I passed on to Spezzia, in a vessel provided by the kindness of Lazarro Conduriotti, at whose house I slept two nights, and where I was treated *en Sybarite.* The Spezziotes, who are a keen and intelligent people, were occupied in the same manner as their neighbours. I had a formal conference with the Primates, and received a letter from them to the same effect as that given to me at Hydra. Having dined with Gika Botasi, brother to the Vice-President, I set out at an early hour on Friday, to visit the celebrated harbours of Portokeli and Vivari, where the Venetians kept their naval arsenals, and arrived here in the evening. On presenting myself to the President and Executive Body, I found them reading a despatch that instant received from General Dimo Scaltza, dated within six leagues of Salona, and giving an account of the repulse and discomfiture of Dervish Pacha, who attempted to advance to that place, for the purpose of opening a communication with Patrass. This victory is the most decisive and important of the campaign, as the Turks had fully calculated on the success of their plans. The first letters of the General, state their loss at 600 in killed alone; other accounts reached the government last night, by which it appears that a thousand of the infidels fell on the occasion, while the main body, amounting to eight thousand, retreated, leaving their baggage, cannon, and standards, in the hands of the Greeks. Owing to the judicious choice of the ground, the loss of the latter did not exceed twenty men in killed and wounded! Nothing can exceed the exultation of the government and people at the successes at Marathon and Salona, as the schemes of the enemy are thus in a great measure frustrated. The whole attention of the Executive is now directed to preparing for defensive and offensive operations on a large scale.

"You have heard of Mehemet Ali's expedition. Though considerable, it is by no means sufficiently so to induce a belief of its being intended for the Morea. We all think the Egyptian tyrant intends to occupy Candia, whence he doubtless imagines there will be great facilities for carrying his ulterior designs into execution. The affair of Ipsara, though disastrous in every point of view, has, however, roused Greece, and great things may be expected from her;

but circumstances have arisen which render the support and interference of England more urgent and necessary than ever. You have seen the note of Russia; I was very remiss in not telling you ere this, that the conduct of certain foreign naval officers in the Levant, has been most flagitious during the last four months; they are, in fact, the active allies of the Turks, and doing their utmost to sacrifice the unhappy but heroic people of Greece. I am preparing a letter to Sir F. Adam on this subject, which will, I trust, be forwarded to Mr. * * *. Tricoupi and myself dined with the President and his charming family to-day. I had previously a long conference with the Executive, and settled every thing about my departure. A vessel is ordered, and I hope to embark in a few days. I shall do all I can to find out Sir H. Neale, and represent to him the scandalous violation of our neutrality, as well as that of the other powers, in allowing their vessels to be employed in conveying the troops of Mehemet Ali. There are no less than thirty Maltese, and about seventy or eighty Austrians, Neapolitans, Spaniards, &c. Surely Mr. * * * * must have paid but very little attention to the wishes of ministers, in thus suffering these sordid wretches to prostitute our flag to the basest purposes! God grant that you may not be sleeping in England! Now that the enemies of the cause have thrown off the mask, the fate of this country depends on us—if we betray or abandon her . . . . !

"The late law in favour of public credit authorized the executive to send home some produce with me, but seeing the importance of not losing any time, I have made a communication, stating, that I felt assured the creditors would be perfectly satisfied to wait a few months longer, until the oil and currants of this year are collected, so that the articles I proposed, might be sent home in November or the following month. In other respects, the papers and documents of which I hope to be the bearer, will, I feel assured, give great and general satisfaction. The Greek youths, who seem most anxious to profit by the offer of the Quakers, are ready and will be embarked immediately. The vessel I have chosen is a fast sailing schooner of Hydra. They offered me a ship. Hastings goes home with me on a special mission.

" It is high time to inform you that the first instalment reached this from Zante a week since—90,000 dollars have already been paid over to the fleet. The rest is distributing to the army. The employment of the whole will, I am convinced, give the utmost satisfaction. What I am most anxious about is, that every possible effort should be made to rouse the Government and country to a sense of what is passing on the continent with regard to the East of Europe. If strong and energetic measures are not taken, we shall be completely duped, and incur the stigma of sacrificing another people within one short year!

" Should this letter reach you in any reasonable time, it will be adviseable to see about the best means of obtaining supplies of every kind. The deputies must know what is wanted. I ought to mention, that it is doubtless to Mr. Barff's zeal and activity the arrival of the money here is due. I need not say that notwithstanding the irreparable disasters occasioned by the delays already so often deprecated and deplored, the advantages to Greece of its coming even so late in the season are altogether incalculable. If you have determined to stop the remittances from motives of prudence, for God's sake continue to send supplies, and let the other matters be managed so as to occasion as little delay as possible. I will not enter into any farther details at present, though I have much to say. Pray occupy yourself with the means of procuring supplies, and believe me to be, &c.

(Signed) " EDWARD BLAQUIERE."

" P.S. The situation of the Ipsariots calls loudly for a subscription. Those families who have been saved from the Turkish knife, have taken refuge in Napoli di Malvasia—their condition is indescribably wretched! Pray tell Orlando I paid a visit to his family, and found them well, though in despair at his absence. As it may be a satisfaction to him to receive a letter given to me by his wife, I enclose it.

No. XLIV.

PHILANTHROPIC SOCIETY.

Address of Nicolas Jeracaris, of Scio, delivered to a Meeting of Patriots convened at Napoli de Romania, on the 10th of August, 1824, to discuss the propriety of forming a Philanthropic Society in Greece.

"Friends and Fellow Countrymen!

"Convinced of the patriotic zeal and humane sentiments which animate all those whom I have now the honour to address, it affords me great satisfaction to have an opportunity of submitting the following facts for your consideration; satisfied that whatever may be the result of this day's meeting, they will be received with candour and indulgence.

"It must be well known to you, that after the breaking out of our revolution, and the cruelties which preceded and followed the event, great numbers of families took refuge in the Morea, both on account of its having become the seat of Government, and because it would afford a safer asylum than any other point of the confederation. It would be an act of injustice to the national character, were I to say, that all who had any means of ministering to the wants of the fugitives, most of whom came here in a state of the greatest destitution and wretchedness, did not do their utmost to alleviate the sufferings of their fellow citizens on that occasion. When the nature of the contest is considered, I need hardly say, that the number who could stretch forth the hand of charity was very limited, while the more important duties of conducting the naval and military operations, precluded the possibility of the Executive devoting its attention to the subject. The natural consequences of this state of things has been, that independently of thousands having become the victims of poverty and disease, during the early stages of the war, the spectacle of wretchedness exhibited in various parts of the Peloponnesus at this moment, is not less heart-rending than it has been at any former period. This is occasioned by the recent influx of not less than fifteen thousand fugitives from Livadia, Negropont, Candia, and Ipsara. These unhappy fugitives, of whom three-fourths are women and children, have taken refuge at Epidaurus, Malvasia on the adjacent coast of Maina, and in this place. When I state that by far the greatest portion of these poor creatures, are suffering under the double calamity of want and sickness, without adequate food or raiment, and obliged to live in the open air, I feel assured that no more is required to prove the necessity of the present meeting, or excite the sympathy of every man who professes a spark of benevolence and Christian charity.

" So far as our self-interest, independent of every other consideration, is connected with our duty on the present occasion, I shall only mention two points, which cannot fail to strike the most superficial observer. So long as no steps are taken to relieve the distresses of our fugitive countrymen, how can it be expected that they will abandon their helpless families to enrol themselves in our fleets and armies? Thus it is, that numbers of brave soldiers and seamen, whose presence would be of such utility in the field of honour, either die neglected, or lead a life of sloth and misery. But what will be the fate of the other sex, if nothing be done to show the national sympathy in their favour? It is true, the Greek women have as yet borne up against their accumulated misfortunes with the most heroic constancy, preferring death itself, to any dereliction of their duties as wives and mothers. But it is for you, my friends and fellow countrymen, to reflect on the possible consequences of withholding charity, or betraying indifference to our suffering countrywomen!

"Impelled by the crying necessity of the case, and anxious to insure the co-operation of government in forming a Philanthropic Society, I have already addressed a memorial on the subject to the Executive, pointing out among other matters, a mode by which a sum of two thousand dollars per month, might be raised in this place alone, without interfering with the public revenues. As I shall do myself the honour of laying a copy of my memorial before you, it is unnecessary to make any farther allusion to its contents in this place.

"Should the above most desirable association be formed at the seat of government, I feel assured the example will be followed by the formation of branch societies throughout all the provinces. Without dwelling on the mass of human suffering which must be removed by such a beneficent establishment, what better reply can we give to the detractors of our national character. Called by Providence to take our place among those nations of Europe, which knows to what an extent our ancestors contributed to modern civilization, we are no less bound to shew those nations who have so generously received the Greek patriots in their bosom, that notwithstanding all the calamities of our revolution, we are also alive to the duties of humanity and benevolence. I am satisfied too, that the proposed measure, if carried into effect, will be highly gratifying to the nations who have in various ways sympathized in our eventful struggle; but more especially to those foreigners, who abandoning their own country, have come to share in our misfortunes, and even die in combating for our holy cause.

Memorial addressed to the Provisional Government of Greece, relative to the formation of a Philanthropic Society, and to which reference is made in the preceding address.

"Were those who govern the people, even gifted with the hundred eyes of Argus, such is the multiplicity of concerns which constantly occupy their attention, and the cares to which they are exposed, that it would be impossible for them to think of every thing that is required for the benefit of the governed. This is one powerful reason, why it is the privilege of every lover of his country, except in despotic governments, to observe the sufferings of their fellow citizens, reflect on the means of alleviating them, and lay his suggestions before the proper authorities. These are, on the other hand, in duty bound, to take such suggestions into consideration, and if found beneficial, to carry them into effect without delay. The consequence of treating propositions for the general good with indifference or neglect is, that it proves the rulers to have deviated from the social compact, while it renders them deservedly unpopular, if not unfit to govern.

"Convinced, as I am, that the Provisional Government, is most anxious to diminish those evils, inseparable from the war, and which have fallen upon a large portion of the population, and that the variety, as well as importance of other matters, have alone prevented it from taking the subject more immediately into consideration, I humbly beg leave, respectfully to offer my sentiments, as to the best and speediest means of alleviating some portion of the public misery, which continues to aggravate the other horrors so inseparable from the war of regeneration.

It is well known that thousands of my countrymen, who were enabled to escape from the hands of our blood-thirsty tyrants, have taken refuge in the Morea, hoping here to find profitable employment and the relief of their distresses, distresses which have deprived great numbers, as it threatens to deprive others, of that existence which the Almighty had preserved, in order that they might one day have an opportunity of avenging the murder of their wives, children, and parents! With every disposition to aid their unfortunate fellow-citizens, such is the number of those who possess no adequate means of sustaining life, that it has been impossible to prevent the miserable spectacle of whole families perishing from absolute want, while others are at this moment exposed in the open air, without any hopes whatever of relief, except through the prompt aid of Government or those of their countrymen, who are enabled to come forward. Seeing, therefore, that it is impossible for the executive to withdraw any part of its attention from the great objects of the war, while individual charity only requires a proper impulse to become general all over the confederation, I beg leave to offer the following suggestions, as those, which are, in my humble opinion, best calculated to provide a proper remedy for the distress to which I have thus alluded. It is proposed—

" 1st. That a Philanthropic Society be formed at the seat of the Provisional Government, and an immediate appeal be issued by it, to all classes of the citizens, calling on them to come forward in aid of the poor and necessitous.

2nd. That each shop-keeper be called on to contribute the trifling sum of from 4 to 8 paras, 2½d, daily to the Philanthropic Fund.

"3rd. That the ministers of the gospel be requested to make collections in their respective churches for the same object.

"4th. That a small box be placed at the Custom-House, and another at the entrance of the fortress, to receive such donations as those who return from sea and land journies may be disposed to give.

"5th. That a small additional duty be levied on imports for the above purpose.

"6th. That a trifling sum be retained from the pay of all public functionaries, for the said fund.

"7th. That the Priors of Monasteries be invited to contribute a certain sum annually to the Philanthropic Fund.

"With these aids, and the sums arising from voluntary subscriptions, the Society would be enabled to form such an establishment, including medical men, purveyors, and other attendants, as may be requisite to carry the objects of the association into active effect.

"Such is the object to which I would entreat the support and encouragement of the Provisional Government. This is, indeed, all that is required, not only to insure the success of the Society here, but lead to the establishment of branch associations throughout the confederacy; thus proving to the whole civilized world, that in practising the fundamental principles of Christianity, the Greeks are worthy of the sublime destinies to which they aspire.

(Signed) "NICOLAS JERACARIS, of Scio.

"Napoli di Romania, Aug. 1st, 1824."

No. XLV.

Letter addressed by the Deputation of the Philanthropic Society of Greece, to Joseph Hume, Esq. M P., William Allen, Esq. Treasurer and Secretary to the Committee of Friends, in favour of Indigent Greeks; Jeremy Bentham, Esq. and John Bowring, Esq. Hon. Secretary of the Greek Committee: enclosing a Copy of the Rules of the new Society, together with a power to act for it in the United Kingdom.

"Napoli di Romania, August 12-24th, 1824.

"GENTLEMEN,

"The number of fugitives pressing into liberated Greece, from those points which are still cursed with the presence of our late sanguinary tyrants, added to an epidemic disease, the natural result of such a struggle as that in which we are engaged, having produced the greatest distress among a large portion of the population, while thousands are thus prevented from going forth against the enemy, and our youth left without instruction, a meeting lately convened for the purpose of taking the above important subject into consideration, with a view of adopting ulterior measures, resolved at once to form themselves into an association, to be called the Philanthropic Society of regenerated Greece, the organization of which we have the honour to transmit, not doubting that you will appreciate the advantages of such an institution at a moment like the present.

"Although the success which has attended the early efforts of the Society at the seat of government, far exceeds what we had anticipated, while it leads us to entertain the most sanguine hopes for the future; yet such are the accumulated wants of our suffering population, and the multifarious objects proposed to itself by the society, that it would be preposterous to expect that all the funds required could be raised in Greece. Calculating, therefore, on the sympathy which has been shown towards the Greek cause, it has been determined to appeal to the Christian world of every denomination and sect, in behalf of an association, established for the express purpose of fulfilling that great maxim of our common faith, which the Saviour of mankind sought to impress on his followers as the first of duties, and affording the best claim to the approbation of heaven.

"As the objects of the association are fully detailed in the accompanying papers, it only remains for us to solicit the favour of your becoming the agents and representatives of the Society in Great Britain, where Greece has already experienced such proofs of sympathy and benevolence. It was indeed but natural for us to appeal more especially to a country which is covered with charitable institutions; and if we have selected you, Gentlemen, to be the medium of this appeal, it is because your names have been mentioned to us as being closely connected with the formation of two societies established for the express purpose of relieving our suffering countrymen, or aiding us in the struggle for independence.

"Leaving the mode of carrying the objects of the Society into effect, in the United Kingdom, to your better judgment, all we would request is, that you might be pleased to transmit regular lists of all those who become patrons of the association, in order that the people of Greece may know, through the medium of the public press, who are their benefactors.

"When it is considered that an institution like the present, if encouraged and brought to maturity, while it ministers to the wants of thousands now, may, at no distant period, become the means of extending civilization far beyond the limits of Greece, the undersigned feel it would be altogether superfluous to offer any apology for the liberty they have taken in soliciting you to promote the objects of the Society, and receive contributions for it in England.

"With expressions of heartfelt gratitude for your exertions in favour of Greece, the undersigned avail themselves of this occasion to offer you the assurance of their highest consideration and respect.

"NICOLAS JERACARIS, Chairman.

"N. KALERGI.

"GEORGIUS GLARAKES.

"JOANIS THEOTOKIS.

(Signed) "DEMETRIUS DESILLAS.

"T. NEGRIS.

"J. CLASSIS.

"NICOLAS FLOJAITES, Hon. Sec."

No. XLVII.

ORGANIZATION
OF THE
PHILANTHROPIC SOCIETY OF GREECE.

Sect. I.
Of the Society in General.

I. Individuals of every nation and condition are eligible to become members of the Philanthropic Society.

II. The members of the Society are to be divided into three classes.

1. The first class is to consist of persons who have contributed to the funds of the Society, and afford personal assistance.
2. The second class to consist of those who only contribute to the funds.
3. The third class to consist of persons who, not being able to contribute to the funds, would feel disposed to afford their personal services.

Sect. II.
Objects of the Association.

III. The Society will occupy itself with,—

1. The clothing and supporting the poor, sick, widows and orphans.
2. The education of orphans and destitute children.

IV. The Society will be fixed and hold its meetings whenever the seat of government may be established.

V. The affairs of the Society shall be managed by a deputation.

1. The deputation shall consist of seven members, to be chosen out from the first class only.
2. The deputation shall be under a president, who is one of the members chosen by ballot, and elected monthly from the number.
3. The deputation shall keep records. It shall have a secretary, an accountant, apothecaries, and their clerks.

Sect. III.

Of the general Assemblies.

VI. The members of the Society, personally present, shall elect the deputation by a majority of votes.

VII. The functions of the said deputation are to be continued for two years. Half the number to be changed at the end of the first year; that is to say, the secretary, treasurer, and store-keeper, to be also chosen by ballot, will thus be changed at the end of the first year.

VIII. The general assemblies of the Society will be composed of the first and second classes, including the members of the deputation. The discussions to take place under the president for the time being.

IX. In the general assemblies, (see article 6) the members of the Society and of the deputation are on a perfect equality as to the right of voting.

X. The members of the first and second class, collected at the central station, are under the obligation of attending at all the ordinary and extraordinary meetings of the Society, except when prevented from an admissible cause.

XI. Every member of the Society has a right to publish his speeches or opinions, through the medium of the press.

XII. The seal of the Society shall be a head of Apollo, with this inscription, "Philanthropic Society of regenerated Greece."

Sect. IV.

Duties of the Deputation.

XIII. The assemblages of the deputies will be regarded as complete, whenever two-thirds of the members, with the president, are present.

XIV. The resolutions of the deputies will be regulated by a majority of votes.

XV. All the written documentary proceedings shall be signed by the president, and countersigned by the assembled number of the deputation, and the secretary shall cause the seal of the Society to be affixed to them.

XVI. It will appoint agents or correspondents in the provinces or abroad.

XVII. It will keep up a correspondence with the foreign members resident out of Greece, and in reference to objects coming within the views of the Society; but always, however, with the concurrence of the members present.

XVIII. It will convene the members present to attend the ordinary weekly meeting, to consider and resolve on the various objects which may arise for their consideration; and it will unite them to meet once a month, to render a special account of the diversified objects which have occupied their attention; the result to be made public through the medium of the press.

XIX. It will promulgate, by means of the public press, the names of all new members, as well as specify the amount of their contributions.

Sect. V.

On the Duties of the Secretary.

XX. The secretary of the deputation shall prepare and preside over the correspondence, keeping up the degree of order and punctuality necessary in the receipt and dispatch of all documentary proceedings.

XXI. He will publish regularly the report of meetings, containing a minute account of all that occurs either in them, or as connected with the affairs of the Society.

SECT. VI.

Duties of the Treasurer.

XXII. The treasurer shall keep registers of all sums received and disbursed, seeing that the entries are carefully and promptly made.

XXIII. He shall make no issue of monies, without a legal order in writing from the deputation.

XXIV. All the vouchers of the accountant shall be signed by him, and countersigned by the clerk who keeps the books of his department. The accountant shall receive all sums tendered to him, and shall issue the necessary receipts or vouchers.

XXV. At the end of each month, he shall return the deputation an exact account of all the receipts and disbursements.

SECT. VII.

Duties of the Dispensers.

XXVI. All the written orders of the dispensers shall be signed by the clerk, to whose department the voucher be consigned; he shall keep regular and appropriate registers of the same.

XXVII. The dispensers are to receive all the articles or items of money received by the Society, and they are to give proper receipts for the same.

XXVIII. The apothecaries are not to deliver the most

trifling article, without a legal written order from the deputation.

XXIX. They are to render a monthly report of every thing received and delivered by them.

SECT. VIII.

Of Admission.

XXX. As soon as they have paid their contributions to the accountant or dispensers, the members of the first class shall receive a written acknowledgment as a receipt of the same, which they are to present to the deputation, upon which they will receive a written diploma of their admission, and be thus recognised as members of the Society.

XXXI. The admission of members of the second class will be regulated in the same manner.

XXXII. Members of the third class are admitted merely by a written diploma from the deputation.

SECT. IX.

Of Contributions.

XXXIII. The contribution of each member cannot be less than fifty piasters.

XXXIV. The contributions may be either in specie or in articles useful and necessary, and signified to be receivable by the deputation.

SECT. X.

XXXV. The Society places itself under the controul of the laws and of the government, and it invokes the approbation and support of the philanthropists of the whole civilized world.

XXXVI. The undersigned organizers of the present Society, take upon themselves its entire management, until the number of members shall have increased to thirty-one of the first and second classes; and the first general meeting of the Society will be convened, in order that it may proceed to the election of the deputies, and the subordinate officers, according to the foregoing plan of organization.

Given at Napoli di Romania, 1-13th August, 1824, IN THE FOURTH YEAR OF GRECIAN INDEPENDENCE.

(Signed) D. DESILLAS.
DEM. GOUZELES.
P. A. ANAGNOSTOPOULO.
JOANIS THEOTOKIS.
N. JERAKARIS.
N. KALERGI.
GEO. GLARAKES.
F. NEGRIS.
E. KALERGI.
N. NIKITOPOULOS.
N. THESEUS.
T. VALIANO.

(True Copy) N FLOGAITES, *Sec.*

No. XLVII.

Extract of a Letter from M. Gropius, Austrian Consul at Athens, relative to the present State of the ancient Remains in that City.

"Athens, April 15th, 1824.

"You will have heard that, in 1821, Athens was exposed to a bombardment for three months, by the Ottomans, who were shut up in the Acropolis, which was in its turn battered by the besiegers, who occupied the adjacent heights. Nor is it unknown to you that, during the invasion of Omer Vrione, in August of the same year, all the Christian temples of the city, as well as a great part of the Greek and French houses, and several villages, were consigned to the flames; and that after this catastrophe, and the Pacha's retreat, the Greeks having renewed the siege of the Acropolis, it was cannonaded a second time, when several hundred shells were thrown into its precincts. I am, however, enabled to inform you, and it is with the utmost satisfaction I do so, that notwithstanding all these risks, the ancient monuments have not suffered by any means so much, as was justly apprehended at the time. That which has been most damaged, is the precious Choregiac monument of Lysciratus, vulgarly called the *lanthorn*. The greatest part of this ruin was incorporated with the French convent, which enclosed the church, so that the Turks did not fail to make it share the fate of all the rest, by setting fire to it; the heat of the conflagration, after causing some figures on the frieze to crack and fall, brought down several pieces of the grand circle forming the architrave and frieze, enriched with bas-reliefs. This circle formed but one piece, and is of marble, like the whole of the edifice. The fragments which fell in the greatest quantities, was exactly in the spot where the sixth column was wanting to sustain the *circle*, so that the whole was threatened with total ruin. In order to prevent such a calamity to art, a column was brought from another spot and substituted in its place. The insterstices under the frieze of the other columns, were also filled up by small pieces of lime-stone, whereon they had fallen. Care was at the same time taken, to demolish the walls of the late convent, which pressed on the monument, and whose fall would have brought it down also. The hospital wall on the side of the street was also rebuilt, to prevent its being exposed to injury in that direction, as well as impede the too near approach of carts or animals. Thus arranged, this beautiful remain now presents a much more interesting aspect than formerly, when not more than a third of it could be seen. The repairs are due to the generous zeal of M. Digean, charged with the duties of the French Consul-general, in the absence of M. Fauvel. The expences were borne by the consulate, as the convent ground on which it stands belongs to France. I had the direction of the workmen, and superintended the restorations, but we could only think of the solidity of the building ; at a future day, it is hoped the work will be completed in a manner more worthy of the object in view.

" The whole of the other monuments, whether of the city or in the Acropolis, have happily escaped ; this most fortunate circumstance, is doubtless due to the fact of their either not being devoted to religious worship, or filled with any combustible matter to attract the flames. The temple of Theseus has only remained intact from the last named cause.

" The grand Corinthian Colonade of the Pœcile, in the centre of the town, was spared because it formed a part of the residence of the late Voivodes. The Society of Philomusæ, charged with the preservation of ancient monuments, has just proposed to the government, to take down the line of shops which is built up against this magnificent remain, and which almost conceals it from the view, as well as threatens it with total destruction, in the event of a fire. The town would gain a fine open space by this trifling sacrifice. The matter is still undecided, but we hope our request will be granted.

"With respect to the temple of Theseus, it should be observed, that on the 13th of May, 1821, a few days after the occupation of the town by the peasants, its north-west angle was struck by lightning, which carried away five or six feet of the cornice, and descending through the angular column, completely split the fourth tambour, that of the centre, separating one part from the other several inches, so that the sky can now be seen through the opening, though no material injury has been done to the general strength of the edifice. One of the pieces forming the architrave of this angle, and facing the west, was thrown out of the line six or eight inches, together with its trighlyphe and metope, in which state it remains. The first lateral metope, was also removed from its place, and continues to lean over on one side; after causing this damage, the lightning went down through the foundation of the same angle, shivering the block of marble which forms the upper step of the ascent towards the entrance of the temple, and shaking several of the lower blocks from their places.

"Finding some respectable looking tombstones in the temple of Theseus, and Capuchin convent, the avidity of the Arnaut soldiery, made them fancy there must also be treasures concealed under them; they were in consequence all opened, and their contents scattered about. This sacrilege was effected at the temple without injuring the marble slabs, but in the convent they were forced to break them to pieces.

"The Tower of the Winds, which had been formerly converted into a *Tèkè*, or dervish's chapel, has not suffered any injury. The houses built up against it, happening to be Turkish, were not burnt; but they are now sharing the fate of others, that is to say, of being demolished; which is at least useful to the arts, since their removal will prevent the possibility of communicating fire to this monument, which is one of the most interesting at Athens.

"The Propyleums of the Acropolis have not experienced the least damage. The Parthenon has suffered some additional injury, but this has happily only extended to the flat walls on the sides of the edifice, and which the besieged pulled down, to obtain the lead which secured the iron cramps that hold the blocks together. The same thing has occurred to the temple of Minerva Polias, and Erectheus, though in a less degree.*

"We have not as yet been able to get the powder removed from the old magazine established by the Turks, which is, as you know, in the fine vestibule of the temple of Erectheus. The matter is decided on, but money to construct the new magazine is wanting. I need not say how anxious the society is to rescue this master-piece of art, from the total ruin with which it is hourly threatened. Upon the whole, the Acropolis has gained in picturesque beauty, as a number of wretched looking houses have been demolished, thus leaving a free passage over the interior, and greatly facilitating the access to its splendid remains. The new bastion, constructed by order of Odysseus, besides its securing the precious spring lately found under the right angle of the Propyleum, also adds greatly to the effect from without, as well as these portions of the ancient bastions which have been rebuilt, and where the mine had

* The temple of Apollo Phigalian, in Arcadia, owed its demolition to the same cause, as could be plainly seen during the excavations of 1811.

thrown down the small tower before the site of the Temple of Victory.

"The wall which enclosed the paved way leading to the first gate of the Acropolis, as also the houses in this part of the upper town, have been demolished, because they were too near, and thus interfered with its defence. It is proposed to convert this space into an esplanade and public promenade, commencing at the temple of Bacchus and terminating at the cave of Pan. A new entrance will be made to the town, between the rocks of the Areopagus and the new bastion, the wall is also to be taken a little farther out. It is also intended to open a second gate, between that on the north side and the Morea, near the isolated column of St. John.

"The large Téké, which was formerly on the top of the theatre of Herodius Atticus, having been considered as injurious to the defence of the Acropolis, has been demolished, as well as that called Carababa, and the mausoleums at the Turkish cemetry. In the town, all the minarets have been taken down or destroyed; the mosques have had various destinations: that which faces the corn market, has been converted into a Lancasterian school. Thus much for the present, concerning the ancient remains here. I hope, however, to be enabled to inform you in a future communication, that the labours of the society have recommenced under more favourable auspices than ever.

No. XLVIII.

Address from E. Blaquiere to the Legislative Body, and of which a Romaic Translation was read to the Assembly by Mr. Tricoupi, on the day after its date.

"Fathers of your Country!

"Having, when I last had the honour of addressing you, stated the object of my second visit to Greece, I cannot depart without expressing the heartfelt satisfaction with which I hope shortly to tell my countrymen, of the perseverance and patriotism which the representatives of the Greek people continue to display, in supporting the glorious cause in which they are engaged ; as well as the confident hope I entertain of your ultimate triumph.

" In all that I have hitherto published on the state of Greece, it has been my principal study to prove, first, the justice of her cause ; secondly, to refute the calumnies of her enemies ; and thirdly, to demonstrate the capability of this country to become great, prosperous, and happy. The more I see of Greece, the more I feel convinced that there has been no exaggeration in any of my assertions.

" Among the statements which I am anxious to communicate to the British public, I feel assured that none will afford more satisfaction to your friends, or be so beneficial to Greece, than the measures taken by your august body to sustain her public credit in England, while I am bound to offer it as the opinion of the wisest politicians in Europe, that the success of your endeavours to establish your independence, depends on the maintenance of good faith and punctuality with those capitalists who have so generously come forward to aid the Provisional Government, at the most critical period of the contest. It is, I trust, unnecessary for me to entreat in the name of those friends, that the salutary measures to which I have alluded, may be scrupulously carried into effect. If they are, I do not hesitate to promise the continued support of your English friends ; nor is there any doubt of their having a most favourable effect on the political relations of the confederacy in other quarters.

" When it is considered, that the history of the world presents no phenomenon so extraordinary, as the resuscitation of a people who had suffered so many centuries of tyranny and oppression, and that such unworthy efforts have been made to impede your holy cause, even by those who were bound by the ties of religion and humanity, to give it their utmost support, who can wonder at the difficulties Greece has had to encounter from without, or that a few passing clouds should have occasionally darkened the horizon of her hopes at home.

"The result of the observations made during my present visit, and which I shall hasten to communicate to the European public, is, that the people of Greece have been progressively advancing in knowledge and civilization, ever since the commencement of their arduous struggle; that they are unanimous in their desire to enjoy the blessings of freedom under a regular government; and that, in point of natural resources, no country on earth possesses more ample means of attaining the sacred objects for which you are contending.

"It has already been unanswerably proved, that the Greek contest has nothing in common with those commotions which have agitated other countries of Europe; since, therefore, the foregoing fact is no longer denied, while the justice of your cause is universally admitted, I cannot possibly persuade myself, that there is any serious intention of depriving Greece of the advantages she has gained during this most unequal struggle. If this be really the case, I feel assured that the wisdom, prudence, and firmness of your agust body, aided by an active, intelligent, and paternal executive, will defeat every project which has a tendency to bring about the ruin and degradation of your country.

"If the obstacles connected with the former condition of this beautiful region, and those inseparable from the nature of the war, have rendered it impossible for your august body to give full effect to the social and political system, happily traced out at Epidaurus, the friends of Greece look forward with pleasing confidence, to your future labours in the field of legislation. In the mean time, it is truly gratifying for them to reflect, that you possess in the above celebrated law, a charter which places Greece on a level with the freest states of Europe.

"With respect to the most effectual mode of promoting your sacred cause, if any difference of opinion has existed heretofore, it is now agreed by all parties, that the paramount and exclusive object of those who wish well to Greece, should be that of devising the best and speediest means of driving the enemy from her soil. As, independently of other considerations of the highest political importance, it will be totally impossible for the legislature and executive Government to establish any permanent plan for disseminating knowledge, or availing themselves of the national resources, while the infidels are in possession of points, which enable them to keep the neighbouring districts in a state of continual inquietude and alarm.

"In the report which I propose making on the actual state of the confederacy, I cannot adduce any greater proof of a determination on the part of your august body, to prosecute the war with becoming energy and vigour, than by pointing out the steps that have been taken to organize a regular army, and national marine, without which it would be vain to calculate either on a prosperous issue of the contest, or the recognition of your independence by foreign powers.

"Here I should be neglecting an important and imperative duty, were I to omit stating to your august body, that previously to my leaving England, the friends of Greece, for whom I am acting, instructed me to urge in the most earnest manner, the improvement of your municipal system, by which the peasantry of Greece, whose excellent qualities are now fully known to my countrymen, may be protected from the excesses to which they have been hitherto unavoidably exposed, and thus be enabled to appreciate the advantages of the late providential change. Considering that this country is destined, from its extensive resources, to become a naval power of considerable importance, and that it is of the utmost consequence, to avoid giving cause of complaint to neutral states, the friends of Greece are most anxious to hear of the establishment of an office for the registering of ships and seamen, and above all, an Admiralty Court, for the adjudication of captures, as well as the punishment of crimes committed on the high seas. On the importance of establishing tribunals, hospitals, sanitary regulations, and posts, it is unnecessary for me to dwell, convinced that these objects already occupy the attention of your august body.

Having determined not to withdraw your attention, or that of the executive, from the great and paramount duty of driving the infidels from your country, I shall defer offering any suggestions of my own for the present. When, however, the above grand object is attained, I shall perhaps also take the liberty of frankly stating whatever seems likely to improve the condition of Greece, whether it relates to the dissemination of knowledge and virtue among the people, or adding to the national resources. Next to the establishment of a good fiscal and financial system, one of the very first points I should be induced to propose to your august body, would be to grant a piece of land on which to establish an *English farm*. This spot will be under the immediate auspices and protection of the government. Its sole object, that of introducing into Greece the numerous agricultural improvements which have been made in England during the last century ; as well as to serve for the cultivation of the various fruits, vegetables, flowers, shrubs, and even forest trees, we possess, to be thence distributed and transplanted to every part of the confederation. In addition to recommending the introduction of our diversified breed of cattle, sheep and horses, unequalled in any other country, I shall, when the proper time arrives, strongly urge the propriety of introducing the Spanish Merino into Greece. Having already made some enquiries on this subject, it is evident that there is no part of the confederacy in which the above celebrated breed would not thrive as well as in its native clime. When once introduced, it will soon become a source of incalculable wealth to Greece.

"It would, in fact, be easy to multiply suggestions like those I have named; but as there is no possibility of carrying them into effect under present circumstances, they had better be deferred for a future day. In the meantime, I can safely assure your august body, that what the friends of Greece are most anxious about is, to see union among the people, and strength in the Government; to witness the increase of good institutions and wise laws: as with these, there can be no doubt of your making the most rapid advances towards wealth and knowledge.

"Unlike all the other nations of Europe, the legislators and citizens of Greece, have not to seek for models and examples abroad: her own annals are replete with lessons of wisdom and virtue, which have served at once as the impulse and guide of succeeding ages. If strangers, therefore, have profited so much by those sublime precepts which were taught in the Academy, and the no less admirable examples of valour and patriotism displayed at Marathon and Mycale, what ought not Europe to expect from the descendants of the sages and heroes who bequeathed such examples to the world?

"Finally, what the friends of your sacred cause wish to see, is, that every citizen of Greece shall constantly keep in mind his glorious ancestors, and while he avoids the errors which caused so many calamities in their days, that he should recollect *regenerated Greece* forms but ONE FAMILY, united by the strongest ties of religion and duty, and that whatever inconveniences he may now suffer, or however great the sacrifices he is called upon to make, the prospect for him and his posterity, is one of the brightest and most cheering ever opened by Providence to any nation!

(Signed) "EDWARD BLAQUIERE.

"Napoli di Romania, August 18th, 1824."

No. XLIX.

*From Prince Mavrocordato, to E. Blaquiere.**

"Ligovitzi en Acarnania, le 18-30 Août, 1824.

"Je viens de recevoir votre lettre obligeante du 8-20 Août. Vous voici enfin porteur des meilleures nouvelles à Londres. Vous vous plaigniez de votre retard; mais je crois que vous n'en étes gueres repenti. Je suis plus que sur que votre mission réussira parfaitement. Vous n'aurez pas aussi de preuves plus convaincantes que celles de faits mêmes, pour faire entendre à tout le monde, combien vous aviez raison lorsque vous vouliez utiliser l'emprunt, et combien ceux qui l'ont pour ainsi dire séquestré, ont eu tort. Cassos et surtout Ipsara, ces deux boulevards de notre marine, auraient aujourd'hui existés, comme Samos existe. La flotte Turque auroit été mise en déroute bien avant le depart de la flotte Egyptienne. L'exemple de sa défaite aurait renversé tous les projets ambitieux du Satrape d'Egypte, et nous n'aurions pas eu aujourd'hui des nouveaux risques à courir, des nouvelles dépenses à faire; mais ce qui est fait, est fait. Si je répéte souvent mes objections sur le passé, c'est pour que de pareilles choses ne sa renouvellent plus.

* This letter was received about six weeks after my arrival in England.—E.B.

"Vous êtes déja assez intruit, cher ami, tachez d instruire également les autres. Nos opérations dans le pays d'Arta reussissent parfaitement. Omer Pacha se trouve au desespoir; il n'ose pas quitter la position de Carvansarà, ce qui me disespère aussi. J'ai tâché de lui tendre un piège et le faire avancer du coté de Dragomeste; lá il ne m'aurait pas echapé; mais soit qu'il est mieux guidé dans cette compagne, soit qu'il a pu connaitre notre plan, au lieu de s'avancer comme, Je l'ai espéré un moment, et que je lui avoit laissé même le passage libre, il s'est tout à fait retiré derriere Carvansará: que fera-t-il la? sans doute rien; mais il pourra se retirer sur Vonitza sans une grande perte, en se faissant protéger par sa cavalerie, et en embarquant ses effets et ses malades. Si nous avions une petite force seulement dans le Golfe, il étail immanquablement perdu. Adieu, cher ami, ecrivez mois le plus souvent que vous pourrez, et rappelez moi au souvenir de tous nos amis. Faites agréer mes respects au digne Capitaine Hastings, et conservez toujours votre amitie pour votre devoué.

(Signé) "A. MAVROCORDATO."

TRANSLATION.

"Ligovitzi, in Acarnania, Aug. 18—30th, 1824.

"I have just received your obliging letter of the 8-20th instant. Behold you at length the bearer of better news to London; you complained of the delay, but I think you are not sorry for it. I am fully convinced your mission will completely succeed; you cannot have any proofs more convincing, than the facts themselves, to satisfy every body, how correct you were in wishing to render the loan useful, and how much those by whom it was, as it were sequestered, were wrong. Cassos, and above all, Ipsara, these bulwarks of our navy, would have existed this day, as Samos exists. The Turkish fleet would have been defeated long before the departure of the Egyptian fleet; the example of its defeat would have overturned all the ambitious projects of the Satrap of Egypt, and we should not now have to run new risks nor fresh expences;—but what is done, is done. If I often repeat my objections as to the past, it is that similar things may not occur again. You are already sufficiently informed, dear friend, endeavour to inform others also. Our operations in the district of Anta succeed perfectly. Omen Pacha is in despair: he dare not quit the position of Carvansarà; which also makes me despair. I have tried to lay a snare for him and make him advance to Dragomeste—once there, he would not have escaped me; but whether it is, that he is better guided this campaign, or that he has found out our plan, instead of advancing as I hoped at one time, he has retired altogether behind Carvansarà. What will he do there? doubtless nothing; but he may retire to Vonitza without a great loss, by causing himself to be protected by his cavalry, and embarking his effects and sick. If we only had a small force in the gulph, he would be irretrievably lost. Adieu, dear friend, write to me as often as you can; remember me to all our friends; make my respects acceptable to the worthy Captain Hastings, and always preserve your friendship for

"Your devoted Friend,

"A. MAVROCORDATO."

No. L.

Extract of a Letter from E. Blaquiere to John Bowring, Esq., Honorary Secretary to the Greek Committee.

"London, Dec. 18th, 1824.

"THE principal object of the present communication is to suggest the propriety of answers being forwarded to Greece, in reply to the various letters I brought from the seat of government, more particularly those addressed to the Committee by the Philanthropic Society, formed at Napoli di Romania, and the Ipsariot deputies. There was also an application from M. Theotoki, the minister of justice, for a small selection of such works, on international law and jurisprudence, as the Committee might judge best calculated for extending a knowledge of those subjects in Greece. Another letter from a distinguished patriot, Schilitzi Homeride, of Scio*, solicited the patronage of the Committee to a small pamphlet in MS., suggesting a plan of civil and political organization for the confederacy, and which he is desirous to circulate among his countrymen. I have written to our friends at Napoli, to say that they might expect an early decision on the part of the Committee, touching all the above points. Perhaps, in alluding to the law books, it will be as well to apprize the Com-

* The object of M. Homeride's addressing the Committee, was to solicit its patronage for a small pamphlet, in which the author has pointed out the defects of the present political organization of Greece, and suggested such improvements as he thinks more likely to insure the happiness of his country.

My friend, who is one of the best intentioned patriots I met with at the seat of government, insists more particularly on the necessity and importance of education and moral improvement, without which he conceives it will be impossible to consolidate the social edifice. When I quitted Napoli di Romania, M. Homeride was busily occupied in projecting a national Pritanæum.

mittee, that M. Meyer, the editor of the Greek Chronicle, published at Messolunghi, is labouring very sedulously to establish a public library there. If the Committee were induced to present a few standard works to the municipality of that town, I feel assured it would be rendering a very important service, and one which would greatly increase its popularity. I should imagine, that, with little more than a sum of 50*l.*, both the above objects might be carried into effect.

"I have great pleasure in being able to submit specimens of the writing of the Greek youths, who came home in the Amphitrite, for the inspection of the committee; and I am happy to add, that there is every prospect of their making a rapid progress in every other useful acquirement. You are aware of the desire expressed by the Society of Friends, to confer with the Committee again, relative to the best mode of defraying the expenses of educating these interesting youths. I should imagine that the monies about to be raised at Birmingham might be made available for this object. Should the Committee not deem it advisable to authorize your reminding the gentlemen of that place of their promises, I should make a point of addressing a letter on the subject to Parkes. Our indefatigable and zealous friend, Barker, of Thetford, writes to say, that he is convinced any appeal, having the education of these youths for its object, cannot fail to be met in a liberal spirit by the public. The last suggestion which I have felt very anxious to have an opportunity of offering to the committee, relates to the importance of conferring some mark of distinction on the naval and military chiefs, who have so highly distinguished themselves during the fourth campaign. Knowing the Greek character, as I think I do, there is no point to which I would call the attention of the Committee with more solicitude than the above; nor have I any hesitation in saying, that a few *swords*, presented to the leading men at the end of each campaign, would produce the most salutary effects. Those who have contributed most to the successes of the late campaign, are the Generals Dimo Scaltza, Stornaris, and Gouras, on shore; and the naval chiefs Miaoulis, Canaris, and Sactouri. If the funds of the Committee were in as flourishing a state as they ought to be, I am almost sure it would enter into this project without hesitation.

"You will oblige me greatly by letting me know whether any thing is decided respecting the foregoing points; and pray believe me, &c.

(Signed) "E. BLAQUIERE."

No. LI.

Extract from the Minutes of the Greek Committee, on the day the foregoing Letter was presented.

"Greek Committee Room, London, 18th Dec. 1824.

"JOSEPH HUME, ESQ. M.P. in the Chair, read a letter from Mr. Blaquiere, dated 18th Dec. 1824.

"Resolved,

"That in the opinion of this Committee, it is very desirable that an association should be formed for advancing the moral and intellectual improvement of Greece, by annual subscriptions, separate and distinct from this Committee.

(Signed) "JOHN BOWRING, Hon. Sec."

No. LII.

Extract from the Minutes of the Greek Committee.

"Greek Committee Room, Crown and Anchor,
"London, 1st November, 1824.

"JOSEPH HUME, ESQ. M.P. in the Chair. The Report of Mr. Blaquiere being read,

"Resolved,

"That the Committee are fully impressed with the activity and zeal with which Mr. Blaquiere has exercised his best energies for the aid of the Greek cause, since his departure from England; and they cannot but offer him the testimony of their admiration, for the generous devotion with which he rendered himself personally responsible for the pecuniary aid he was the instrument of procuring to the Greek Government, at a crisis of great difficulty and peril.

(Signed) "JOHN BOWRING, Hon. Sec."

No. LIII.

[It affords me very sincere pleasure to be enabled to add the following powerful address just put forth by the Education Committee mentioned in my Narrative, and I would have gladly subjoined that of the Ladies' Society, formed at Edinburgh, had it reached me.—E. B.]

"*An Appeal to the Public, from the British and Foreign School Society, on the Subject of Education in Greece.*

"AMONG the most interesting events to which the attention of the Christian and the philanthropist has been of late directed, those which have recently occurred in Greece hold a distinguished place. That country, once the most renowned in the annals of civilization, the fountain-head of literature, and arts, and science, after having been completely overwhelmed by invading barbarians, and after ages of severe suffering, has again arisen from its degradation, full of hope and promise. That people, whose ancestors received the maxims of our holy religion from the lips of its earliest Apostles, after being oppressed for centuries, has again been admitted to the free exercise of their Christian faith, and to the free and unmolested worship of the God of their fathers.

"But whether the present situation of Greece be contrasted with its former intellectual glory or its religious privileges, the degradation which a long-enduring despotism has introduced, must awaken the strongest desire in every benevolent heart to counteract and remove its baneful influence. To secure and to perpetuate the blessings of freedom, ignorance and superstition must be superseded by knowledge, judiciously applied, and by that education which can eradicate the causes and the consequences of a devastating misrule.

"To England, then,—to England, great in her means of benevolence, and mighty in her philanthropic influence—this interesting country turns, and implores assistance to carry forward the good work of improvement. It is our duty to answer the appeal: and it cannot but be a matter of high satisfaction to reflect, that we may thus be enabled to pay to the children of Greece some portion of the debt we owe to their illustrious progenitors.

"That, in order to act with effect upon the human mind, education must combine itself with the truths and with the sanctions of the Gospel, can hardly be doubted by those who have watched the growth and the aberration of the moral feeling! and, in this persuasion, it is deemed of the highest importance that a knowledge of the Holy Scriptures should be an object of the most prominent attention.

"To form the heart, and to regulate the life—to fit men for the discharge of their personal and their relative duties—to create a spirit of private and of public virtue—in a word, to raise the human character to its highest standard, religious instruction will be found the most efficient, or, in truth, the only instrument: and if the state of barbarism into which a great mass of the Greek population has been plunged, be contrasted with the extraordinary aptitude which has been uniformly exhibited by those to whom the blessings of education have been communicated, the highest possible encouragement will be found for our exertions—the most satisfactory security for our ultimate, our great success.

"Though, among the highest classes of Greece, the preliminary forms of instruction have been generally and widely extended—and of late years men have appeared to purify the language, and to revive the literature of their country—yet the want of any general system of education, arising, first, from the intolerable severity of Turkish oppression, and, secondly, from the terrors and the anxieties of a desolating war, has left the mass of the people in a state of lamentable ignorance. The present moment appears peculiarly favourable for attempting to establish among them plans of extensive good. Several philanthropic societies have sprung up at Nauplia, Athens, and Messolunghi; and possessing some peculiar facilities for carrying our plans into complete operation, we only look to the sympathy and encouragement of the British public to enable us to confer the highest and the most lasting benefit on the people of Greece.

"Already the British and Foreign School Society has directed its attention to the claims of Greece. Two Cypriot youths, redeemed from slavery, were sent to England in 1823, and, at the expense of private benevolence, have been educated at the Central School in the Borough Road, and trained as masters: the elder left London for the Morea a few months since, in company with a gentleman, who, from motives of sincere benevolence, is gone to that country, to devote himself to the cause of education:—the establishment of a school on the British system, at the seat of government, would be the first object of their attention.

"The society has since taken on its establishment, to train as masters, two other Greeks, whom a series of providential circumstances has led to this country; and has more recently admitted as scholars, seven lads brought over by Captain Blaquiere, together with a young man, their companion, whom they contemplate training as a schoolmaster. Of these lads, only a part are likely to be prepared for teachers, the others are destined for various employments; but their education in England, if rightly directed, may have an important influence on their countrymen; not only in cementing the future friendly alliance of the two countries, but in advancing the moral improvement of Greece. The school society have also printed in the modern Greek, both in the book and sheet form, the scripture lessons used in their central schools.

"In taking a more comprehensive view of the means to be adopted in promoting the establishment of schools in Greece, the committee of the British and Foreign School Society have seen that, however strongly connected with the object for which they were associated, it was utterly impossible for them, with their present limited resources, to meet the expenses needful to be incurred in the promotion of these plans. The instruction of masters and mistresses in this country; their passage to and from England; the printing of elementary spelling, reading and arithmetic lessons for the schools; and various articles of school furniture, will call for funds of a considerable amount. And in a country where little or no provision for reading in the vernacular tongue is already made, it will be necessary immediately to follow up these efforts by a series of instructive and improving reading in a cheap form, adapted to the capacities of children.

"Through their treasurer, the Committee have already opened a communication with the members of the Greek Government; and from this source, as well as from personal intercourse with the Greek deputies now in London, they feel assured of the most cordial co-operation.

"In an effort, thus made, to advance the cause of Christianity, by promoting a religious education, founded on the principles of Holy Scripture, in a country where the Christian religion has so long been oppressed, the Committee trust that they shall be supported by the friends of religion and truth; and they cannot believe that this appeal will be made in vain.

"Whether we look backward in admiration of the past—or around us to contemplate the vast field which is open to our present exertions—or before us, to anticipate the regeneration of a country, whose mountains and plains, whose forests and rivers, whose towns and villages are associated with the most interesting and the most sacred recollections—we feel persuaded that we shall be assisted to carry forward the good work we have proposed. In that confidence we would again urge the claim upon the public benevolence, and we trust that, under the Divine blessing, we shall be permitted to see in the moral improvement of Greece the noblest return for generous assistance—the best and the highest recompense for all our exertions.

"Subscriptions will be thankfully received by the following gentlemen, viz.—Joseph Butterworth, Esq. M. P. Fleet-street; William Evans, Esq. M. P. New Norfolk-street, Park-lane; Wm. Allen, Esq. (Treasurer,) Plough-court, Lombard-street; Rev. Wm. Broadfoot, Pimlico; Henry Drummond, Esq. Charing-cross; Joseph Foster,

Esq. Bromley, near Bow; Samuel Hoare, Jun. Esq. Lombard-street; Zachary Macaulay, Esq. George-street, Mansion-house; James Nesbitt, Esq. Berners-street; Rev. Josiah Pratt, Doughty-street, Foundling Hospital; Wm. Foster Reynolds, Esq. Great St. Helen's; Rev. Dr. Schwabe, Little Alie-street, Goodman's Fields.

"And by Paul Moon James, Esq. Birmingham; Rev. T. T. Biddulph, Bristol; Rev. William Marsh, Colchester; William Roscoe, Esq. and James Cropper, Esq. Liverpool; Benjamin Braidley, Esq. Manchester; Joseph John Gurney, Esq. Norwich; and Samuel Tuke, Esq. York.

THE END.

LONDON:

SHACKELL AND ARROWSMITH, JOHNSON'S-COURT, FLEET-STREET.

CPSIA information can be obtained at www.ICGtesting.com
Printed in the USA
BVOW06s2148240316

441701BV00016B/80/P

9 781314 096293